Ways Of Writing with Young Kids

Teaching Creativity and Conventions
Unconventionally

SHARON A. EDWARDS
Amherst (Massachusetts) Public Schools

ROBERT W. MALOY
University of Massachusetts Amherst

RUTH-ELLEN VEROCK-O'LOUGHLIN
Orange (Massachusetts) Public Schools

Boston   New York   San Francisco
Mexico City   Montreal   Toronto   London   Madrid   Munich   Paris
Hong Kong   Singapore   Tokyo   Cape Town   Sydney

Series Editor: Aurora Martinez
Editorial Assistant: Beth Slater
Editorial-Production Administrator: Deborah Brown
Editorial-Production Service: Colophon
Composition Buyer: Linda Cox
Manufacturing Buyer: Andrew Turso
Cover Administrator: Kristina Mose-Libon
Text Composition: Publishers' Design and Production Services, Inc.

For related titles and support materials, visit our online catalog at www.ablongman.com.

CIP Data on file at the Library of Congress.
ISBN: 0-205-33714-7

Printed in the United States of America

10 9 8 7 6 5 4 3 2 1   09 08 07 06 04 03 02

Contents

CHAPTER THREE

Poems

CHAPTER FOUR

Stories

CHAPTER FIVE

Mathematics

CHAPTER SIX

Science

CHAPTER SEVEN

Social Studies   220

Preface

Welcome to WOW (*Ways of Writing with Young Kids*), a guidebook for adults who want to assist kindergartners through third graders (ages five to nine) to write:

- *Creatively* as they express their ideas and explore their imaginations using many genres and styles of fiction, nonfiction, and poetry.
- *Conventionally* as they learn purposes of writing, types of genres, rules of grammar, mechanics of punctuation/capitalization/spelling taught in school and assessed on high stakes local, state, and national tests.
- *Confidently* as they discover the power of writing as a means of communication, persuasion, analysis, and self-expression.

We have written this book for *all* adults involved in young children's learning—experienced classroom teachers, new teachers just beginning their careers, student teachers in certification programs, and parents and family members. Using practical ideas and proven strategies in the book, adults can make writing an interest-building, imagination-expanding activity that children are eager to repeat. And while writing with kids, adults can demonstrate and teach what young writers need to know about written language to succeed on achievement tests and in other educational assessments.

There is a specific focus for each group of readers:

- *Teachers*—both veteran educators and those new to the profession—benefit from classroom activities promoting children's imaginative thinking, enjoyment of learning, and understanding of conventions without continual drills of skills. Facing tremendous pressures to achieve literacy success for every student, many teachers are unsure how to integrate writing into all learning. WOW ideas connect writing and reading throughout the curriculum and serve as a writing workshop for students and adults.
- *Student teachers*—and others in teacher certification programs—need practical strategies for teaching their students the required curriculum objectives. WOW ideas not only generate success and enjoyment for children, but also show novices how master teachers use writing across the subject areas to teach essential information that children find meaningful and memorable.
- *Parents and other family members*—with youngsters in public, private, or home schools—want to make writing one of the activities of choice for their children. Using the ideas in this book, families can support and extend what children are learning at school and also offer new ways for younger and older family members to write together.

Features of the Book

- **23 WOWs** (creative ways of writing with kids) that include the genres and forms commonly taught in kindergarten through grade three: alphabets, parts of speech, sentences, letters, signs, poetry, imaginative fiction, comics, plays, nonfiction narratives, research reports, science journals, personal memories, and autobiographies.

- ***Ideas for Teaching Conventions* Unconventionally** use children's interest in creative writing to teach about the use of writing processes, purposes, genres, forms, grammar, punctuation, and spelling—thereby equipping young writers with the skills they need to succeed on high stakes tests.

- ***Writing in Mathematics, Science, and Social Studies*** features activities that extend learning across the curriculum in the major academic areas taught in early elementary school grades.

- ***A Young Writer's Bookshelf*** at the end of each WOW builds a reading connection to writing by identifying notable children's literature—including many multicultural titles—that directly involve kids in each writing idea.

- ***Children's Writing Examples*** are part of every WOW idea to show the creativity of young writers while giving adults concrete illustrations to share with their students.

- ***An Easy-to-Read Format*** explains ideas and strategies clearly and concisely using classroom dialogues, writing games, stories of adults and children writing together, and examples of language and vocabulary to use with kids.

Uniting Creativity, Conventions, and Confidence

"Creativity" and "Conventions" mark a longstanding debate dividing the teaching of children's writing. On one side is the belief that the development of children's potential for imaginative self-expression and love of learning should not be disrupted by an overemphasis on rules and conventions. On the other side is the counter-argument that little is accomplished if children enjoy writing creatively but cannot write clearly using standard language and forms. Meanwhile, teachers and parents wonder how to teach children to develop their talents, learn the skills, and acquire the self-confidence needed to perform successfully in school.

It is a primary goal of this book to show the interdependence between creativity and conventions in the learning and teaching of children's writing. In our view, becoming a writer at any age—and particularly for children in kindergarten through grade three—means connecting with and expanding a child's creative curiosity while simultaneously demonstrating how to use standard forms of written language to communicate with readers. Creativity and conventions are not opposing forces facing each other; they are mutually informing parts of a process where children learn to express ideas, share information, and make meaning through writing.

A second goal of this book is to show adults how to make confidence building a mainstay of all the writing they do with kids. Educator and author Mem Fox (30) has observed that to develop as writers, young children must have "a real purpose, a real audience, and a real investment in their writing." We wholeheartedly and unequivocally agree. When children view writing as personally meaningful and engaging, they enjoy doing it and they want to learn more about it, including the conventions of written language. Our challenge as creators of this book, and yours as teachers of young writers, is to inspire kids to write in schools, homes, or any other place where children and adults learn and play together.

A third goal of this book is centered on helping teachers (and parents) prepare children for success on high-stakes tests. Today, most schools follow local, state, or national curriculum standards for what children need to learn in the English/language arts, and, in thirty-four states, tests measure the reading and writing skills of third graders. Forty states test the achievement levels of fourth graders (*Education Week* 17). To succeed on the tests, children who are confident of their abilities must think creatively while using written language conventionally.

Every Child Is a Writer, Right Now

"Children learn from the company they keep," asserts researcher and writer Frank Smith. In his view, children learn to read and write by reading and writing, gradually acquiring essential knowledge, specific skills, and a self-identity as a reader and a writer. In so doing, kids become functioning members of the "literacy club." Teachers and parents play crucial roles in this process: Says Smith (26), "First someone shows you what can be done then helps with whatever you want to do yourself."

Consider how young children learn to read. Initially, adults spend time reading *for* an infant child. As the youngster gains knowledge and confidence with language, adults are reading *with* the child. Before long, the child is reading independently, enjoying the company of book authors and magazine writers. While reading, children naturally and inconspicuously learn about language and its conventions: "how to recognize words; the meanings of words; their spellings and grammatical relationships to other words; and the way words are organized into sentences and paragraphs, and into poetry and drama" (Smith 26–27).

A similar process can happen with writing using the ideas in this book. Children draw on knowledge of language they have heard or read as the foundation for what they write. Reading builds writers and writing builds readers. Just as children join the reading club by reading, they enter a writing club by expressing themselves in written language using genres, forms, and styles. Using written language in personally meaningful ways, children immerse themselves in the ways writers employ words to communicate information and ideas. They gain knowledge of the conventional by exploring the creative.

Writing plays such a powerful role in children's literacy learning because, by its very nature, it comes from the *inside out*, the polar opposite of most academic experiences. When children listen to someone speak, they get information from the *outside in*; when they watch television or go to the movies, the same pattern repeats—images come from the *outside in*. Reading also involves *outside in* as the reader responds to what others have written to create meaning from text.

Writing, by contrast, starts and sustains itself from the *inside out*. The writer decides the ideas, images, feelings, and information to share with others. The *inside out* nature of writing explains much of its potential as a learning force for children. Writing is a vehicle for expression and communication in an adult-dominated world where kids are dependent on others for information and guidance. Writing gives children the time and reflection necessary to make sense of their experiences. It offers opportunities to create new meanings using one's own individuality. Writing lets children exercise ownership and control of learning and as a result offers a unique way for children to succeed.

Every teacher, parent, daycare provider, or babysitter recognizes how children's attention may waver considerably when information comes from the outside in. How many times have we repeated a direction or restated a request that a child seems always to forget? Children's connection to learning from the inside out is far more lasting. By connecting assignments and learning activities to the context of children's writing, the natural investment that writers have in their own ideas and words helps propel the learning of the skills and information that teachers, parents, and employers deem important.

For writing to unleash the power of learning from the inside out, kids must write a lot. To do so they need an abiding sense of personal confidence in their abilities and a fascination with what their minds can produce for learning and entertainment. Confidence in oneself as a writer involves a process of mutually reinforcing experiences, beginning with adults assuring kids that "they are writers, right now" with important ideas to share using words, pictures, numbers, colors, characters, dialogue, scenes, and the other features of written language. Sentences, paragraphs, punctuation, spelling, and other conventions are not arbitrary rules, but essential tools that writers use to communicate ideas and information clearly to readers and listeners.

The Meanings of WOW

"Write *with* kids?" you may be asking. "Isn't writing something that children need to do on their own after teachers and parents instruct them how to do so?" Or you might be wondering, "My children don't even like to write—why would they want to write with me?" In this book, we declare that writing is an exciting and engaging, not a solitary or unpleasant, activity for children. We demonstrate how it can be "fundamental" (fun-from-the-mind) and an essential key to school and personal learning.

Through writing, children discover the astonishing power and vast fascination of their thoughts. They learn that language is an always-at-hand tool for critical thinking, problem solving, and information communicating. Writing facilitates children's belief that they are bright, thoughtful individuals with important things to say using written language. But, building an abiding sense of oneself as a writer is not easy for children to achieve by themselves. They need and immensely benefit from adults who can assist them in unlocking the potentials of written communication.

To bring children and adults together as writers, we have chosen the word WOW because it communicates the spirit and essence of the book in the following ways:

- *WOW* captures the sense of delight expressed by teachers, parents, and other adults when a young child shares her or his writing. Youngsters, hearing positive comments from adults, recognize themselves as smart thinkers and good communicators. This book shows adults how to use and go beyond compliments to being supportive coaches of young writers. When adults provide thoughtful encouragement and enthusiastic responses, young children become more creative, conventional, and confident writers, eager to explore the genres and forms of written language.

- *WOW* invites explorations of writing that are unique, powerful, thrilling, and endless. Engaging children's imaginations leads to their discovering the connection existing between self-expression and literacy learning. The strategies and suggestions in this book open the treasure chest of ideas, information, and inspiration that all young writers possess.

- *WOW* is a habit of mind children develop as they write their ideas in their own ways for their own purposes. The book showcases the enjoyment and learning that occur when young writers are transported by written words from the commonplace surroundings of school or home to realms of adventure, wonder, and imagination. As children choose what to write and how to write it, they establish a sense of uniqueness and voice in their writing. They take pride in what they have to say, verbally or in print. They exhibit the confidence of expressive communicators whose learning is accompanied by a core belief in oneself and one's abilities to succeed.

WOWs happen when creativity, conventions, and confidence blend together the "write" way—from engaging, wonderful writing experiences, with thoughtful adult support, and children's sense of themselves as eminently capable young writers.

Teaching Conventions Unconventionally

The book's subtitle, "Teaching Creativity and Conventions *Unconventionally*," expresses our goal of showing adults how to use children's creative engagement with writing to explore and explain the conventions of written language. To correctly use and remember the *rules* of writing, youngsters must also understand the *roles* that genre, process, grammar, punctuation, spelling, and other mechanics play in written language. Conventions make far more sense when young writers see the purposes of these devices in written language.

Throughout the book, we consider conventions in their *roles before rules* so children can see how standard forms are useful devices that enable a writer to communicate more effectively her or his ideas to others. For example:

- Capital letters are the required way to start a sentence or a proper noun because they provide an attention-getting signal to readers. Their role is to catch people's eye, telling them to LOOK and PAY ATTENTION to something of importance in the writing (names of people, places or things; the beginnings of sentences or phrases; essential messages).

- Verbs are indispensable parts of a sentence because they power the other parts of speech into action. Verbs make people, places, and events come alive by showing their individuality, purpose, and emotion.

- Periods, commas, semi-colons, question marks, exclamation points and dashes are mechanical features of written language that provide speed control for readers, directing when to continue along, slow down, or stop entirely. As stop signs and traffic lights on roadways promote safety, punctuation symbols promote readers' understanding of a text.

Exploring conventions *unconventionally* means connecting specific writing conventions to each of the creative writing activities in the book. Acrostic poetry offers an opportunity to emphasize the importance of standard spelling. Comic strips display how speech bubbles are used to show the dialogue of the characters. Plays and performances demonstrate the value of revising and editing written material before sharing it with an audience.

Blending creativity and conventions broadens the focus of writing instruction from *what to write* (a writer's idea or topic) to *how to write* (the ways writers organize their thinking and then use genres, grammar, and mechanics to get their ideas across to readers). In this way, creativity and conventions become paired topics for investigation between children and adults as they write together. Young writers discover how creative ideas and conventional features are parts of written language and how to incorporate both in their own writing.

How to Use This Book

Ways of Writing with Young Kids is an ideas and activities book organized around many different ways for adults to write with kids. Typically, activity books feature lesson plans, worksheets, and assessment strategies. We believe that adults need models of inspiring writing activities to build successful writing partnerships with kids.

We have coached all the writing activities in this book ourselves many times with children in schools, child-care centers, after-school programs, and family writing workshops in urban, suburban, and rural communities. Our challenge as authors is to describe these ideas so that adults are able to see themselves doing them with kids.

To showcase each WOW in action, we combine classroom stories and original writing by children with literature that inspires kids to write. Our descriptions vary in length from brief to detailed, but our goal is to take readers far enough into each idea so they feel ready to try it themselves. To balance "how to" guidance with letting readers adapt ideas for themselves, we include sections called "Extensions" that offer more ways to write with kids.

This book has two organizing structures—one highlighting creative ideas, the other addressing writing conventions. Teachers can choose a creative writing idea to open ways to teach conventions or identify a convention to teach and find a writing activity that supports learning about it. The two structures work in the following way.

Starting from the Creative

Creative writing ideas (WOWs) are arranged in seven chapters: "Language," "Communications," "Poems," "Stories," "Mathematics," "Science," and "Social Studies," as shown on the following chart.

Chapters of the Book	*Creative Writing Ideas or WOWs*
Chapter 1: *Language* connects writing to the building blocks of the English language: letters of the alphabet, words and meanings, and the construction of sentences.	• WOW 1: Child-Made Alphabets • WOW 2: My Words Abound and Surround • WOW 3: 676 Sentences and Thousands More
Chapter 2: *Communications* focuses on different forms of communicative writing where writers share different forms of "news" with personal and public audiences.	• WOW 4: We've got Mail: Letters, E-mail, and Mailboxes • WOW 5: Signs Are Billboards for Persuasion • WOW 6: What's the Forecast? Short Reports about the Weather • WOW 7: What's for Lunch? The Menu May Not Be Real
Chapter 3: *Poems* explores the creative possibilities of reading and writing poetry to stimulate inventive, expressive writing by children.	• WOW 8: Making Moments for Poetry Every Day • WOW 9: What's Hiding in Acrostic Poetry? • WOW 10: Concrete Poetry: Sketching and Sculpting Words into Pictures • WOW 11: Voices of Poetry
Chapter 4: *Stories* presents story-writing ideas for children to express themselves imaginatively while learning how writers use both facts (nonfiction) and make-believe (fiction) in their stories.	• WOW 12: From Oral to Written Tales • WOW 13: Words for Pictures and Performances • WOW 14: New Versions of Old Tales • WOW 15: Fiction/Nonfiction Story Writing
Chapter 5: *Mathematics* introduces creative writing ideas that use both fiction stories and nonfiction reporting to promote math exploration throughout the year.	• WOW 16: Math Riddles • WOW 17: Doug's Graph: Children Conducting Surveys and Polls

Chapter 6: *Science* links creative writing to the scientific activities of asking questions, conducting research, formulating explanations, and presenting findings in research reports.

Chapter 7: *Social Studies* explains how writers explore the past, present, and future as well as their own roles and responsibilities as members of different communities.

- WOW 18: Garfield Meets Fibonacci: Math Comics by and for Kids
- WOW 19: Thinking and Acting as Scientists
- WOW 20: Investigations and Discoveries
- WOW 21: Attention-Grabbing Science Reports
- WOW 22: A Child's EncycloMEdia
- WOW 23: Community Rules!

Throughout the seven chapters are the genres and forms of writing commonly taught from kindergarten through grade three, encompassing the reasons or purposes writers have for writing. Each WOW idea:

- Activates a child's intrinsic motivation for writing—exploring ideas, entertaining an audience, and communicating something of interest to a reader.
- Propels further investigation of genres and conventions through creative activities.
- Engages children with writing many times over because each activity is interesting when repeated.

Starting from the Conventional

The following Index of Writing Conventions lists the conventions discussed in the book. Taken collectively, these conventions are the common rules and understandings of written language that writers use to convey ideas and information. All represent essential terms that young writers are expected to know and use appropriately by grade three. We developed the list by consulting the "Standards for the English Language Arts" prepared by the National Council of Teachers of English and the International Reading Association (1996) as well as state and local standards selected from around the country.

When many adults hear the term "conventions," they often think only of punctuation, capitalization, and spelling—the readily apparent surface features of written communications. Writers broaden the scope to include four other structural dimensions of writing conventions:

- *Strategies/Skills:* terms related to the processes of writing and reading.
- *Genres:* forms of written language that have their own content, style, or rules.
- *Devices:* features that writers use to convey ideas and information with interest and clarity.
- *Grammar:* structures of language used by writers.
- *Punctuation/Spelling*

Index of Writing Conventions

Strategies/Skills	*Location in the Book*
Explanation and Analysis	Chapter Six: Science (WOWs 19, 20, 21)

Using the Templates

To further aid readers, both organizing structures—creative and conventional—are paired in *templates* at the beginning of each WOW idea. The templates show how creative writing activities launch the exploration of different conventions. For example:

- WOW 5 (Signs Are Billboards for Persuasion) explores how words are used to *persuade* people to do things through the use of *capital and lowercase letters*.
- WOW 9 (What's Hiding in Acrostic Poetry?) opens a treasure chest of ways to understand and enjoy practicing *conventional spelling*.
- WOW 18 (Garfield Meets Fibonacci: Math Comics by and for Kids) features the story ingredients of *characters*, *dialogue*, *storyline*, and *tension* as well as mathematical skills.
- WOW 21 (Attention-Grabbing Science Reports) and WOW 22 (A Child's EncycloMEdia) demonstrates how *factual reports* convey newsworthy information to readers.
- WOW 23 (Community Rules!) shows the structure and function of different types of *sentences*.

Multicultural Learning

Writing is multicultural. It promotes self-expression by every writer, whether conveyed through stories, poetry, nonfiction, drawings, or oral conversation that is written down by others. Self-expression builds self-confidence, letting the writer's voice be heard while fueling a desire to write more.

Writing for self-expression is supported by children's literature that is inclusive of ages, genders, skin tones, family structures, countries of origin, home languages, individual differences, and socioeconomic backgrounds. To open children's understandings and widen the scope of their writing, we have included books about diverse peoples, cultures, and experiences as part of writing activities and in the *Young Writers' Bookshelf* located at the end of each chapters. It is our intention that African American, Latino, Native American, Asian, and Anglo children read and write about topics they know well and about topics that are different from their experiences.

Adults can identify hundreds more multicultural resources by consulting *Language Arts*, the journal of the National Council of Teachers of English; *Social Education*, the journal of the National Council for the Social Studies (and its yearly listing of Notable Social Studies Trade Books for Young People); and resource books by Frances Ann Day: *Multicultural Voices in Contemporary Literature*, updated and revised (1999), and *Latina and Latino Voices in Literature for Children and Teenagers* (1997).

Creative writing ideas supported by a wide-ranging selection of multicultural books directly support students who are learning English as a new language. Multilingual children are striving to become biliterate learners, confident and competent in more than one language. Like monolingual speakers, many multilingual children find the conventions of written English language difficult to master. The terms for genres, grammar, spelling, and punctuation can be difficult to remember because they carry few familiar associations on which to build new knowledge. Plus, the structures of many children's home languages do not follow the same patterns as English.

Kid-Friendly Language

Our focus on "roles before rules" to explain writing conventions is useful for multilingual speakers, who like native English speakers, find the names of many writing conventions context-less and unmemorable. An exclamation point or an interrogative sentence offers no frame of reference for understanding the term or using it appropriately in written language.

Learning the conventions is greatly aided when adults restate terms in *kid-friendly language*. Here are some examples to which you can add others:

- Capitals are *Attention-Getting Letters*. Capital letters flag attention to the beginning of sentences, names and proper nouns, and the main idea in headlines, signs, and announcements.

- Periods, commas, and question marks are *Traffic Signs*. Their job is to regulate the speed of readers moving through the text, signaling when to slow down, pause, or stop so readers will understand what they read.

- Exclamation marks are *Excitement Marks*, traffic signs that signal more than a regular stop. They exert more emphasis than a period so there is more to them—a vertical line above a dot.

- Quotation marks are *Conversation Marks*. Quotation marks set off talk by characters in stories or by people in reports and interviews. As conveyors of conversation, they resemble tiny telephone lines in the text.

- Standard spelling is *Book Spelling*. Because few people are 100 percent certain of every word that they spell in their personal writing, especially in English with its extensive and diverse spelling patterns, everyone makes mistakes. We explain to kids that there is kid spelling, adult spelling, and book spelling because everyone is learning standard spelling all of the time.

- Interrogative sentences are *Question-Asking Sentences*. When interrogating someone, you ask questions. But interrogate is not a common word. So when we say interrogative sentence, we also say, a question-asking sentence.
- Acrostic poems are *Word Mysteries* because unbeknown to the audience a word is hiding inside them.

Kid-friendly language works because it redefines standard terms to build a memory of the function or role that each convention plays in written language. It gives children a context for understanding and for recalling the terms as they write or when they encounter them in tests or writing assessments. Teaching "role before rule" builds new ways to look at and to talk about conventions that support children's natural inquisitiveness throughout the learning process.

Acknowledgments

Before we could write a book about children and writing, we had to spend thousands of hours writing with kids in classrooms, workshops, and families. Those kids have been our writing teachers just as we have been theirs, and we stand in awe of the powers of their intellect and creativity. We have filled this book with their words so that other children and adults can be inspired by what they read. Thank you to each and all of them.

We want to thank family members and friends for supporting us through the long process of writing the book with helpful comments, constructive suggestions, and loving support—Flora Edwards, Peg Maloy, Dennis O'Loughlin, Michael and Mary Verock, Bob and Ruth O'Loughlin, Emily Lehtomaki and family, Hope Sisson, Lucy Verock, Leah Mermelstein, Aaron Longo, Andrea Atkins, Monty and Laurie Haas, Cellastine Bailey, Eshu Bumpus, Michelle Cote, Irene LaRoche, Jodi Bornstein, Amy Ryan, Nicole Guttenberg, Kacie McCollum, Sean Warner, Lauren Kosky, Jane Riley, Amy Estes, Linda Fitzgerald, Fran Arena, Mary Ann Binkowski, Jenn Harris, Amy Wolpin, Shelley Bryon, Sue Hunt Apteker, Barbara Russell, the Thibeault family, and the Sweeney family.

We have continued to learn about how to build schools around a vision of success for every child from Patrick Sullivan, Irving Seidman, Kenneth Parker, Atron Gentry, Richard J. Clark, John Coster, Rob Shumer, Mario Cirillo, Kathleen Gagne, David Hart, Tom DelPrete, and Andy Hamilton.

We also wish to thank the following reviewers: Christopher Atang, Anderson College; Robert Infantino, University of San Diego; Jolene C. Martin, Alamo School; Michele E. Menchaca, Highlands Elementary School; Barbara Morgan-Fleming, Texas Tech University; and Sandra Wilde, Portland State University.

Finally, we thank our editor, Aurora Martinez, and her entire team for their assistance and support in guiding this book to publication.

Language

Entering their classroom one ordinary morning, Sharon's students noticed an empty space on the wall where the last letter of the alphabet had normally resided. "Z is missing!" declared Christina. As the children searched the room for Z, they discovered a note that read:

> Dear Friends,
>
> You didn't seem to care,
> If I were here or there.
> So now I'm there, not here.
>
> Signed,
>
> Z

Amazed, intrigued, convinced that Z had left this note for them, everyone voiced an opinion about the mystery. Four girls concluded that Z had gone to sixth grade to join Ms. Harris, last semester's student teacher who was now teaching in the upper grades. One youngster suggested that Z left because it was jealous of the other letters that were more frequently used, like Y, its alphabet neighbor. Giving no clues herself, Sharon read aloud *The Story of Z*, a picture book in which Z, upset at being the last and least-used letter, decides to leave to organize an alphabet of its own.

The next day, the first child in the room looked at the alphabet, dropped her backpack, and declared, "Oh, No! More letters are gone. I wonder if they left a note?" C, K, and N were missing from the alphabet wall. A second note said:

> Dear Friends,
>
> Gone with Z as you can see.
> Too bored to stay, so gone away.
>
>   Signed,
>
>   N, C, K
>
> P.S. Till you put us to use, we're out on the loose.

The next two days, Sharon placed notes in different easy-to-spot places. T, P, and B wrote to the class, "Don't expect us at noon, we won't be back soon." After some of the other remaining consonants left, a note read:

> You can see we're gone, but don't be sad.
> We want to say we're not being bad.
> We're sending you a real live clue.
> So now you know what you'll have to do.

For the kids, the messages became the most highly anticipated feature of the mystery. Everyone wanted to find the hidden note to read aloud at morning meeting. To some extent, most of the children assumed that the letters had actually written these communications. The class, therefore, was part of an evolving puzzle that it was vigorously attempting to solve.

The expanding mystery surrounding the unknown whereabouts of the letters was the context for reading aloud two poetry alphabet books. In *The Disappearing Alphabet*, former Poet Laureate Richard Wilbur imagines what words and names might sound like if certain letters were missing (without the letter "T," you might be eating "shredded whea" for breakfast). *The Sweet and Sour Animal Book* by poet and novelist Langston Hughes features a rhyming poem for each letter of the alphabet. Written during the Harlem Renaissance, the verses remained unpublished for decades before children from the Harlem School for the Arts made paper and clay images to illuminate each poem.

With the excitement of the activity came the need to resolve the mystery of the letters' disappearance. By good fortune, coincidence, or creative assistance (or all three) a resolution as unique and unbelievable as the mystery itself appeared—an unexpected visit by Aaron Longo, the teaching intern from the previous year.

"Do you know where our alphabet went?" queried Mariel, referring to the final note that said "We are sending you a real live clue."

"Yes. It's in Virginia in my classroom," Aaron replied. "The letters said you were not using them enough, so my class is using them for their writing."

Aaron's explanation emphasized the importance of the letters of the alphabet in the children's minds. "A," "B," "C," and the rest were not merely a group of marks on the wall, but the irreplaceable tools and symbols of the English language. With the letters of the alphabet writers build words, and with words they craft sentences to express ideas and share information to readers and listeners.

For children to become confident and competent users of written language, they must acquire a feeling of personal ownership of letters, words, and sentences.

Chapter One: "Language" gives young writers different ways to explore all of these in written communication while accruing literacy knowledge through practice and creative self-expression. As kids write, they experience letters as "my letters," words as "my words," and sentences as "my sentences," each one crucial to making writing become "my writing."

- **WOW 1: Child-Made Alphabets** presents several alphabet learning activities that illustrate how letters represent sounds in English, a key to reading and writing words in the language. As kids create their own alphabets, they learn letter names, letter formation, and the concept of alphabetical order. "Extensions: Inventing the Alphabet" explores the historical origins of alphabets and the reason for their revolutionary impacts on human communication.
- **WOW 2: My Words Abound and Surround** develops reading, writing, and spelling with a strategy called "Key Vocabulary" originated by Sylvia Ashton-Warner. Kids learn about language by writing words that interest them and by collecting them in favorite word folders and child-made dictionaries. "Extensions: Interest Fuels Learning about Spelling" details spelling activities that expand children's knowledge of letter/sound relationships in words.
- **WOW 3: 676 Sentences and Thousands More** introduces a writing game called "676 Sentences" that lets kids compose dozens and dozens of sentences by pairing subjects and verbs from the phrases they create for the letters of the alphabet. "676 Sentences" opens ways to teach the "parts of speech" using the analogy of a movie or television show to demonstrate how different words convey action, emotion, and imagery to readers.

Child-Made Alphabets

Child-Made Alphabets	TEACH	These Conventions *Unconventionally*
Alphabet Learning Activities		Role and purpose of the alphabet
		Alphabetical order
		Letter names
		Letter features and formation
		Left to right reading
		Phonemic awareness
Types of Alphabets		
• Personalized Photo Alphabets		Possessive apostrophes, adjectives
• Alphabet Searches		English syntax
• Alphabet for Nouns, Adjectives,		Description
and Possessive Apostrophes		Parts of speech
• Alphabet for Theme Study		Math, science, social studies, health
Extensions: Inventing the Alphabet		History of the alphabet
		Early writing systems
		Alphabetic writing

The alphabet is an essential building block for reading and writing in the English language. By first grade, children are expected to recite from memory the twenty-six letters from A to Z, to recognize and name them, and to know how to match letters with sounds. These are prerequisites for the appearance of conventionally spelled words arranged in meaningful sentences.

Despite the alphabet's importance, not every youngster easily learns letter names, sounds, and formations. Most preschool and elementary classrooms, and many homes, display a commercial version of the English alphabet. While the alphabet may be "up there" on the wall, it is not always "in there" in the children's minds. Letters and pictures on commercial alphabets are not intrinsically interesting to children. Kids did not choose the items, write the words, illustrate the pictures, or display the poster in the room. Adults did.

Children's interest heightens when they experience creating (or re-creating) the alphabet using their own ideas and images, as Sharon's students did after the letters mysteriously disappeared from the classroom wall. Children learn letter sounds, letter formation, and spelling through involvement and study of the letters. This is why creating an alphabet is an attention-focusing, thought-promoting method for teaching virtually anything about written language.

Alphabet learning investigations can be repeated numerous times during the school year because choosing letters, making illustrations, and examining language conventions changes how children think about the alphabet. Group collaboration and problem solving transform students from passive observers to active linguists, artists, and anthropologists. Children and adults can discover where letter symbols originated, who invented them, and why we are still using these ancient symbols today. The alphabet reveals itself as an organized, purposeful system where letters represent sounds that are blended together to form the words and sentences through which writers communicate, inform, and entertain readers and listeners.

Composing an alphabet is an interest-building way to introduce conventions that children must use in their writing. The familiar structure of the alphabet guides new learning. When kids feel assured that they will learn unfamiliar information with ease, their confidence smoothes the way to quicker success.

Alphabet Learning Activities

Constructing more than one child-designed alphabet throughout the school year maximizes the alphabet's literacy learning power. As two reading specialists observed, children "do not first learn to name the letters and then learn to write them. Instead, naming and writing letters go hand in hand." Making many different kinds of alphabets gives youngsters creative reasons to look at, talk about, and write letters while gaining "knowledge of letter names as well as more sophisticated understandings of the role of letters in reading and writing" (McGee and Richgels 224). In so doing, kids can focus on various conventions: parts of speech, possessive apostrophes, contractions, compound words, and sentence structure.

Ideas and strategies for designing child-made alphabets start with kindergartners and continue through third grade.

Types of Alphabets

Personalized Photo Alphabets

What do five-to-nine-year-olds easily read, repeatedly re-read, and endlessly delight in? Photographs of themselves, things with their names on them, and objects of personal interest like toys, vehicles, dinosaurs, or make-believe characters; these interest-attracting, idea opening, memory-making elements are featured in photo alphabets for beginning readers and writers.

Kindergartners and first graders create photo alphabets with a camera (regular or digital), favorite toys or objects, and a photograph album. Included in these alphabets as kids make choices about illustrations are three conventions:

- Using a possessive apostrophe
- Matching capital and lowercase letters
- Categorizing objects as nouns.

In *Charlie's ABC*, a fine literature connection, author Nona Hatay has created an alphabet book for her son with black and white photos highlighted by her hand coloring. Charlie is photographed with objects that begin with each letter. For a class photo album, children can first choose an item they like and want to be photographed with, or they can pick a letter out of a hat. If they pick a letter out, they then identify objects that could be in the photo. Next, each child paints, colors, or stands next to an upper and lowercase letter as the background for the picture. If Wayne chooses a toy truck, he stands or sits next to capital and lowercase *T* while he holds or pretends to move his truck.

Photographs are versatile. They vary in size, are inexpensively duplicated, and fit into personalized photo albums, making them easy illustrations for different alphabets throughout the school year; for example:

- Recess play: *Chantel and Zachary's snowfort* for *S*
- Classroom performances or parties: *Bruna's lion* for *L*
- Favorite lunches: *Michael's pizza* for *P*
- Daily curricula activities: *Quitze's book* for *B*.

Second graders might begin a school year with noun phrases on their photo alphabet: *Sasha's bright red bicycle* for *B*; *Julio's goalie mask* for *M*; *Quitze's high-bouncing pogo stick* for *P*. Third graders could compose sentences: *Sasha's bright red bicycle has wide wheels; Quitze's favorite toy is his high-bouncing pogo stick; Julio wears his goalie mask at the soccer games.*

Photo alphabets have numerous advantages. Photographs attract children's attention to literacy learning by making them the stars of the activity. A photo alphabet affixed to the wall at a child's eye-level can be changed easily, even seasonally. These alphabets may be displayed throughout the school in a classroom, hallway, bathroom, gym, lunchroom, library, or entranceway. At the end of the school year, individual photos of kids can become part of personal memory books that each one creates and takes home. Photos taken with digital cameras copy easily and economically, so that each student can have her or his own copy of a class-made alphabet.

Alphabets could contain children's own drawings and artwork with the photographs. Eight-year-old Ola composed a combination photo/drawing alphabet book for his four-year-old sister Lily. He illustrated letter *T* by drawing a shark's mouth with large teeth. When Lily found the image too frightening, Ola revised his original drawing, changing the round circle of the mouth and its sharp teeth into a turtle's shell (Figure 1.1). Everyone was pleased, and brother and sister had a book they enjoyed reading together again and again.

Children can illustrate letter posters or pages with brightly colored markers highlighted with sparkle glue and glitter.

A child-made alphabet creates a lively contrast when displayed with a school or district-mandated commercially published alphabet. Looking at the alphabet on the classroom wall one day, Ruth asked her first graders: "Do you think that this is an interesting alphabet? Can we make a more eye-catching version?" The children were eager to try. Each student chose one let-

Figure 1.1
Ola's drawing.

Figure 1.2

Jimmy's "outrageous otter pool."

ter, brainstormed nouns beginning with the letter, listed adjectives to pair with each noun, and produced a poster illustrating and describing his or her letter. For the letter "O," one first grader composed "Jimmy Oliva's outrageous otter pool for the outdoors" (Figure 1.2).

On the completed alphabet, all the words were conventionally spelled and the drawings and text were visible from every angle in the room.

The students were surprised that they could read so many of the words. Ruth, too, was surprised by the attention and interest the children had brought to the process of designing their alphabet and to how often they began using nouns, adjectives, and possessives correctly in their writing thereafter.

Child-made alphabets focus children's learning on conventions they need to know when writing and reading:

- Names are the first word in the phrase or sentence, cueing kids to read from left to right.
- Possessive apostrophe ('s) show ownership (Figure 1.3). Including apostrophes in their alphabet helps kids to recognize the possessive apostrophes in environmental print: "McDonald's," "Wendy's," "Today's Schedule."

Figure 1.3

Chris's example.

- Color, number, and size adjectives are sight words for kindergarten and first grade readers. "Red," "green," "black," "brown," "big," "little," or "one," "two," "three" included in a photo alphabet caption increase children's opportunities to recognize and read these words. In the phrase, *Ryan's little black dog*, color and size adjectives add interest to the noun and increase reading practice.

Alphabet Searches

Second and third graders long to be detectives with magnifying glasses, notebooks, and a mystery to solve. They want to investigate without being noticed, to wonder over the clues they discover, and to experience the thrill of a mystery solved by their sleuthing. Children's interest in unlocking a secret or figuring out an odd occurrence is the power that adults can steer into investigating language conventions via an alphabet search.

A search involves small groups of kids investigating ordinarily overlooked objects (inside or outside of school) to feature on a classroom alphabet. Common objects—walls, lights, signs, windows, doors, and books—are similar to those illustrating the short poems found in *A Helpful Alphabet of Friendly Objects* by John Updike and his son David. This book opens and guides the process of a class alphabet search, from choosing letters to displaying their photos to writing their own descriptive poems.

To begin discovering, photographing/illustrating, and publishing the alphabet, children choose a letter from a hat. In groups of two, three, or four, kids search for objects beginning with the sounds of their letters that may be in front of their eyes, but are unconsciously overlooked. The question they are investigating is "What is hiding in front of our eyes that we could include in our alphabet?"

Before embarking on their investigations, children consider what they have noticed in their surroundings beginning with the letters of all of the search party members. A few letters require more than one object to illustrate its sounds: *G* might be the gym (soft *g* sound) and the grass (hard *g* sound); *c* might be a calendar and a cymbal, or a few cents. Kids may consult dictionaries or alphabet books for ideas of possible items to photograph or illustrate before leaving with paper, pencils, notebooks, or clipboards to stroll through the school building and grounds or the neighborhood to identify persons, places, or things that begin with their letters.

After selecting and photographing objects, students compose their poems individually or collaboratively in different styles—voice, acrostic, picture (see Chapter Three, "Poems"). Then they read their poems aloud to the search team for ideas and revisions. When completed, the poems are printed in book spelling by kids or by computer, and premiered publicly. One team each day reads their poems and displays their photos in front of the class. Thus a few letters are added into the alphabet daily in random order, adding a final small mystery to the activity: "When all of the alphabet is displayed, how will it look?"

Alphabet for Nouns, Adjectives, and Possessive Apostrophes

Kindergartners and first graders do not know that everything around them is a noun, even though they learn letter sounds by associating nouns with letters—*B* is for "bird," "bear," "boy," "block," "butterfly," or "baseball bat." Many alphabet books use clearly identifiable nouns as illustrations for easy reading. It always amazes and pleases youngsters to find out that they can answer the question, "What is a noun?" by naming things around them as they play with and learn about the alphabet.

Adjectives, another unknown term, are constantly employed in kids' conversations. "Loud," "soft," "bigger," "littler," "more," "less" distinguish one thing from another. Through specific descriptions, kids transform generic items into unique objects. A clever opener for explaining "adjectives" is Stan Mack's alphabetical tale, *The King's Cat is Coming*, where every letter is an adjective: The king's cat is "elegant, fat, and gigantic." Equally useful is Carolyn Lester's nonfiction *Spots: Counting Creatures from Sky to Sea* where adjectives describe all kinds of animals with spots.

Food offers an experiential way for teachers to elicit adjectives. Mini-marshmallows, multicolored and white, can be distributed to each child, to inspire responses to questions using the five senses to describe the treat:

- "What do you notice about the marshmallows?" elicits color and size adjectives: "pink," "green," "blue," "white," "large," "small," "big," "little," "tiny," and "regular."
- "How do they smell?" garners descriptive phrases: "sweet like sugar," "like cotton candy," or "like my cereal at breakfast."
- "How do they feel?" receives answers like "soft," "squishy," "gooey," "rubbery," or "airy."
- "How do they sound?" gets responses from "silent," "like nighttime," or "they're sleeping" to "windy" or "whispery."
- "How do they taste?" prompts kids to say "sweet," "delicious," "yummy," "sugary," and "good enough to eat right now."

An interesting and amusing adjective extravaganza is Judi Barrett's book about superlatives, *Things That Are the Most in the World*. Children grin, giggle, and groan at these outlandish descriptions and inventive illustrations, and are inspired to compose their own wacky superlative phrases.

Alphabet for Theme Study

Theme alphabets are an interdisciplinary creative writing idea for elementary school students who are learning to formulate open-ended questions, conduct observations and experiments, get information from books and other sources, and draw well-founded conclusions based on their investigations. Theme alphabets that illustrate a specific topic or unit link the learning of language to the required science, mathematics, and social studies curriculum.

Any part of the curriculum might be used for a theme alphabet to highlight key terms and concepts that students must learn for local and state tests. In constructing a theme alphabet young writers get to

- Show what they know about a topic or area of study based on their in-school learning and out-of-school observations.
- Display information they find intrinsically interesting so that it is likely to arouse everyone's interest in learning more.

Teachers can choose to make a theme alphabet with a class early in the year to open up an area of study, in the middle to expand on what has already been learned, or toward the end as a form of test preparation and review.

Sharon chose her district's "Earth Changes" second grade science unit for a theme alphabet. In New England, with its four distinct seasons and often wildly changing weather patterns, "Earth Changes" is a fascinating year-long process of investigation and discovery. The children learn how the tilt of the earth toward the North Star causes seasonal change, how day and night happens as the earth spins on its axis every twenty-four hours, how the earth orbits around the sun every 365 and one-quarter days, and much more information about the characteristics of winter, spring, summer, and fall (see WOW 19 for more on seasonal change). To begin writing an "Earth Changes" alphabet, Sharon listed a group of key concepts and test vocabulary she wanted to review and reinforce in the children's minds. The children then chose one or two terms to research and illustrate for the alphabet.

EXTENSIONS

Inventing the Alphabet

As children build literacy by learning to write and read, they are recreating the same processes that people all over the world have done for thousands of years ever since the first marks appeared on the walls of caves. The purpose of writing is to communicate with others using a system of symbols called language (Goodman 12). Broadly speaking, language includes the parallel processes of writing and reading/speaking and listening. As children engage in early literacy learning, they are doing what our ancient ancestors did when they invented and sustained oral languages.

Every human society uses some form of oral language to express sounds that convey meaning to listeners. When the same sounds are used over and over again to mean the same thing, the pattern develops into amazingly rich and complicated communication systems. Worldwide, people speak some 6,800 languages, although due to the effects of war, famine, and genocide, linguists estimate that 50 percent to 90 percent of all languages could become extinct in the next hundred years.

The evolution of spoken languages into written languages can be traced back nearly five thousand years. As the size and complexity of those early human societies increased, oral forms of communication became limiting. People needed ways to relay information beyond face-to-face interactions. Goodman (14) notes that drum signals, yodeling, blowing air into rams' horns or conch shells, ringing bells, or whistling extended the range of human oral communication across physical distances. A person did not have to be standing next to the communicator to receive and understand the message. Many of these ancient forms are with us today as bells call the faithful to worship or a foghorn warns ships of impending danger.

Anthropologists now date early writing systems back to 3400 B.C. when Mesopotamians, needing ways to keep track of trade records, "started marking symbols for numbers and items in clay tablets," a system of writing called "cuneiform" that rapidly spread throughout the Middle East (Samoyault 4). Soon thereafter, Babylonian and Assyrian societies developed "written correspondence, a postal service, and even clay envelopes" as well as one of the earliest recorded literary text, *Epic of Gilgamesh*.

Writing systems developed in other parts of the world with

- The Harappan people in the Indus Valley of India (2800 to 1900 B.C.) and in China (1200 B.C. to present).
- Ancient Egyptians (3200 B.C. to A.D. 394), who used hieroglyphics that combined pictorial and sound signs to create new words. To communicate a message, writers combined one hieroglyph with another; for example, pictorial representations of a bee and leaf would come together to create the word "beeleaf" or "belief" (Der Manuelian 1991). Hieroglyphs were written on long sheets of papyrus left to right (as in English), right to left (as in Hebrew and Arabic) or top to bottom (as in Chinese).
- The Maya of southern Mexico (A.D. 250 to 900) recorded key mathematical and astronomical information using glyphs on bark and stones, although their written language included some phonetic signs as well.

Recent discoveries of carvings on stone walls at Wadi el-Hol, a site in the Egyptian desert north of the Valley of Kings, suggest that the first alphabet appeared there between 1900 and 1800 B.C. (Wilford 10). Some 300 years later, around 1500 B.C., an alphabet was used in Ugarit, an ancient port city on the Euphrates River in what is now modern-day Syria. Traders who came to Ugarit from all over the Middle Eastern and Mediterranean worlds found it difficult to exchange goods and materials using pictorial writing systems where many different symbols represented words.

The early Middle Eastern writing systems used signs or pictures to represent words, a form called "ideograms." To create less complicated ways of using and recording information, the Ugaritarians, and later the Phoenicians, created "symbols that represented the *sounds* in their words. When put together and sounded out, the symbols created the sound of the word in the spoken language" (Samoyault 1).

Connecting letters to sounds through an alphabet prompted a communication revolution throughout the globe. Many more words could be easily created and used. A writer or reader need only know the sounds rather than try to remember hundreds of symbols for an entire message.

Over the past 4,000 years, different cultures have constructed different alphabetical systems. At first, alphabets contained only consonants as Arabic and Hebrew still do today. The Greeks were the first to include both vowels and consonants. During the Roman Empire, new letters and new sounds were added to Latin that became the basis for many words in English. Eventually, most world alphabets connected vowels and consonants in different ways to produce more sounds. Some Japanese and Indian alphabets, for example, are "syllabic" (consonant and vowel sounds together) while English and modern Cyrillic (used in Russia and parts of southeastern Europe) represent vowels as sounds in words.

Abstract Alphabet: A Book of Animals by Paul Cox is a visual puzzle that engages kids in thinking what the alphabet would be like if symbols represented objects. Readers of the book must match the different shaped and colored figures with a list of letters to decode the animal described on each page. Memorizing the symbols instead of the letters seems an enormous task, but it would be a far larger task if English letters did not have sound/symbol associations connected to them.

Young Writers' Bookshelf for Alphabets

Jambo Means Hello: A Swahili Alphabet Book. Muriel L. Feelings. Illustrated by Tom Feelings. Dial Books for Young Readers, 1992. This award-winning alphabet book introduces children to African scenes and teaches Swahili words for every letter.

Gathering the Sun: An Alphabet in Spanish and English. Alma Flor Ada. Illustrations by Simon Silva. Translated by Rosa Zubizarreta. Lothrop, Lee & Shepard Books, 1997. Honoring Mexican migrant farm workers who annually harvest the crops, every letter has a lavish illustration and a short poem in Spanish and English that explains or describes food, places, and people.

I Spy: An Alphabet in Art. Devised and selected by Lucy Micklethwait. Mulberry Books, 1992. Objects that begin with the letters of the alphabet are found in paintings by Pablo Picasso, John Singer Sargent, Francisco Goya, and other artists.

Tomorrow's Alphabet. George Shannon. Illustrations by Donald Crews. Scholastic, 1999. Instead of pairing letters of the alphabet with words that begin with that letter, this book uniquely refocuses the perspective: "B is for eggs—tomorrow's birds."

The Alternative Alphabet Poster for Little and Big People published by the Syracuse Cultural Workers powerfully presents the themes of freedom and equality in a large poster-size visual display. The letter *R*, for example, features the words *recycle, reduce, re-use,* Paul Robeson, *read, revolution, roots, river, rain-*

bow, and Ray. Diverse people and key concepts from United States and world history inform every letter.

The Rebellious Alphabet. Jorge Diaz. Illustrated by Oivind S. Jorfald and Ivind Jorfald. Henry Holt, 1993. When an illiterate general gives orders to destroy all reading and writing, a word lover creates a clever way to give print back to the townspeople.

Books Cited in the Text

The Story of Z. Jeanne Modesitt. Illustrated by Lonni Sue Johnson. Simon and Schuster, 1990.

The Disappearing Alphabet. Richard Wilbur. Illustrated by David Diaz. Voyager Books, 2001.

The Sweet and Sour Animal Book. Langston Hughes and Harlem School of the Arts. Oxford University Press, 1997.

A Helpful Alphabet of Friendly Objects. John Updike. Photographs by David Updike. Alfred A. Knopf, 1998.

The King's Cat is Coming. Stan Mack. Random Library, 1976.

Spots: Counting Creatures from Sky to Sea. Carolyn Lesser. Harcourt Brace, 1999.

Things That Are the Most in the World. Judi Barrett. Illustrated by John Nickle. Atheneum, 1998.

Abstract Alphabet: A Book of Animals. Paul Cox. Chronicle Books, 2001.

WOW 2

My Words Abound and Surround

"My Words"	TEACH	These Conventions *Unconventionally*
Collecting "My Words"		Sylvia Ashton-Warner's "key vocabulary"
		Vocabulary building
		Letter formation
		Reading left to right
Becoming a Language Detective		Words convey meaning
		Sound/Symbol relationships
		Word building patterns
		Phonemic awareness
Extensions: Interest Fuels Learning about How Words Are Spelled		Spelling knowledge
		Interest, observation, and effort
		Encoding and decoding

*A*lphabet Soup by Kate Banks is the story of a young boy and a helpful bear who discover the power of words through a series of amazing adventures with narrow escapes. The action begins as the boy reluctantly sits down to lunch. Annoyed with his mother, he spells b-e-a-r with the letters in his soup. Unexpectedly his word comes alive, and he is face-to-face with a large friendly bear who invites him on an exciting journey. In their travels, the new companions encounter a fierce ogre, a lake too wide to swim across, a wave that capsizes their boat, and a loud thunderstorm. At each new problem, spelling a word creates a solution as when h-o-u-s-e provides them with a warm and cozy shelter from the rain. Words, the boy and the bear learn, create predicaments but solve them, too.

"My Words," a year-long language study, is introduced by this tale. Its goal is for children in kindergarten through grade three to investigate the meaning of words, to learn spelling patterns, to practice recognizing sound chunks or small words inside bigger words, and to use a dictionary and thesaurus easily. Our inspiration for "My Words" derives from the literacy work of renowned educator and philosopher Sylvia Ashton-Warner as described in *Teacher* (1986), a book about the innovative methods she developed to instruct New Zealand Maori children to read and write.

"My Words" releases the enormous powers of children's self-chosen words to describe, delight, convey, convince, report, and reward through writing and reading. Ashton-Warner (32) called self-chosen words "key vocabulary" because they come from children's own interests and emotions. In her view, every child has "two visions, the inner and the outer" and "of the two the inner vision is brighter," meaning that viewing from the outside involves seeing through other people's eyes while viewing from the inside means feeling through one's own emotions. The words that adults choose for children to learn to read and spell "can be meaningful and delightful." But it is children's own expressions "that have the power and the light" to propel a youngster's desire to read and write.

Young children, Ashton-Warner observed (33, 44), have inclinations toward "destructiveness" and "creativeness" and as the creative expands, the destructive declines. In the development of a child's personality, words "are no less than the captions of the dynamic life itself, they course out through the creative channel, making their contribution to the drying up of the destructive vent." Key vocabulary unites children's outer and inner visions of learning in intensely personal ways. In teaching, "no time is too long spent talking to a child to find out his key words, the key that unlocks himself, for in them is the secret of reading, the realisation that words can have intense meaning."

Our introduction to "My Words" is designed to activate children's curiosity about language. We distribute empty 8′ × 10′ mailing envelopes to kids. To contrast the pristine, unadorned envelope with what it will become, Sharon explains, "You are holding a treasure chest in your hands."

"Treasure chests?" the kids ask in astonishment, peering inside or flipping these bland receptacles to see if they missed something on the other side. "How can this be a treasure chest?"

"It does not look like one because nothing valuable is inside, but it soon will be," Sharon assures them. "Once you fill it, it becomes a door to your imagination, which will be more valuable to you than a pot of gold. You spend gold and it's gone. What you put in your envelope you can use over and over again—a million billion times! It's always ready for you to open and find something new."

"Your treasure will be different from everyone else's and it will amaze you every time you use it. It will give you a way to become whatever you would like to be: teeny, huge, invisible, funny, a queen, a bunny, a bird, a dinosaur. Your envelope is like having a magic lamp!"

"What are we putting in this?" someone inquires wonderingly.

"Words and pictures!" Your own words and pictures!" replies Sharon.

Looks of disbelief abound in the room. Words are more precious than gold and also have magic powers? "You will be amazed by the power your own words give you," Sharon tells the students. "Words can be as powerful for you as they were for boy and bear in *Alphabet Soup*."

The children remain unconvinced:

"Our words can't come to life like that!"

"That's a story. It's not real!"

"How can they be as powerful?"

"Words have more power than anyone truly understands," replies Sharon. "You will find out as you use them."

"You want to collect important words: Big, little, funny, sad, wonderful, scary, and magical words. Let's start. I can't wait to discover what your words are and to tell you mine."

"You have words, too?" the children ask.

"Everyone does," answers Sharon, waving her envelope in the air, "but the power of words comes from what you do with them and the adventures they create. That's why they are a treasure."

Collecting "My Words"

When children are just beginning to learn how to read, "My Words" propels learning sight words, spelling, and correct formation of letters. Self-chosen words promote excitement about learning letter sounds, identifying small words hiding inside bigger words, reading from left to right, counting syllables, recognizing rhyming words, and recalling spelling patterns.

Selections from Seven-Year-Olds' "My Words" Folders

banana	tarantula	tiger
helicopter	monster truck	motorcycle
scorpion	calf	diamonds
kitten	pumpkin	continental shelf
jack-o-lantern	unicorn	world
rainbow	Disney	wizard
books	September	bucket
jewelry	princess	unicorn

"My Words" works best as a regular literacy learning activity. Initially, it is necessary to do "My Words" at least three times a week while the children fill a folder with their choices. This schedule can increase or decrease as time allows, but once begun, children expect and await this language activity. Kids can add to their collection of words while working with a teacher or on their own whenever new terms, favorite phrases, and wonderful word creations appear in books or conversations.

Besides manila folders, the materials needed for "My Words" include

- Paper—scrap, copy, white art paper or cardstock, lined or unlined and cut into different lengths for small (2–4 letters), medium (5–7 letters), and large (8–12 letters) words.
- Markers, colored pencils, or colored pens draw children's attention to the word structure.
- A paper dictionary for each child.
- An electronic "talking" dictionary as part of a collection of dictionaries, pictionaries, and word books for classroom or home use.
- Write-on/wipe-off boards with pens and erasers (or chalkboard with colored chalk and erasers).
- A basket, box, or container for collecting children's words before each child stores a new word in a personal envelope.
- A "Treasury" display of children's words listed alphabetically or categorized as parts of speech.

Because each child needs individual attention when choosing words, "My Words" is easier to accomplish with small groups of children. Sharon divides her class in half. While one half works on math, drawing, computers, and blocks for fifty minutes, Sharon divides the other half in half again, making two groups of four to six children. One of these small groups does "My Words" with her while the other group reads aloud to one another, practices spelling, plays word games, or writes. After completing "My Words" with the first small group, those kids read aloud, spell, and write while Sharon does "My Words" with the other small group. At mid-morning, she switches the activities and repeats the schedule with the other half of the class.

Sharon's introduction to "My Words" is similar to Sylvia Ashton-Warner's explanation that everyone has words he or she thinks are special or important. These are the words people want to read and to spell. They are different words for different people; we do not all choose the same words.

After the first few times of doing "My Words," kids are familiar with the process and often arrive with a word in mind. It is essential that children freely choose whatever word they want. As Ashton-Warner (33) observed, "pleasant words won't do, respectable words won't do. They must be words organically tied up, organically born from the dynamic life itself. They must be words that are already part of the child's being." Initially, this may mean words from computer games, everyday slang, or TV entertainment.

To the children in her small group, Sharon inquires, "Who has a word?" As kids voice their choice, Sharon writes one word on the write-on/wipe-off easel for everyone to see. Then the children announce whatever they recognize in their classmate's word:

- the beginning sound(s)
- little words hiding inside the words (no, up, it, is, if, on, at, out, end)
- chunks of sounds: *er*, *th*, *ch*, *or*, *ing*, *un*
- *s* or *y* at the end of the word

Sharon points out anything that is unrecognized or that she wants to teach. Then children choose one word from their envelopes to pair with this word. While Sharon records the new word on a piece of paper for the child requesting it, the others create phrases to read aloud with their words and the new word.

If little words or sound chunks are inside a child's word, Sharon records them in different colors. For the word *train*, Sharon writes *t* in brown, *rain* in red, and uses purple to underline *in*. "You've got four words in one!" she exclaims, folding and bending the paper strip to reveal the little words in *train*—*a*, *in*, *rain*—and then unbending it to display the entire word.

Next, the other members of the group hold up their words to the left or the right of the new word to show some interesting combinations and phrases they have made. *Train* might be joined with *rocket* to create *rocket train* or *train rocket*. The word *umbrella* might be added to form *rocket train umbrella* or *umbrella train rocket*. The phrase expands as each child's word is added to what is already on display.

These child-created phrases draw surprise and laughter about the interesting, comical, or nonsensical combinations that occur when other children place their words to the left or right of a new word. Rearranging the order of the words lets everyone hear and see how a phrase sounds with small changes. Meanwhile, left to right reading practice is occurring and spelling knowledge is accruing while the group plays with different word combinations.

Other language lessons that accompany the writing of children's words include:

- Noting whether a capital or lowercase letter begins the word. Proper nouns naming a specific person, place, or thing always capitalize the first letter. Discussing capitalization is a powerful daily reminder of the rule and its role.

- To model the formation of letters, first in manuscript, and later in cursive, Sharon combines visual and oral cues to build children's memories of correct formation. For *m* in manuscript, she sings or says, "Move your pencil down, up and over, up and over" as she writes the letter while the student observes. For *m* in cursive, she sings or says "slope up, down, up, down, up, down, done," while forming the letter. Then, Sharon holds the child's writing hand and uses the forefinger to trace over the letters while saying cues for forming it. When tracing is finished, the child spells and reads the word aloud. Either the word is deposited into a container for later read aloud to the whole class (before children put their words into their envelopes) or it is written in a personal dictionary and then added to the child's word envelope.

To build lasting interest in learning words, kids must begin the process with their own word selections, even if some of these are unfamiliar to adults. When children ask, Sharon writes words they do not know how to spell even if she has not heard them before (as in the names of characters from video games or cartoons). Writing the requested words produces a bond between adult and child that would not exist if Sharon had discarded the words because she did not recognize or know how to spell them conventionally.

"Will you go home and write these words and bring them to school so *I* can see how they are spelled?" Sharon asks. After writing words they find personally interesting, children begin building connections to words in books or on school vocabulary lists. In this way, terms like "evaporation," "percent," or "ancient" become choices in "My Words."

In our experience, children have not requested inappropriate words such as swears, bathroom functions, insults, or hate words. If anyone did, Sharon would explain that words have the power to embarrass, frighten, or anger people. Words need to be considered thoughtfully since all of us may read and spell everyone else's words. Causing discomfort with words, intentionally or unintentionally, is never the purpose of "My Words."

Becoming a Language Detective

Adults and children read words differently, as in the following story:

> After finishing morning snack at a fast food restaurant, Sharon and her four-year-old nephew, Ryan, cleared their table, gathering leftover paper plates and cups to empty in a nearby wastebasket.
>
> Pointing to the words on the container's swinging top, Sharon said: "This says 'Thank You'."
>
> "No it doesn't!" declared Ryan emphatically. "It says Trash Can!"

Children, astute observers and thinkers, learn quickly that symbols make letters, letters make words, and words make sense. Ryan's purposeful interpretation of the words on the lid reveals his emerging literacy knowledge and skills as a reader and writer. In the context of print on a container for garbage, "Trash Can" makes sense. "Thank You" does not.

Words, the building blocks of language learning and meaning making, unite singular letters of the alphabet to form our system of written language. As they enter school, most children, like Ryan, stand poised to gain full entry into an ever-expanding universe of written language. From their experiences as members of a print and symbol-filled society, youngsters already know a tremendous amount about the purpose and appearance of written words.

Investigating words together enables adults to employ a kid-focusing way to advance the development of young children's literacy knowledge. Kids are intensely interested in discovering how words look when they represent something a kid is interested in or wants to know. Whether it is dinosaurs, jewelry, foods, toys, or sports, youngsters have words they really want to learn. Moreover, they want to write those words so that other people can read and understand them, as teachers and parents know after hearing "How do you spell . . . ?" from kids.

Every word in a "My Words" envelope can be a focus of study by children and adults working as team of language detectives. Investigating words serves as a personally meaningful way to explore word building patterns and recognize phonemic sound/symbol relationships as in the following story of two language detectives in action.

When Ruth and first grader Sam teamed up one day, the boy chose *book* as his word. Ruth wrote it on a paper strip and invited Sam to think of other words he knew that sounded like "book." Sam said "look," "took," and "cook." As he said each word, Ruth made it appear by folding the paper to cover the *b* so each new letter could be attached to *ook* to reveal the new words. The one-word paper now held four words with the addition of the three new initial letters: *l*, *t*, and *c*.

The discovery of this rhyming pattern is a huge "ah-ha" moment for beginning readers who now realize they know how to read and spell many more words than they previously thought. By learning to look beyond the first letter to see the other letter combinations, kids discover how common sound chunks make many words. For example, in *jump*, the power pattern is *ump*. Knowing that pattern makes it easier to recognize and spell *bump*, *lump*, and *dump*.

When Sam proposed "wook" as a word, he and Ruth discussed how *w* and *ook* do not form a conventional word, but by changing just one letter the common word *work* appears. Then, Sam found *boo* hiding in *book*. Ruth covered the *k* to show *boo* as part of *book* even though people do not say *booo-k* when pronouncing the word.

The following day, Sam chose *mummy*, which led to the rhyming word *dummy*. This caused him to ask about *dumb* and then *Dumbo*. In so doing, Sam brought to attention the silent letter *b*, one of the spelling anomalies of English. A silent *b* also appears in *climb* and *comb*. English has many such unusual features in its word structures, one reason why learning words is so interesting. *Dumbo* pronounces the sound of *b* with the addition of *o* at the end of the word. Letters are sometimes silent and sometimes heard, depending on the other letters around them. Word detectives discover these patterns.

Adults often assume that child-generated words will contain too many disconnected patterns for kids to remember at one time. While this is sometimes the case, many times it is not. "My Words" brings the power of curiosity and novelty to the study of words; kids remember what interests them. Combinations like *mummy*, *dummy*, *dumb*, and *Dumbo* may not appear in a language arts workbook or spelling list, but as Sam and Ruth demonstrated, unique and unexpected learning occurs when children and adults create interest-building language lessons together.

Learning about the words that interest them are opportunities for youngsters to show everyone what they know about spelling. When Sam sees the name "Dumbo" on television or in a book, he will point out what he now knows about its spelling. An adult could extend his knowledge with an advertisement for "combo" sandwiches at *Subway* to introduce another example of the same rule. Removing the *o* from *combo* reveals *comb* with a silent *b* at the end.

Writing "My Words" on paper strips enables adults to add, subtract, and change letters quickly, transforming one word into many and making word study engrossing. Every choice a child request directs word study in many directions:

- Switching beginning letters makes rhymes: *ake—cake*, *shake*, *flake*.
- Changing a vowel makes the word sound different: *ike/like*, *ake/lake*.
- Finding little words inside bigger words as *in* and *side* make *inside* or *pump*, *in*, *kin* make *pumpkin*, helps make "sounding out" words a word recognition strategy.
- Identifying sound chunks such as *at, am, it, an, up, ing, er, ar, or,* and *all* make spelling bigger words easier: *ring*, *has*, *hat*, *art*, *her*.
- Adding letters to the ends makes plurals or variations: *make/making*, *like/liked*, *mom/mommy*.
- Recognizing silent letters helps word pronunciation: *knock*, *climb*, *block*, *gauge*.
- Defining unknown words or prefixes increases vocabulary for speaking and writing: the word *kin* in *pumpkin* when by itself means family members and relatives.

Baloney, Henry P. by the innovative author/illustrator team of Jon Scieszka and Lane Smith is a surprising opener for language detective activities with second and third graders. Framed as a transmission from another planet in outer space, the story begins with a young boy explaining to his teacher why he is late for class again. Henry's story is a tall tale misadventure, and in telling it to Miss Bugscuffle, he uses 20 words from different Earth languages ("deski," Swahili for "desk"; "uyarak," Inuktitut for "stone"). To figure out the meaning of these unfamiliar words, readers must be language detectives, deducing from the wonderfully expressive illustrations and the rest of the English language text what each word means or "look them up" in the dictionary decoder in the back of the book.

EXTENSIONS

Interest Fuels Learning about How Words Are Spelled

Preparing for a trip to the supermarket, Sharon asked her five-year-old nephew Kyle to write a list of what he wanted her to buy. Needing a battery for his remote control monster truck, Kyle asked, "How do you spell battery?"

"Write it the way you think it is spelled, like you do in your stories," Sharon replied.

"That's for pretend. This is for real!" objected Kyle, declaring in no uncertain terms the knowledge that he had accrued about spelling—when you want someone to understand your message without any doubt, conventional spelling is significant.

Children want to know how to spell words conventionally when the words mean something to them personally. For Kyle, the spelling of "battery" was very important, for without one, his toy truck would not run. This is why he feared that his invented spelling might not be read accurately when Sharon got to the store. Then his battery would not be purchased.

Learning to spell involves learning how to crack the different codes of the English language patterns. To do this successfully, kids need both decoding and encoding practice. Decoding is what we do when we read a book; we interpret the code of letters and words to derive meaning from the text. Encoding is what we do when we write words on paper. It makes sense that children get better at reading (decoding) by writing (encoding). Learning to read one's own writing gives kids a personally meaningful way to practice the skills readers need to understand written text.

Decoding and encoding involves phonemic awareness about the English language:

- There is a phonemic code matching sounds to letters.
- The phonemic code changes with combinations of letters (*th* says something different than *t* or *h*).
- Some words have multiple spellings to differentiate meanings (*to, too, two/there, their, they're/I'd, eyed*).
- Words with non-phonemic English spelling patterns have been incorporated from other languages: **phonemes**, **night**, **knock**, **tortilla**, **pizza**.
- Adding endings (*s, es, ing, ed*) changes spellings of some words.

To remember and correctly use the assorted rules and tools for spellings, kids need what Kyle and Sylvia Ashton-Warner's Maori students possessed—interest in words. Interest fuels observation and effort. The combination of interest, observation, and effort propel and support children's learning to spell conventionally. By *interest,* we mean a child's personal involvement and desire to learn. **Observation** refers to seeing, hearing, reading, and writing language repeatedly in all kinds of situations. **Effort** is another term for repeated practice. Of the three, interest is the one that fuels the others to expand and build competence in spelling throughout a lifetime of writing and reading.

Interest, observation, and effort are present whenever young children read and study words to increase their knowledge of language. Standing in the cafeteria line one day, a first-grade boy glanced at the word "lunch" on the daily menu sign and remarked, "So that's how it's spelled." He wanted to check his own spelling and his interest spurred his observation and effort.

Spelling begins with children constructing personal systems of encoding. What adults call spelling "**errors**" are actually children's efforts to make sense and to use what they have learned about written language. As they proceed through school, children's spelling becomes more and more conventional especially through occasions to use written language in real situations. It takes years of practice to spell more and more words conventionally.

Words spelled irregularly and inconsistently increase the difficulty for a reader trying to make sense of a text. Writing words accurately and consistently is essential for writers who want to clearly communicate their messages to readers. As kids gain knowledge about language, successful decoding and encoding requires readable spelling. Adults have a vital role to play in helping children to learn "conventional spellings," understand "common spelling patterns," and develop "strategies for changing temporary spellings to conventional spellings in final drafts" (Weaver 67).

When "My Words" is included as a daily activity, spelling becomes a lively, energizing study that kids find enlightening and worth their attention. Learning the spelling of words is not only desirable, it is a topic of daily conversation among kids who are expanding their use of words to communicate with readers and listeners.

YOUNG WRITERS' BOOKSHELF FOR MY WORDS ABOUND AND SURROUND

Eye Spy: A Mysterious Alphabet. Linda Bourke. Chronicle Books, 1991. Readers see four picture puzzles for each letter of the alphabet to discover two words that sound the same but have different meanings.

*Baby Buggy * Buggy Baby*. Harriet Ziefert. Illustrated by Richard Brown. Houghton Mifflin, 1997. Lift the flaps of this delightfully framed book and explore amusing phrases and words with multiple meanings. Also see *Night * Knight* by the same author, offering a lift-the-flaps look at many common homonyms.

The Circus of Words: Acrobatic Anagrams, Parading Palindromes, Wonderful Words on a Wire, and More Lively Letter Play. Richard Lederer. Illustrated by Dave Morice. Chicago Review Press, 2001.

*There's an Ant in **Ant**hony*. Bernard Most. Mulberry Books, 1992. Every time Anthony finds a word with the letters "a-n-t" inside it, as in his name, he puts *ant* in a collecting jar.

Can You Find It? Bernard Most. Harcourt Brace, 1993. Colorful pictures and spelling patterns ask you to find *it* in our daily activities.

Opposites, More Opposites and a Few Differences. Richard Wilbur. Harcourt Brace, 2000. Words and their opposites appear in short, humorous verses.

Taxi: A Book of City Words. Betsy Maestro. Illustrated by Giulio Maestro. Clarion Books, 1990. Wide-angle illustrations add wonderful imagery to this book of words found in cities.

Frindle. Andrew Clements. Illustrated by Brian Selznick. Aladdin Paperbacks, 1998. When fifth grader Nick decides to create a new word for "pen," he starts a trend among his classmates, faces an argument from his teacher about the dictionary, and ultimately learns how words' meanings are determined.

Martha Speaks. Susan Meddaugh. Houghton Mifflin, 1995. When a dog named Martha eats alphabet soup, the letters go to her brain instead of her stomach, making it possible for her to talk. See other books in the *Martha, The Talking Dog* series, including *Martha Calling*; *Martha Blah Blah* (1996); *Martha Walks the Dog* (1998).

Miss Alaineus: A Vocabulary Disaster. Debra Frasier. Harcourt Brace, 2000. A fifth-grade girl's homework assignment first turns into an embarrassing mistake and then a winningly creative idea—all from her misunderstanding of a vocabulary word.

676 Sentences and Thousands More

676 Sentences	TEACH	These Conventions *Unconventionally*
676 Sentences Revealed		Parts of sentences Subject and predicate Sentence structure
Extensions: Lights, Camera, Grammar: A Whole Look at the Parts of Speech		Sentence construction Parts of speech • Nouns, verbs, adjectives, adverbs, pronouns, prepositions, interjections, and conjunctions

When does 26 and 26 not equal 52?

Would the answer 676 seem possible or impossible?

This surprising answer is revealed when kids compose twenty-six subjects and twenty-six predicates for their own sentences—one for each letter of a child-made alphabet.

A sentence, by definition, is a group of words that communicates a thought using grammatically complete language. Writer Patricia T. O'Connor (87) likens a sentence to a superhighway, "a triumph of engineering: the stately capital letter, the procession of words in their proper order, every arch and tunnel, bridge and buttress perfectly fitted to its job."

To be a sentence, either a single word or a group of words must have two parts—a subject ("who or what is doing the action") and a verb or a predicate (to "show action or a state of being"). Groups of words that lack either a subject or predicate are not sentences, but sentence fragments, acceptable in oral communication but considered incorrect in most written language.

Amazingly, sentences in English appear in all shapes, sizes, and lengths. With an infinite number of possible sentence constructions available, young writers need to learn how to compose sentences that readers can easily understand and appreciate. Crafting interesting, varied sentences occurs as much during revising as during drafting, so sentence construction is often sentence reconstruction. In a writing process fit for a child, we want youngsters to write their ideas and read them for meaning to structure sentences for clarity, style, and purpose. To introduce this idea, and to help writers recognize the difference between phrases and sentences, kids compose 676 sentences for a classroom alphabet, an activity that produces astonishing results every time.

676 Sentences Revealed

Imagine displaying two rows of 12″ × 18″ white construction paper, twenty-six sheets in each row, top sheets directly above bottom sheets, somewhere in a classroom. Top and bottom papers, although not connected, touch each other, making an optical illusion of 12″ × 36″ posters on display. The posters are arranged so they can be easily switched around from their original positions—either by fastening them onto two cords with clothespins or by attaching them to the wall using tape or velcro.

The top row displays subjects of sentences; the bottom row displays predicates of sentences. The top features a possessive apostrophe ('s) on each child's name to designate ownership, a noun communicating the letter's sound, and adjectives describing the noun. The bottom shows a verb or action phrase that forms a predicate, adverbs describing the verb, and a period or exclamation point punctuating the end of the sentence.

Combining the top and bottom sheets of each letter creates twenty-six sentences, written and illustrated by the class members. The list below shows subject/predicate posters composed for the letters *B*, *R*, *T*, and *W* by children in Sharon's room (Figure 1.4 is an original text example).

Children's Subject and Predicate Posters

Bb	Rr	Tt	Ww
A'Kieli's yellow school bus	Gabrielle's colorful bright over the clouds rainbow	Marco's rainbow haired tiger	Izzy's high blue watery waterfall
goes bump, bump, bump, bump, bump every second on the way home to his grandmother's house.	rises in the glorious baby blue and white sky.	gobbles hamburgers with macaroni and cheese inside them.	rushes swiftly down the huge bumpy rocks.

Read together, subject and predicate posters make sentences:

- A'Kieli's yellow school bus goes bump, bump, bump, bump, bump every second on the way home to his grandmother's house.
- Gabrielle's colorful bright over the clouds rainbow rises in the glorious baby blue and white sky.
- Marco's rainbow haired tiger gobbles hamburgers with macaroni and cheese inside them.
- Izzy's high blue watery waterfall rushes swiftly down the huge bumpy rocks.

These sentences show that one solution to the riddle "When do 26 and 26 not equal 52?" is "When 26 halves and 26 halves make 26 wholes!"

But this answer to the riddle is incomplete until someone realizes that the 26 tops and the 26 bottoms can be reassembled to create 676 different sentences (26 × 26 = 676). This fact amazes kids—hundreds of sentences, sensible, funny, or ridiculous, all constructed from the 26 tops and 26 bottoms they created together!

Kids are intrigued by the possibilities of combining top posters with bottom posters to compose sentences. While enjoying humor associated with language play, they practice the essential elements of sentence construction—noun with verb or subject and predicate. When A'Kieli pairs his subject with other predicates, the following sentences emerge:

- A'Kieli's yellow school bus rises in the glorious baby blue and white sky.
- A'Kieli's yellow school bus rushes swiftly down the huge bumpy rocks.
- A'Kieli's yellow school bus gobbles hamburgers with macaroni and cheese inside them.

Figure 1.4

A'Kieli's subject and predicate poster.

Lest you think the possibilities of mixing twenty-six tops and bottoms is quickly completed, kids can add more descriptive language to the tops or to the bottoms to compose more complex sentences. In the following examples, youngsters use adjectives, adverbs, and even dialogue to expand the subject or the predicate of the sentence (Figure 1.5 is a child-written example).

Children's Expanded Subject and Predicate Posters

Bb	Gg	Kk	Mm
Katherine's soaring, gliding, breathtaking brilliant baby butterfly	Rachel's brown fuzzy gorilla	Jacob's furry golden bashful kitten	Allie's huge bunch of beautiful mermaids with green hair and green tails and purple lipstick with brown eyes
flutters and mutters "I am the most beautiful silvery blue winged butterfly on this earth."	swings through the air as fast as a cheetah on a beautiful vine with red speckled roses that were just blooming.	plays with a ball of yarn, throwing the ball in the air and catching it with its paws.	sit on silver rocks.

Figure 1.5

Jacob's expanded subject and predicate poster.

Expressed as sentences, these expanded descriptions read as follows:

- Katherine's soaring, gliding, breathtaking brilliant baby butterfly flutters and mutters, "I am the most beautiful silvery blue winged butterfly on this earth."
- Rachel's brown fuzzy gorilla swings through the air as fast as a cheetah on a beautiful vine with red speckled roses that were just blooming.
- Jacob's furry golden bashful kitten plays with a ball of yarn, throwing the ball in the air and catching it with its paws.
- Allie's huge bunch of beautiful mermaids with green hair and green tails and purple lipstick with brown eyes sit on silver rocks.

The purpose of a 676-sentence alphabet is to extend wordplay to sentence play, interesting and involving kids in considering how words work together to communicate a thought, idea, emotion, or action. If children connect a subject with two different predicates or two subjects with one predicate to make new versions of their original sentences, 676 becomes a low number of possible sentence constructions!

Ruth Heller's picture books about the parts of speech are resources of ideas and information for making and remaking 676-sentence alphabets throughout the year. Appreciating the lavish color illustrations in *Merry-Go-Round: A Book About Nouns*, kids easily identify the nouns surrounding them in the classroom as they read the nouns in the book. Hearing the adjective choices from *Many Luscious Lollipops*, kids are inspired to combine two or three to describe their noun. The results are often playfully funny: "Tom's little, exploding, gold and white skateboard."

When kids finish composing adjective/noun phrases, *Kites Sail High: A Book About Verbs* and *Up, Up and Away: A Book About Adverbs* initiate the process of composing verb/adverb phrases to accompany their adjective/noun phrases. *Behind the Mask: A Book about Prepositions, Fantastic! Wow! and Unreal! A Book about Interjections and Conjunctions,* and *Mine, All Mine: A Book about Pronouns* show the roles other parts of speech play in sentences.

EXTENSIONS

Lights, Camera, Grammar: A Whole Look at the Parts of Speech

The term parts of speech is confusing to kids and adults for obvious reasons. First, most of us do not associate "speech" with written language unless it is dialogue. Second, the names of the different parts of speech—nouns, verbs, adjectives, adverbs, pronouns, prepositions, interjections, and conjunctions—are unusual in everyday conversations. Yet, despite their unfamiliar names, parts of speech compose our communications with others and form our thought processes. Kids are amazed to learn that all day long they are using the parts of speech in speaking, reading, and writing.

A toddler's first words are nouns and verbs that express needs or desires: "mama," "dada," or "out." Preschoolers acquire an astounding array of nouns and verbs from family, television, games, playmates, and computers, and they understand the different role of each in communicating meaning. Accumulating this knowledge about parts of speech in oral language happens through daily use without naming or defining the terms. In conversation, speakers learn to formulate sentences and fix language mistakes.

Learning to identify and use parts of speech correctly in writing is not as easy as doing the same in conversation because people talk more than they write. If we wrote half as often as we speak, we would all acquire vast knowledge about sentence formation in written communication. Pointing out the connection between talking and composing sentences informs kids that without realizing it they have spent years practicing oral sentence construction. Knowing how to communicate orally is a foundation for composing written language and understanding the roles of the parts of speech.

Through teamwork, parts of speech work together in sentences to make meaningful communication. Individual words alone cannot always produce a whole effort. The same is true in everyday life where group activities—like an orchestra performance, operating a school, or making a movie—need everyone's contribution to be successful. We could spotlight any collaborative effort as a metaphor for constructing sentences, but we use a movie set because of kids' familiarity and fascination with this form of entertainment. The analogy of a director creating a motion picture builds a bridge between children's experiences as English speakers and their need to learn the roles and rules of the parts of speech in writing.

A Young Writer as Movie Director

Imagine the activity on a movie lot sound stage filled with creative energy, endless possibilities and nervous excitement. Setting up are makeup artists, set designers, technicians, and other members of the production team. Everyone is busy rehearsing a story from a written script. The director, as head of the production, makes decisions about what will happen and what each person will do during the day. The director oversees all of the parts—lighting, camera angles, and timing—and what the stars and supporting cast are doing. The director decides how the film will ultimately communicate the story.

Envisioning a sentence as a short movie, the sentence writer serves as the director in charge of the production. Instead of commanding actors and technicians, the writer arranges and rearranges words (parts of speech) to form sentences. As a director watches the result of each shoot to decide whether to film the scene differently, the writer rereads sentences to determine to his or her satisfaction whether they are interesting, dramatic, compelling, descriptive, or humorous enough to convey the desired image. Here is how the parts of speech might appear on a movie set.

Nouns: Main characters

Pronouns: Stand-ins

Verbs: Action-Generators

Adjectives: Set designers

Adverbs: Special effects

Prepositions: Stage directions

Interjections: Dramatic or mood music

Conjunctions: Extension cords

Words are what create movies, videos, cartoons, plays, skits, and television shows. All entertainment happens because someone writes the scripts that give the characters personality, individuality, and motivations to move about the set. Without words and sentences there would be no show. All the elaborate electrical circuitry and technological equipment would illuminate silent pictures and stationary figures. In the sentence-writers-as-movie-directors analogy, the movement happens in the theater of the mind as writers imagine the action that their words generate. Children and adults activate theaters in their imaginations as they write—seeing scenes and situations in their mind's eye and conveying those images to readers by combining words, phrases, and descriptive language in sentences.

Envisioning sentences as a movie or TV show with writers as the directors-in-charge teaches children about their power as authors. A written language sentence cannot occur until a writer arranges the words in a certain order. In fact, the success of the sentence depends on how well the parts of speech work together as a team. Like the movie or television show's director who commands "Lights! Camera! Action!" the sentence writer/director declares "Lights! Camera! Grammar!"

Exploring Parts of Speech in Sentences

Each time children write they realize only a tiny fraction of their potential as written language communicators. Ideas and pictures in a young writer's head possess no boundaries; the challenge is how to get those thoughts on paper in ways that audiences understand and enjoy. There are an almost unlimited number of ways to combine words into sentences as linguists

Once upon a time there was a dragon and the dragon ate the mouse. It was the dragon's birthday. Then the dragon went to his mom. She was making the cake and the dragon went to school and the mom was done making the cake. Then the mom went to the store. She bought the dragon presents. Then the dragon went back home and his friends brought their presents to give dragon. Then they had cake. Then they opened the presents.

Figure 1.6 *Zachary's story.*

have shown. In one study by Noam Chomsky, twenty-five people viewed a cartoon and then described in one sentence what was happening. From their twenty-five sentences, 19.8 billion different grammatically correct sentences could be created (Cogswell 61).

While grammarians and linguists study parts of speech and construction of sentences as part of their professional work, kids do not converse about or explore written language construction unless they acquire interest in the topic. The image of the movie set and the idea of an audience watching a movie establishes a personal context for grammar study because children want others to read and to understand what they have composed. The idea of audiences coming to "see" their production gives immediate purpose to revising and editing their written work.

Many youngsters have richly textured and descriptive images in their minds that they speak aloud. But when writing, these same children compose spare, "just-the-facts" sentences, using common verbs, few adjectives or adverbs, and giving little attention to sentence length and style, similar to what Zachary did in his story about a dragon, a mouse, and a birthday cake (Figure 1.6).

Once children regard themselves as movie directors who are sentence makers, a universe of writing possibilities opens up before them. Thinking like a moviemaker gives kids a recurring image or model to guide them as they write.

- What is my movie going to show?
- How can I best devise it so other people will watch it?
- What is going to happen next?

Helping Zachary to think of himself as the director-in-charge of his own movie gives him reasons to "view" and revise his text collaboratively with kids who are the audience. First, he might examine the nouns (*mom, dragon, cake, presents*, etc.) through the eyes of an illustrator or costumer. Is the dragon "small, purple-spotted and spiked from head to tail" or "a furry fire-breathing, gigantic, striped, creature"? What kind of cake did everyone enjoy—a "double chocolate layer cake" or an "orange castle cake sprinkled with tiny sugar crystals glistening like jewels"?

Zachary and his classmates could compose descriptions of these nouns using adjectives and adverbs. No two children will craft matching descriptions, thus showing the endless variety of possible combinations from different imaginations. Before or after choosing their describing words, kids may draw or illustrate the ideas they have in mind.

Zachary can reconsider the verbs that regulate the power source, making action faster or slower, louder or softer, powerful or gentle. His choices are important to the overall effect. Classmates may suggest alternate choices to describe the action—the dragon "lifted his wings and sailed home to his mom" or the dragon "breathed fire and puffed smoke out of his mouth." This process of exploring choices identifies words that add the eye-popping, ear-catching, odor-sensing details to the scene. Doing so creates interest in examining how other writers power their sentences.

With lists of nouns, verbs, adverbs and adjectives in view for their use in composing sentences, children will talk with each other about how their sentences can be revised and improved by changing parts of speech. A movie director often rehearses dozens and dozens of times before a scene is ready for recording on camera. Young writers too can rehearse their sentences by writing them, reading them, and changing them to determine if they like the new version more than the previous one.

As writers, children do not need to ponder every word or phrase in an effort to get something just right every time they put a sentence on paper. Revising and editing is an opportunity to view and review what has been written to change it for clearer, more effective image making. Rewriting explores possibilities and allows young children to consider other versions before deciding which is the "final" version of their writing. They consider feedback from others, think about what has been written, and determine the sentence movie that best conveys what they want for their audience. The writer, as movie director, decides when to stop making changes and call it a "wrap."

Young Writers' Bookshelf for 676 Sentences and Parts of Speech

Watch William Walk. Ann Jonas. Greenwillow Books, 1997. A whole story expressed in short alliterative sentences features William, Wilma, Wally the dog, Wanda the duck, and all sorts of other words that begin with *W*.

New Nonsense from the North. Willowisp Press, 1996. Third graders from one school in British Columbia highlight ten letters of the alphabet in alliterative question-asking sentences about the animals that live in the Canadian wilds.

Animalia. Graeme Base. Puffin Books, 1986. Lights, camera, grammar in alphabet book form where alliterative sentences make widely imaginative images come alive for the reader.

Nouns

A Mink, a Fink, a Skating Rink: What Is a Noun? Brian P. Cleary. Illustrated by Jenya Prosmitsky. Carolrhoda Books, 1999. Rhymes about nouns with illustrations of people and places found all over town.

Verbs

Hop Jump. Ellen Stoll Walsh. Harcourt Brace, 1996. Frogs hop, jump, twist, and leap as they begin to dance and experience other verbs.

To Root, To Toot, To Parachute: What Is a Verb? Brian P. Cleary. Illustrated by Jenya Prosmitsky. Carolrhoda Books, 2001. Rhymes about verbs featuring comical cats.

Adjectives

Hairy, Scary, Ordinary: What is an Adjective? Brian P. Cleary. Illustrated by Jenya Prosmitsky. Carolrhoda Books, 2000.

Things that Are the Most in the World. Judi Barrett. Illustrated by John Nickle. Atheneum Books for Young Readers, 1998. Learn about superlatives in this imaginative and humorous adjective book where "heaviest," "hottest," "stickiest," "longest," and more are defined in never-before-seen situations.

Prepositions

The Wonder Thing. Libby Hathorn. Illustrated by Peter Gouldthorpe. Houghton Mifflin, 1996. Prepositions connect a riddle of places before revealing water as the element they all have in common.

Window Music. Anastasia Suen. Illustrated by Wade Zahares. Puffin Books, 2000. Prepositional phrases create the rhythm of the train wheels and descriptions of scenes along the journey.

From Apple to Zipper. Nora Cohen. Illustrated by Donna Kern. Macmillan, 1993. Letters' shapes portray images ("P is for Pencil to write down a riddle") that are described in sentences with prepositional phrases.

All About Where. Tana Hoban. Greenwillow Books, 1991. Lists of prepositions and color photographs invite readers to write descriptions of all the different things they see happening in the picture.

Ruth Heller's Books Cited in the Text

Merry-Go-Round: A Book about Nouns. Putnam & Grosset, 1990.

A Cache of Jewels and Other Collective Nouns. Putnam & Grosset, 1998.

Kites Sail High: A Book about Verbs. Ruth Heller. Putnam & Grosset, 1988.

Up, Up and Away: A Book about Adverbs. Putnam & Grosset, 1991.

Many Luscious Lollipops. A Book about Adjectives. Putnam & Grosset, 1989.

Behind the Mask: A Book about Prepositions. The Putnam & Grosset, 1995.

Fantastic! Wow! and Unreal! A Book about Interjections and Conjunctions. Puffin Books, 2000.

Mine, All Mine: A Book about Pronouns. Puffin Books, 1999.

CHAPTER SUMMARY

Chapter One, "Language," focuses on letters, words, parts of speech, and sentences as essential building blocks writers use to express ideas and share information. Letters stand for sounds in English, creating a vast number of words for writers to choose from when expressing ideas in print. Words acquire meanings that identify objects and actions, giving writers a way to communicate with many people. Parts of speech assign different roles to words when they are put together in sentences, letting writers compose written explanations and expressions about virtually any topic.

Like artists and craftpersons in many fields, children become competent and confident users of writing's building blocks by using them. Child-made alphabets, definitions and spellings of personally chosen words, short sentence movies using the parts of speech, and information-carrying, idea-conveying, image-expressing sentences give children practice using written language to express, entertain, and persuade.

As children write words and sentences creatively, they learn the roles of many conventions: alphabetical order; sound/symbol relationships; standard spelling; meanings of nouns, verbs, adjectives, adverbs, and other parts of speech; the pairing of subjects with predicates in structuring sentences.

Communications

At age four and five, Kyle was fascinated by the telephone. It was a magical machine that carried his voice to everyone he knew: his aunts, grandparents, playmates, and his mom or dad when they were traveling away from home. Once on the phone, he would tell whoever was listening about his day's activities. First, he might describe how he rode his bike up and down the small hill next to his house. Then, pausing only so briefly, he would declare, "You know what?" and launch into another topic—going swimming with his sister and brother, burying his dump truck in the front yard, discovering the broken toys his mother had hidden after cleaning his room. It was nearly impossible to get a word in edgewise when Kyle was broadcasting his news.

Like Kyle, young children enjoy sending and receiving news—on the phone, through the mail, or in face-to-face communications. For kids, daily experiences and discoveries have vibrancy and immediacy, so they happily report what they learned, what they did, what they are going to do, and who said what to whom. Astute kidwatchers and kidlisteners gain instant access to this information by tuning in to a readily available broadcast channel: "Kid News Reported by Kids." "Kid News" is always on-the-air (at least during the waking hours) and never seems to run out of material.

Since most children are instantly engaged by the idea of what is "new," the WOWs in Chapter Two, "Communications" explore how to write about the different kinds of news in people's lives. Writing personal news, weather, or information about the school and the community dramatically enlarges how kids think about sharing daily nonfiction facts with audiences. Kids learn that the purpose of news writing may be:

- *Personal communications*—news communicated to small audiences of family members and friends, or
- *Public communications*—news communicated to wider audiences of readers and listeners.

Throughout the chapter, we broadly define news as whatever is new or previously unknown to listeners or readers. For the reporter who participates in or personally witnesses an event and writes about it later, the event is no longer "news," but "olds." But to everyone who was not there in person, it is still news. Informing people about what they do not already know makes news especially meaningful writing for children.

The WOWs proceed from personal to public communications:

- **WOW 4: We've Got Mail: Letters, E-mail, and Mailboxes** features forms of communicative writing taught in most elementary schools. Writers use letters and e-mails to communicate with personal audiences and, sometimes, with wider audiences. Classroom mailboxes encourage writing and help kids learn the parts of a standard letter (heading, greeting, body, closing, and signature).

- **WOW 5: Signs Are Billboards for Persuasion** highlight examples of public writing whose purpose is persuasive; that is, to convince readers to do what the sign tells them to do. "Extensions: Capitals are Attention-Getting Letters" explores the role of capital letters in text.

- **WOW 6: What's the Forecast? Short Reports about the Weather** combines daily writing with the study of mathematics, science, and social studies. As kids track temperatures, investigate meteorological events, and learn geography, with the assistance of a daily newspaper or the Internet, they practice incorporating factual information into short nonfiction report writing. "Extensions: Using Sentences to Report the Weather" offers sentence templates for kids to use in constructing their weather reports.

- **WOW 7: What's for Lunch? The Menu May Not Be Real** is another occasion for news reporting to which kids can add fictional elements, descriptive writing, and humor. Deciding "What Is the *real* Menu?" introduces the concepts of fiction and nonfiction in a humorous way. "Extensions: Writing to Entertain" discusses how writers use humor to enliven their text.

We've Got Mail: Letters, E-mail, and Mailboxes

Letters, E-mail, and Mailboxes TEACH	These Conventions *Unconventionally*
The Excitement of Letter Writing • Letters with Riddles and Jokes • Letters to a Group • Letters to and from a Fictional Character • Letters of Protest/Petitions for Change • Personal and Business Letters	Genre: Letter writing Personal communications, friendly letter, business correspondence
Creating Classroom Mailboxes	Parts of letters • Heading, greeting or salutation, body, closing, signature Spelling
Electronic Mail	

Arnold Lobel's stories about the adventures of two friends, Frog and Toad, are much-loved classics among children and adults alike. In "The Letter," from *Frog and Toad Are Friends*, Toad is unhappy about never receiving mail. Frog decides to cheer up his friend by writing him a letter. He gives the letter to Snail, the letter carrier, and then goes to Toad's house to await its delivery. By the time the letter arrives days later, Frog has already divulged his surprise along with its contents to Toad. Even knowing in advance did not alter Toad's excitement about receiving mail from his friend.

Mouse Letters by Michelle Cartlidge, a very small book (only 4″ × 4″), also features the joys of letter writing as its theme. On every page is a tiny envelope holding an even tinier letter, 1¼″ × 2″ in size. Each letter gives a clue about where a present from the mouse fairies is hidden at the end of the story. Accomplished and beginning readers want to read these little letters despite their teeny print. They inspired one first grader to write a very small letter to her teacher with a 1¾″-tall pop-up bear inside.

After reading these stories to small groups of children in her class, Sharon asked how they would feel if they never had any mail in their mailboxes. "Sad!" was the unanimous response. Sharon then invited kids in each group to write a letter on a postcard to another child in the class.

The Excitement of Letter Writing

Child-made letters (and notes and cards, too) are an instantly effective way to introduce children to writing as a form of personal communication. Who does not look forward to receiving written messages that might contain surprises as well as greetings? Kids certainly do, and they also enjoy writing letters for many purposes:

- Saying hello to friends
- Sharing the family or neighborhood news
- Requesting information
- Asking or answering a question
- Offering an apology
- Publishing their artwork, poems, and short stories
- Giving a unique gift
- Inviting someone to a party or special event
- Expressing appreciation and good wishes.

Letter writing by kids generates its own momentum and expands its scope when adults encourage and support it. Initially, kids lack examples or models for writing letters. Their first attempts are often brief exchanges among friends; for example, inviting someone over to play after school or to a birthday party. But as kids learn how to communicate information and ideas from sender to receiver, and to include poems, songs, illustrations, and jokes, they increase the diversity and creativity of their letters.

Children in Sharon's classroom have written the following letters over the past several years. They illustrate examples of different letter-writing formats because in each the author has a clear purpose—to entertain, to inform, or to persuade. As so often happens, writing by children inspires other children to write when they see real reasons to do so.

Letters with Riddles and Jokes

Kids enjoy the humor of riddles and jokes and tell them over and over again. That same delight can happen when the riddles and jokes are included in letters such as those Allie and Gabrielle sent to friends (Figure 2.1).

Letters to a Group

Letters are often written to more than one person, especially when the writer wants to inform many people of the same information, as in the following letters by Chris and Gabrielle, who penned her message to the class in a memorandum style (Figures 2.2 and 2.3).

Letters to or from Fictional Characters

Letters to or from fictional characters gives kids another way to tell a story, one that shows how writers often build fiction stories from events that actually happened. After a bat was discovered in her classroom one afternoon, Allie composed a letter to Bill, her school bus driver, from the point of view of the bat (Figure 2.4).

Dear Jacob,

J have a riddle.
Why did the skeleton leave the party?
He had no body to dance with.
Here's another riddle.
Why did the bunny cross the road?
The chicken had his Easter eggs.

Love, Allie

p.s. Write back.

5000 Happy Birthday Road
Balloons Galore, Texas
December 18, 2001

Hi, Bob,

J hope you had a great birthday and did you make a wish? Well, if you did J hope it was a good one. What kind of cake did you get? Last year J got a chocolate cake. J wish that you get a good present. Whoops! J was not supposed to tell my wish because then it will not come true. Oh darn.

Happy Birthday,

Gabrielle

Figure 2.1   *Allie's and Gabrielle's letter to friends.*

Letters of Protest/Petitions for Change

Adults write letters not just to communicate information, but to protest injustice or petition for change. United States history includes many such written statements from the Declaration of Independence to Dr. Martin Luther King Jr.'s "Letter from the Birmingham Jail."

Children too can use letters to express their opinions about situations they consider unfair or in need of change. When, as part of a social studies unit, Sharon conducted a reenactment of the famous "Blue Eyes/Brown Eyes" antidiscrimination simulation, many children were moved to protest. Each of them wrote a letter to the principal describing their displeasure about two unusual school days.

At the beginning of the first day as children entered the room, Sharon directed each to pull a number from a hat. At morning meeting, she explained that all odd-numbered children would receive special privileges—a longer recess, no cleanup duties, walking at the front of the line, and recording the baskets made from tossing their hand-wiping paper towels into the wastebasket. Even-numbered children would have a shorter recess, cleanup duties for themselves and for the odds, places at the back of the line, and no record of paper towel shots in the wastebasket. No one knew that the next day, the roles switched. After the first day, Leah was so unhappy that she penned a letter of protest (Figure 2.5) giving the class an opportunity to discuss how written language can communicate feelings of discontent.

Letters to the editor of a newspaper or to public officials offer other opportunities for individuals to state their case for change. Kayla directed her appeal for the protection of endangered species directly to the President (Figure 2.6).

Figure 2.2

Letter by Chris. Translation:

Dear Class,

You should check out the day length. Yesterday the day length was 13:06 and now it is 13:12. And this day length was in December, 2000 which was on the 9th and this is that day length, 9:10 and look how much it has changed. It has changed a lot hasn't it?

Chris

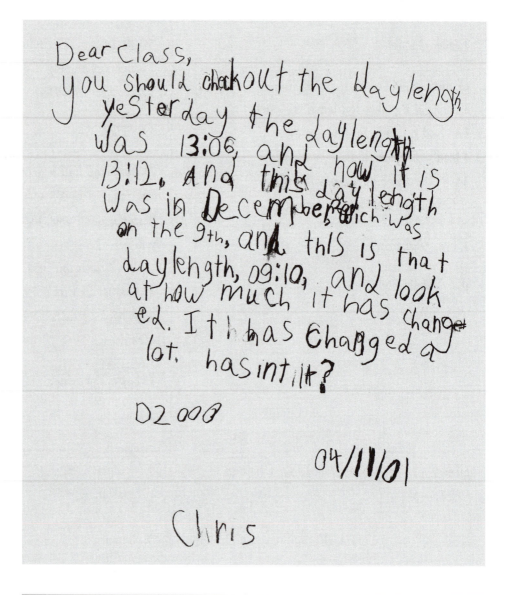

Figure 2.3

Letter by Gabrielle.

To: My Class

From: Gabrielle

Dear Class,

Did you know that Valentine's Day is coming up? Well I do. I hope we can all make Valentine's bags for Valentine's Day. I hope we can have a Happy Valentine's Day. I hope we can celebrate!

Sincerely,

Gabrielle

Figure 2.4

Allie's "Bill the Bat" Letter. Translation:

To: Bill

From: The Bat

Dear Bill,

I hope you remember me. We used to be best best very good friends. I hope you remember me well. I have black hair and beady eyes with white glistening in the middle of them. You believe in bats right? I hope.

Love,

The BAT

P.S. If you write a letter back, give it to Allie and make sure you give it to her!

Figure 2.5

Leah's protest letter. Translation:

Dear Ms. Edwards,

I can't believe you are doing this to us. You said that nobody can hurt people, and now you are hurting us. The odds have extra you choose and the evens can't do the scores for baskets [tossing paper into the wastebasket].

From Leah,

PS. And when I asked Sara how she would feel, she just said she would never have to do it.

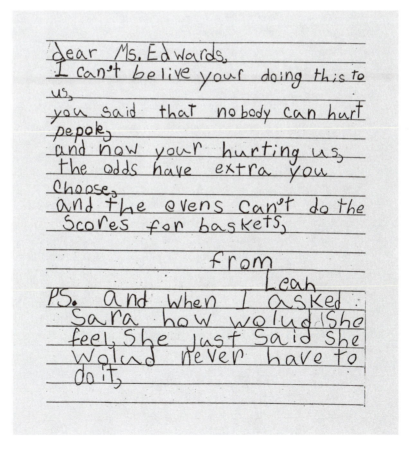

June 8

Dear Bill Clinton.

There are lots of endangered animals. Can you help us save them? We are studying them. Here are some of them. Spanish lynx, leopard, cheetah, golden toad, pandas, chimpanzees, tigers, walrus, orangutan, wooly pink pigeon, polar bear, bald eagle, ocelot, condor, spider monkey, estuarine baboon, flamingo, dolphin, gazelle, lion, crocodile, Australian ghost bat, kiwi, Asian otter, rhinoceros, quetzal, zebra, African wild ass, tortoise, rhinoceros, jaguar, manatee, penguin, whooping crane, grizzly bear, green sea turtle, African elephant, scarlet macaw, brown pelican, giant anteater, camel, Amazonian slot, blue whale, gray wolf, lowland gorilla, giant fruit bat, gray owl, great white shark, ring-tailed lemur, red kangaroo.

p.s.

If you want to write to me, my address is . . .

Kayla

Figure 2.6 *Kayla's Letter to Bill Clinton.*

Writing protest letters can be informed by reading historical biographies of individuals who expressed dissent through writing as part of social action. *If a Bus Could Talk: The Story of Rosa Parks* by Faith Ringgold chronicles the civil rights pioneer and the events surrounding the Montgomery Bus Boycott of 1955–56. *Carter G. Woodson: The Man Who Put "Black" in American History* by Jim Haskins and Kathleen Benson is the story of the man who founded the *Journal of Negro History* and launched "Negro History Week," the precursor of Black History Month. *Malcolm X: A Fire Burning Brightly* by Walter Dean Myers details the life of the civil rights activist.

Children's fiction books also address issues of protest, sometimes in a humorous vein. *Click, Clack, Moo: Cows That Type* by Doreen Cronin describes how a group of cows, dissatisfied with barnyard conditions, send letters to Farmer Brown demanding change. *Ruby Mae Has Something To Say* by David Small features a remarkable invention that enables an otherwise too-bashful Ruby Mae Foote of Nada, Texas, to deliver a call for world peace before the General Assembly of the United Nations in New York City.

Personal and Business Letters

Many letters are person-to-person communications, in contrast to signs, newspapers, weather reports, product advertisements, and other forms of more public writing. Usually a letter is intended to be a private or mostly private exchange between the writer and the person(s) to whom it is being sent (unless it is a letter to an editor for magazine or newspaper publication).

Style guides distinguish between a friendly letter and a business letter because function dictates form in letter writing, an important distinction for young writers to learn. A friendly letter to family members, pals, relatives, and others with whom one communicates on a personal and informal basis is not subject to the same conventions as a business letter that is generally sent to an individual or firm and conveys its message in more formal language and style. A letter between friends is filled with jargon, catch phrases, and funny remarks that communicate informally to the correspondents, while a business letter follows established guidelines and requires sentences, paragraphs, and clarity of phrasing if it is to be taken seriously. To communicate effectively, letter writers must pay attention to their audience and to how they are using language.

To invigorate personal letters, we encourage kids to include artwork and illustrations that add personality and individuality to their letters. But pictures cannot transmit or fully describe the message a writer is conveying—only words can do that! So we invite kids to include poetry, stories, and cartoons as parts of friendly letters.

Receiving letters from a favorite person inspires kids to write back. For example, grandparents, aunts and uncles, and other family members are great writing companions for kids. Imaginary characters can also play this role. Now adolescents, Kyle, Ryan, Emily, and Christina still look forward to letters from "Big Bear," a fictional character we created when they were very young who delivers clues for family treasure hunts.

Creating Classroom Mailboxes

Classroom mailboxes are an exciting way to promote letter writing by young children. The surprise of finding mail in one's box is an experience that kids want to have again and again. An easy way to do this is to establish a classroom mail system with a mailbox for every child. Children fold, decorate, and display their names clearly on the front of paper boxes or envelopes that are mounted alphabetically on a door in the classroom under the sign, "Local Mail."

Stories about letters and mail that introduce mailboxes include

- *Mailing May* by Michael O. Tunnell, the true story of five-year-old May, whose parents spent fifty-three cents in 1914 to send her by railroad train across Idaho to surprise her grandmother. May, weighed and categorized as a "baby chick," rides in the mail car with the postman.
- *Dear Mr. Blueberry* by Simon James, a story told in a series of letters between a young girl and her teacher, corresponding about the whale that she sees in her backyard pond and that he believes cannot possibly be there.
- *The Magic Cornfield* by Nancy Willard, the adventure of Tottem, who, on his way to celebrate the one hundredth birthday of his cousin Bottom, finds a mailbox that magically sends postcards with actual Postal Service stamps depicting historical figures, environmental scenes, and artistic illustrations.

As openers for letter writing, adults may write short notes to every child. At first, the children do not know what to do with the mail. Discussions ensue about writing back to someone who has written to you and the children are given class time to compose replies or write letters to each other. While it is impossible to write twenty-five letters once a week, it is well worth the investment of time to write four or five weekly so each child receives a letter a month. Kids enjoy getting mail from you and they will reply, so adults must have a mailbox too.

A classroom mail system works best when children have weekly in-class letter writing time, even if letters are an option during "You-Choose" time, at recess, or for home practice at night. Writing to kids who at first do not receive many letters from their classmates is important to keep letters from being a popularity contest. Regular mail for everyone is an attainable goal when kids play and work with each other. Kids may draw names from a hat to send a card or letter to a different child every other week.

Classroom mailboxes naturally lead to a discussion of postal mailboxes and the written correspondence that goes in them—personal and business letters. The United States Post Office along with other services like FEDEX and UPS carry millions of letters everyday. These letters are fundamental ways for people to conduct business and maintain friendships and family relationships.

Letters, whether friendly or business, have five essential features: *heading, greeting or salutation, body, closing,* and *signature*. These standard features of letter writing are intended to make it easier for writers to communicate meaning and intent to readers.

- *Heading:* The heading contains the writer's address and the date. In a business letter, it also includes the recipient's address.
- *Greeting or Salutation:* A greeting identifies the recipient of the letter: "Dear Big Bear." Without a greeting, no one can be sure to whom the letter is being addressed.
- *Body:* The body of the letter conveys thoughts and ideas from the writer. If a letter has only a greeting and a closing, but no body, then "no body" will read it.
- *Closing:* A letter writer closes with common phrases that signal an end to the conversation and a farewell—"Thanks," "Best wishes," "Love," and "Sincerely." Kids enjoy closing with inventive and clever statements like: "Hope your wings fly far!" "See you soon, but not on the moon!" "Later, alligator!"
- *Signature:* A signature tells readers who sent the letter. Adult signatures often have distinctive flourishes intended to show the writer's individuality. After all, a person's handwritten signature is used as proof for cashing a check, getting a driver's license, entering a contest, and other legal matters.

Electronic Mail

E-mail—correspondence of the present and the future—provides fast communications, integrates different types of information in a single document, and offers kid-engaging ways to explore writing conventions. It also provides adults with a context for teaching kids about safe activities online.

The arrival of e-mail has extended the scope of letter writing for adults and children. Phone lines, once used primarily for oral communication, are now filled with signals delivering written correspondence that can be read, printed, edited, and passed along with the press of a few keys. Traveling at the speed of electricity and at a fraction of the cost of postal mail, e-mail has become for many the preferred means of information exchange. Most computers include a word processing and e-mailing feature. Many of these programs are appealing to use and easy to learn. This is good news for kids because the easier it is to compose a letter and receive a reply, the more likely they are to want to write another one.

E-messages invite the receiver to reply, promoting a seamless flow of information through virtual conversations between writers. Popular software programs provide tools to communicate in real-time, letting individuals converse with each other as if they were in the same room. Type becomes talk as words appear on the screen. This volley of communications back and forth over the Web adds excitement to sending and receiving mail.

Word processing programs combined with e-mail programs make powerful writing toolboxes. Young writers can use a variety of virtual markers, cans of spray paint, crayons, pencils, paintbrushes, and hundreds of different fonts and sizes to fashion a screen with text and illustrations of amazing clarity and detail. Digital photos from home or in school can be attached to writing and drawing with electronic paper clips. Such tools bring state-of-the-art publishing software to children, adding to the possibilities for creative self-expression.

The unprecedented access to people and private information available on the Internet necessitates teaching kids about safe e-mailing practices. Two basic principles guide safety for kids online:

- Never e-mail alone.
- Use only known e-mail exchanges.

We tell kids that just as you would not give everyone you meet your home address and telephone number, you share your e-mail address with only a few relatives and friends. We facilitate safety by asking kids to develop an e-mail address book. In the beginning of the school year, we ask parents to provide names and e-mail addresses of people they will allow their children to correspond with using the Internet. These are the only addresses that the students send e-mail to from school. If a child's family does not know of any such addresses, they are given the opportunity to compile a list that includes the addresses of the classroom teacher and any of the teaching staff who are willing to receive e-mail from students.

Examining e-mail and web addresses gives kids the opportunity to explore writing conventions such as spelling, compound words, and abbreviations. Many individuals and organizations run two, three or more words together to create a web address: www.poetryalive.com or www.yourdictionary.com/. Sometimes, they use an acronym to shorten their address: www.nasa.gov or insert a capital letter in the middle: happEdays@eworld.com. Kids can practice decoding and creating e-mail addresses, locating small words inside longer titles, and combining separate words into more lengthy phrases.

Kids might brainstorm hypothetical web addresses for themselves or for fictional characters, finding different ways to include their names and personal interests in their e-mail addresses. Bob might choose to combine his interests with his name to create: bobwrite@computer.com or bob@blueskiesgreenfairways.com. An address for a fictional character such as "The GoodWolf" might be Iamagoodwolf@computer.com. Exploring the many possibilities for creating personal e-mail and web addresses involves the brevity of haiku poetry. Every address expresses a compelling message or image in one short line.

Designing a hypothetical website extends even further how kids use Internet technology. Kids might construct a website design for themselves or a fictional character. Many web designers start with written plans that can be easily edited and revised and then applied to web software. They lay out the plan for the entire site and that helps inform how each section is built. Kids can do this on large sheets of paper, then implement their ideas using web design software that can be downloaded free from the Internet. Here is what a website might look like if it were designed for a fictional character, The GoodWolf.

Welcome to the Pleasant Valley Home of "I. M. A. GoodWolf"	*Pictures of my friends*	*Pictures of my dinner guests*
	Wolf pictures go here	Pig pictures go here
My friends		
My foes		
Favorite recipes		
Picture of "I. M. A. GoodWolf" smiling		

I. M. A. GoodWolf's recipe for cooking a pig	Grandma Wolf's recipe for preparing a pork meal	Cousin Wolf's pig recipe
Take one pig	Take one pig	Be kind to pigs! Chew on some salad!
Clean it	Put it in a pot	
Rub it with lemon	Cook it till it is hot	
Put it in the fire	Stir it into some soup	
Let it cool for an hour	Yum yum pig stew!	
Pig Out!		

YOUNG WRITERS' BOOKSHELF FOR LETTERS, NOTES, CARDS, AND MAILBOXES

Love Letters. Arnold Aldoff. Illustrated by Lisa Desimini. Scholastic Trade, 1997. Letters written in poetic verse and accompanied with eye-catching collage and illustrations fill each page with affection (and sometimes disaffection).

Postcards from Pluto: A Tour of the Solar System. Loreen Leedy. Holiday House, 1996. Dr. Quasar and students write about the planets they encounter during their travels.

Hail to Mail. Samuel Marshak. Translated from the Russian by Richard Pevear. Illustrated by Vladimir Radunsky. Henry Holt, 1990. A rhyming poem tells the story of a letter that makes its way around the world.

The Long, Long Letter. Elizabeth Spurr. Illustrated by David Catrow. Disney Press for Children, 1997. Mother's very lengthy letter to Aunt Hetta blows away during delivery and becomes a gigantic snowstorm of paper, covering the whole town in the winter.

Dear Annie. Judith Caseley. Greenwillow Books, 1991. At Annie's house, mail from Grandpa comes once a week, each letter recording an important memory in a growing girl's life.

Arthur's Birthday. Marc Brown. Little Brown, 1999. Arthur and his friends invite Muffy to a surprise birthday party—since they were both born on the same day.

A Letter to the King. Leong Va. Translated from the Norwegian by James Anderson. HarperCollins, 1991. Set in China more than 2,000 years ago, this story recounts how a young girl's letter to a king saves her father from prison and demonstrates that boys are not the only valuable members of society.

Felix Explores Planet Earth: With Six Letters from Felix and a Fold-Out World Map. Annette Langen and Constanza Droop. Abbeville Press, 1997. Sarah's favorite toy rabbit, Felix, sends letters to her from his trip around the world. Also, *Letters from Felix: A Little Rabbit on World Tour* (1994) and *Felix Travels Back in Time* (1995).

Books Cited in the Text

Frog and Toad Are Friends. Arnold Lobel. HarperCollins, 1979.

Mouse Letters. Michelle Cartlidge. Dutton, 1993.

If a Bus Could Talk: The Story of Rosa Parks. Faith Ringgold. Simon & Schuster, 1999.

Carter G. Woodson: The Man Who Put "Black" in American History. Jim Haskins and Kathleen Benson. Illustrated by Melanie Reim. Millbrook Press, 2000.

Malcolm X: A Fire Burning Brightly. Walter Dean Myers. Illustrated by Leonard Jenkins. HarperCollins, 2000.

Click, Clack, Moo: Cows That Type. Doreen Cronin. Simon & Schuster, 2000.

Ruby Mae Has Something to Say. David Small. Dragonfly Books, 1999.

Mailing May. Michael O. Tunnell. Illustrated by Ted Rand. Greenwillow Books, 1997.

Dear Mr. Blueberry. Simon James. Margaret K. McElderry Books, 1991.

The Magic Cornfield. Nancy Willard. Harcourt Brace, 1997.

Signs Are Billboards for Persuasion

Signs	TEACH	These Conventions *Unconventionally*
Signs for All Purposes		Genre: Signwriting
• Daily Attendance Signs		Persuasive writing
• Big Mouth Puppets		Announcements
• Reminder Notes		Notices
		Lists
		Daily attendance signs
		Big mouth puppets
		Reminder notes
Extensions: Capitals Are Attention-Getting Letters		Capitalization of letters
		Uppercase and lowercase letters

Stop!
Watch It!
Do Not Touch!
Look Where You Are Going!
Here is Very Dangerous!
Do Not Pass This Sign!
Don't Get Any Closer!

Where might you find these messages? At a construction site in the city? Next to a precarious location along a mountain trail? Near hazardous materials stored in a science laboratory? Yes, indeed, but also in a second-grade classroom beside domino structures carefully arranged on tables by kids. These young builders, wanting to convey the importance of their work to classmates and viewers, wrote warning signs for all to heed.

Often hastily written, not deliberately crafted to be attractive, with invented and conventional spellings of words scattered across the page, children's signs may appear to be insignificant moments of creative writing and literacy learning. But unconventional surface features camouflage young writers' powerful efforts at persuasion as they inform readers that important matters are underway and warn them to do what the sign says. In one sense, signs are an easy and quick way to ensure that kids will write. At another level, they offer children key insights about how writing enables writers not only to relay messages, but to convince readers to do something as well.

Persuasion is one of the primary purposes for writing. The goal of a persuasive writer is to encourage, motivate, or convince a reader to do something, even to change a reader's mind. Persuasive writing begins with a clear message, then uses different language and presentation strategies to get that message across in ways that cause people to think differently about a subject or situation. Children need to be able to understand persuasive techniques since advertisers, peers, and adults constantly use them to influence kids' thinking or behaving. One way to learn about persuasion is by writing persuasively. Signs offer a kid-sized introduction to persuasive writing, a topic we return to in Chapter Seven with the writing of classroom rules (WOW 23).

Signs for All Purposes

"I don't want anyone to take my block building down," Paul informed his teacher, hoping she would do something to enforce his wish.

"Then you'd better make a sign for the building to tell the kids that," she replied.

Away he went, returning shortly with a paper on which he had traced his hand in a circle with a diagonal line through it. Borrowing from the picture version of the universal "No Smoking" sign, he had inserted his hand in place of the cigarette. His sign set a model everyone else used for the rest of the year for their "Do Not Touch!" pictograms.

Signs start appearing regularly in classrooms when children and adults write their requests instead of expressing them orally. Sarah created a sign after she brought two new tops for the class collection (Figure 2.7); Gabrielle created her sign to promote a puppet show she and her friends were going to do for the class (Figure 2.8).

Other kinds of kid-written signs include

- Messages: *Do Not Erase!*

    Wednesday and Friday Boy/Girl Days (for sitting side by side at lunch)

    Climber is Closed!
- Notices: *Computer Reserved for Rachel at Recess.*
- Requests: *May We Have Glitter Next Week?*
- Advertisements: *Clock Shop. Watches and Clocks for Sale!*
- Lists: *Members of the In-Charge Team for the Week Are . . .*
- Warning: *Do Not Enter!*

Signmaking originates from a child's desire to accomplish a specific purpose—preserving a block construction, reserving the computer, inviting kids to join a recess activity, or urging passersby not to touch a game in progress.

The Signmaker's Assistant by Tedd Arnold opens a discussion of the purpose and intent of signs. In the story, Norman, a young apprentice, left alone in the shop, decides to make more interesting messages on signs all over town. The resulting misinformation creates misadventures for everyone. When children consider signs they might never expect to see, the activity leads to laughter first and then to consideration of why signs are not used to fool or misdirect readers.

Signs are requests to pay attention and act a certain way. In a sense, they are billboards for persuasion, commanding readers to follow the directions. A "STOP" sign has a clear message and a persuasive intent: "Do Not Go Straight Through Without Stopping First." Similarly, "Speed Limit" is both a warning and a request. Please abide by our decision to

Figure 2.7 *Sarah's new tops sign.*

limit your choice of speed on this road, the sign warns, because ignoring the limit may result in a speeding ticket or even worse, an accident.

Children's classroom signs also proclaim their requests for compliance in a succinct and forthright manner. Whether written in the form of announcements, messages, advertisements, or warnings, signs are rehearsals for persuasive writing. A bold presentation along with a clear intent increase the likelihood that what the writer hopes will happen does happen. Of course, adults need to give authority to children's signmaking; otherwise these requests will become merely unacknowledged and unheeded pleas for action and children will stop writing them. But given adult sanction and support, signs demonstrate that pow-

Figure 2.8 *Gabrielle's puppet show sign.*

ers of communication and persuasion are present every time they write to each other in the classroom, and might also be at home as well.

Many varieties of signs, from quickly written to deliberately designed, deliver messages that persuade readers. Here are three to do with kids: Daily Attendance Signs, Big Mouth Puppets, and Reminder Notes.

Daily Attendance Signs

Even daily routines like compiling an attendance list can be an occasion for creative communication through writing, as we discovered unexpectedly as children began using a sign-in attendance board. Sharon placed a 24″ by 36″ piece of write-on/wipe-off paper on the classroom door. She divided it into a large grid with children's names written down the left side and the days of week displayed across the top. Her intent was for children to stop at the door as they arrived in the morning and make a check mark next to their names so whoever was delivering the attendance to the office would quickly know who was absent.

It did not take long before Sheyla devised a more inventive way of marking the daily square next to her name. Pausing at the classroom door one Monday morning, marker in hand, she announced she had a great idea. Next to her name under Monday's column, she wrote "S." She added a letter a day as the week progressed until on Friday with the letters "LA" she had her whole name: *Sheyla*. Other kids followed her lead, and lively discussions could be heard at the doorway about how many letters were in different names, and how many days it would take to display a name with eight, nine, ten or more letters.

As different ways of marking the grid appeared, kids' responses changed the chart from the routine to the unexpected. Using pictures, numbers, and colorful designs to confirm their attendance, children computed simple math equations on the sign board, wrote cartoons, and drew pictures and panoramas, one frame at a time. Each week, the attendance grid displayed many creative ideas:

Examples from the Daily Attendance Sign

	MON	TUE	WED	THU	FRI	SAT	SUN
Tyler	I'm first.	It is nice to see you.	Is it time for school?	I'm not here! I'm not.	Here I am.		
Julian	9	+	9	=	18		
Sheyla	S	H	E	Y	L	A	
Heyley	Hello! Hello! Hello!	Hi Again!	Wow!	Nice Day!	Bye!		

Kids transformed the daily attendance chart into a child-directed communication center, viewed by everyone entering and exiting the classroom. It became so eye-catching that other kids and adults walking by stopped to read and admire the responses. By designing the attendance chart so that kids had creative choices, young writers found ways to persuasively attract the attention of readers. Each unique way of responding on the chart declared "*I am creatively expressing my attendance. I think you'll like it if you look!*"

Big Mouth Puppets

A "Big Mouth Puppet" is a three-dimensional paper pop-out shaped as a large mouth that announces an urgent message or important idea. While the mouth opens and closes, an accompanying speech bubble expresses the text of this live-action sign. The large size of the mouth draws a reader's attention to the sign. Fourth graders made Big Mouth Puppets with speech bubbles to urge water conservation by neighborhood residents. Their talking puppets were so appealing that their signs won prizes in a contest conducted by the city's Water Department.

Easy-to-follow instructions for making all kinds of interesting pop-ups, including what we call "Big Mouth Puppets," appear in Joan Irvine's *How to Make Pop-Ups* and *How to Make Super Pop-Ups*. Directions for the pop-up mouth are on her website: www.makersgallery.com/joanirvine/books.html.

Reminder Notes

Reminder notes are personal signs. Everyone recalls kids' disappointment after asking for something that an adult then forgot to bring or do. Having not remembered the food dyes one student needed for a science experiment, Sharon suggested the child write her a reminder note and put it on the refrigerator where it would be visible at day's end. After that, "Write a Reminder Note!" became a familiar refrain as children wrote notes to themselves about important items to bring to school: backpacks, shoes, boots, library books, snacks, or home practice assignments.

At the outset of the school year, Sharon does not edit the spelling or appearance of these reminders until someone's invented spelling cannot be read without the assistance of the author (who also may not recall exactly what it said). Then the class discusses the usefulness of editing and rewriting to ensure that others understand the message. If certain errors repeat—misspelled words, lack of capitalization, incorrect or incomplete punctuation—they become topics of instruction within the context of why signs need to be instantly clear to readers.

EXTENSIONS

Capitals Are Attention-Getting Letters

Signs open an examination of uppercase and lowercase letters and the roles of each in the rules of capitalization. Capitals are attention-getting letters. They command a reader's eye, which is why they are used on signs, and they can influence a reader's behavior as Ola discovered one day when he sought to reserve the classroom computer for his use the next morning (Figure 2.9).

Ola's desire to get back to the computer shows how the visual and persuasive impact of a sign's message can change depending on the way uppercase and lowercase letters are used in the writing. Of course, book spelling of all the words makes his message more

comepter resefed for Ola in the morning.

Figure 2.9 *Ola's computer sign. Translation: The computer is reserved for Ola in the morning.*

understandable to more readers. But even if he uses invented spelling in his sign, we tell kids that Ola has many choices for how to convey his message:

Choice A: All lowercase letters	the computer is reserved for Ola in the morning.
Choice B: All uppercase or capital letters	THE COMPUTER IS RESERVED FOR OLA IN THE MORNING.
Choice C: Mixed case letters	The COMPUTER is RESERVED for OLA in the MORNING.

Kids and adults can consider the potential impact of choices A, B, and C.

- Using all lowercase letters means that every word looks the same. This diminishes the intended impact of the message. Readers may tend to overlook the fact that Ola has reserved the computer for tomorrow morning because his sign does not use conventions for commanding attention.

- Using capital letters, by contrast, tells readers they need to pay the utmost attention—put all eyes on every word—as in roadway signs like SPEED LIMIT, STOP, RAILROAD CROSSING, or DO NOT PASS. Using uppercase letters is therefore a good choice, but it may also overstate the situation as well, unless Ola has been denied the computer by someone, in which case all capital letters delivers the definitive message of "DON'T USE."

- Having some capitals and some lowercase letters lets a writer put selective emphasis on key information. If readers easily and quickly recognize the important parts of the message, then Ola will find the computer available to him when he comes to school the next day.

Talking with young writers about capitals as attention-getting letters shifts the focus from the rules of capitalization to the roles of uppercase and lowercase letters in writing. By capitalizing the first letter of people's names, organizations, historical events, religions, brand names, nationalities, titles, and geographic regions, a writer alerts readers to the important information following the capital letter. A capital *O* at the beginning of his name declares that Ola is an important person with important things to say. Starting other words with uppercase letters similarly gives a message of importance and significance to a word or phrase.

Capitalizing every letter in a word or phrase is a way to call maximum attention to the term. Capital words in newspaper headlines play this role, calling attention to a story and inviting the audience to read on to find out more information. "WOODS: IRON GAME," declared the *Boston Globe* that day after Tiger Woods won the 1999 PGA golf championship, acknowledging both the steel-nerved athlete and the many fine shots he hit throughout the tournament with his iron clubs. Sign writers, like newspaper headline writers, choose what words to capitalize according to their purposes.

Young writers need opportunities to use the English alphabet to understand the roles of uppercase and lowercase letters in a sentence. One type of letters cannot do all the work of communicating meaning in writing; the two types must work as a team. Capitals, however, cannot be used anywhere a writer wants to put them. They will not perform their role if they are randomly placed in the middle of words and sentences, as Jack Prelutsky has done in his poem "I'm All Mixed Up" from *A Pizza the Size of the Sun*. A capital letter flags people's attention at the beginning of sentences, identifies names of people and places, or makes information STAND OUT within the other print.

But to learn these conventions of capitalization, signs need to appear first as kid statements, using their words, their spelling, their letters. These forms of writing need to be complimented for their purpose—communicating an important message to others—before any changes are suggested or mini-lessons are taught.

Young Writers' Bookshelf for Signs

Do Not Open. Brinton Turkle. E. P. Dutton, 1993. Miss Moody and her cat, Captain Kidd, discover a mysterious bottle on the beach that says "DO NOT OPEN." What will happen if they disregard the instructive warning?

Red Light, Green Light. Margaret Wise Brown. Illustrated by Leonard Weisgard. Scholastic, 1992. People, animals, cars, and trucks all move back and forth around the Stop and Go signs of a traffic light.

The Signmaker's Assistant. Tedd Arnold. Dial Books for Young Readers, 1992. After the master signmaker leaves for the day, Norman, his young assistant, paints signs that cause confusion and misadventures all over town (cited in the text).

A Pizza the Size of the Sun. Jack Prelutsky. Illustrated by James Stevenson. Bantam, 1999 (cited in the text).

What's the Forecast? Short Reports about the Weather

WOW 6

Weather Reports	TEACH	These Conventions *Unconventionally*
See the USA, Every Day		Genre: Weather report writing
		Spelling: Weather words
		Days of the week and months of the year
		Names of states
		Alphabetical order
		Geography of the United States
Reporting the Weather		Short report writing
		Clarity in sentence construction
		Past, present, and future tense
		Apostrophes and contractions
		Proper nouns

Imagine a one-stop, child-friendly learning resource that connects reading, mathematics, science, social studies, and news writing in an easy-to-read, attractive-to-kids format—all for fifty cents a day or for free on the Web. "Impossible?" This multi-purpose resource is available Monday through Friday at stores near you on "The Weather Page" of the national newspaper, *USA Today*. It is an invaluable part of children's ongoing study of the weather and how writers use weather reports to communicate meteorological and environmental news to readers and listeners.

See the USA, Every Day

USA Today's weather page opens endless opportunities for creative learning of reading, writing, spelling, geography, and mathematics:

- A half-page, color-coded map charts temperature ranges and weather predictions across the contiguous United States, southern Canada, northern Mexico, Cuba, Puerto Rico, and the Bahamas.

- Insert maps of Alaska (with nine months of thirty-degree temperatures in parts of the state and often three to five different temperature ranges in a day), Hawaii (with year-round tropical conditions), and Puerto Rico (with the central rainforest region cooler than the surrounding coast) provide sharp contrasts with the seasonal temperature changes in the contiguous states.

- Temperatures from below ten to above 100 are color-coded incrementally so, as young readers compare cold to cool with whites, purples, blues, and greens and warm to hot with yellows, oranges, and reds, they read a chart and count by tens.

- The map of the continental United States is like a geographical puzzle. Major cities and state capitals are displayed but state names are not. By comparing the *USA Today* weather map with other maps or puzzles, kids learn to recognize the shapes and positions of states and the spellings of their names.

- Daytime high and nighttime low temperatures of major U.S. and world cities are highlighted with predicted weather in an abbreviation-code (*s, pc, t, sh*). Learning the code shows kids that beginning letters of words correlate with their abbreviations—*s* is *sunny, pc* is *partly cloudy, t* is *thunderstorms, sh* is *showers*.

- Alphabetized lists of cities around the world from Acapulco, Mexico, to Zurich, Switzerland, and thirty-six major U.S. travel destinations—from Atlanta to Washington, D.C.—showcase world weather temperatures and forecasts for today and tomorrow.

USA Today's on-line weather site—www.usatoday.com/weather—has enhanced features supported by colorful graphics, including

- Daily maps for precipitation and high- and low-pressure systems.
- World forecasts by region: Canada, the U.S., Mexico, the Caribbean, Central and South America, Europe, the Middle East, Africa, Asia, and Australia and the South Pacific.
- State-by-state five-day forecasts plus weather radar images and movies.
- National and international satellite images for all parts of the globe.
- Weather news and analysis with links to other sites (U.S. Geological Survey, National Weather Service, Geographic Names Information System).

In Sharon's room, weather reports are written by groups of two to six children for presentation on the "Before Noon News," a class meeting time held daily before lunch. Each child chooses one or two states, outlines them on the *USA Today* weather map, and then writes states' names, weather conditions, and temperatures in their individual reports. Kids use different colors on the map to denote their states—Sam's are red, Donashas's are green, Jose's are blue, and so on.

When each reporter reads the weather report aloud to the class, one of the other weather writers points to the states on the map. "What color are you?" asks the pointer before the reporter begins reading her report.

"I'm red," replies the reporter.

If two states are outlined in red, the pointer adds for clarification, "Alaska's first" (letting the reporter determine the order of presentation).

For children, writing weather reports combines accurate reporting of meteorological facts and language-rich imaginary descriptions of weather conditions. Here are two examples, first Siobhan's report on the weather (Figure 2.10) in Alaska followed by Izzy's make-believe report of weather in the Northwest (Figure 2.11).

Today's weather is warm and cold in Alaska. It is in the below 10s, 10s, 20s, 30s, 40s, and a little bit of the 50s. It is partly cloudy, cloudy, sunny and rainy. It's warm for a change in Alaska for now.

Figure 2.10   *Siobhan's report. [Her map of the state is color coded to the temperatures displayed on the USA Today Weather Page.]*

Today's weather in the northwest is hopping with hot dogs (woof woof) and flower power. It is raining frogs and snowing eyeballs. There is a chance of raining baby faces too. BYE.

Figure 2.11   *Izzy's report.*

Identification of state names and positions on the map happens every day during weather reporting (Figure 2.12). At the beginning of the school year, children's favorite choice of locations include

- Their home state, Massachusetts
- Large states (Texas, California, and Alaska)
- The island state of Hawaii or the island commonwealth of Puerto Rico
- States that have a connection to someone in the class because of relatives living there or having lived there previously themselves.

After the first few months of children choosing states, Sharon widens their choices by requesting that they find

- a hot and a cold state
- a warm and a cool state
- a northern and southern state
- an eastern and western state
- a northeast and southwest state
- a midwestern (or Great Plains) state with any other state

These requests expand children's geographic vocabulary and understanding of map terms. Soon, children are able to find one of the following choices:

- two cool states
- two warm states
- one cool and one warm state
- one state that has three temperature ranges

Figure 2.12

Ian's report on Texas.

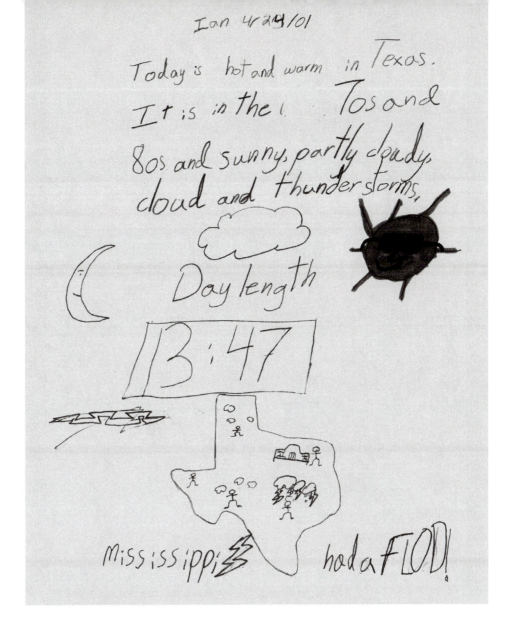

- one state that has no temperature ranges
- two states with two different temperature ranges
- a desert state and a mountain state
- an ocean-bounded state and a landlocked state

Reporting the Weather

Weather reports for first and second graders begin with fill-in-the-information sentence templates:

- "Today's weather in (*geographic location*) is (*type of weather*)." Type of weather is described using familiar weather words: sunny, hot, cloudy, windy, cold, partly sunny.
- "The temperature is in the (*range of temperature*)." The temperature range is described by including numbers in sentences: for example, the temperature in Florida is in the 70s and 80s.

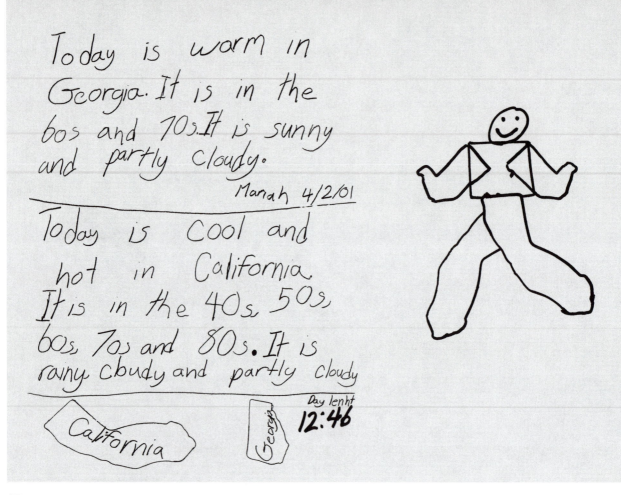

Figure 2.13   *Mariah's report.*

The sentence templates are easily combined with learning how to read the temperature chart, the precipitation symbols, and the length of day (listed in a local newspaper or online). As kids gain confidence with weather report writing, they extend this basic format in creative ways, including Mariah's summary of conditions in Georgia and California, with a weather reporter drawn from the shapes of the states (Figure 2.13).

Sentence templates in weather reports show the roles of many language conventions by:

- Illustrating that weather reports seek to communicate considerable information in few words using easily understood language. Adult readers of weather reports expect quick information and accurate facts so they can prepare for outside conditions. Writing weather reports for daily broadcast is a way to practice forming clear informational sentences.

- Acquainting children with geographic locations and terms that they need to learn: continents, countries, regions, states, and cities. Most children are unfamiliar with maps of the United States and where their home state is in relation to the rest of the country. Daily map reading and weather reporting generates repeated lessons about the geography of places without sacrificing students' interest in the topic.

- Promoting standard spelling of common weather words: rain, snow, warm, cold, hot, dry, cool, sunny, cloudy, and so on. Writing reports about different places teaches standard spelling of state and city names. In addition, kids see that names of countries, states, and cities begin with capital letters.

- Demonstrating present, past, and future tense in writing. Today's weather is described in present tense since it is happening right now; yesterday's weather is reviewed using the past tense because it happened in the past; tomorrow's weather is forecast in the future tense because that weather has yet to occur: Today's weather *is*; yesterday's weather *was*; tomorrow's weather *will be*.
- Showing how numbers are included with words in weather information. Kids also learn to include a degree sign with numbers to indicate a temperature reading.
- Demonstrating that an apostrophe in "Today's weather" indicates a possessive— the current weather is happening today. Similarly, yesterday's or tomorrow's weather belongs to the past or is forecast for the future.

Gradually, other types of information become part of the writing of weather reports. For example, very hot and very cold places always attract children's attention. High and low daily temperatures can be added to the reports. The *Boston Globe*'s weather page gives the length of daylight for each day so children chart how many minutes of daylight are being lost or gained as the seasons change and include this data in the weather reports.

As weather reports become a regular feature of classroom learning, kids enjoy adding more interesting facts to their written presentations. As a result

- Including states and cities that are not usually part of their reports gradually helps kids learn the names of the fifty states and their locations on the map.
- Saving a summer map to contrast with a wintertime map (and vice versa) shows how temperatures differ greatly in some spots depending on the season of the year.
- Adding local information to their reports, available from newspapers or online— length of day, times of sunrise and sunset (or moonrise and moonset), the hours of high tide and low tide—increases the usefulness of the weather page and adds to the kids' knowledge.
- Writers begin to use adjectives to create more descriptive reports. "Today in 'hot-enough-to-fry-an-egg-on-the-sidewalk Tucson', it is 100 degrees" adds poetry, humor, and wordplay to the facts.

YOUNG WRITERS' BOOKSHELF FOR WEATHER REPORTS

Wild, Wet and Windy. Claire Llewellyn. Candlewick Press, 1997. A volume on weather from the SuperSmarts science book series.

On the Same Day in March: A Tour of the World's Weather. Marilyn Singer. Illustrated by Frane Lessac. HarperCollins, 2000. The weather all around the world featuring sixteen locations with warm and cold temperatures from all six continents.

The Weather Sky. Bruce McMillan. Farrar, Straus & Giroux, 1991.

Pictures of clouds and sky taken in the "thunderstorm alley" section of Maine help to show how meteorologists use weather maps in their forecasts.

The Cloud Book. Tomie dePaola. Holiday House, 1995. An introduction to weather through a study of cloud formations.

What Will the Weather Be? Linda Dewitt. Illustrated by Carolyn Croll. Scott Foresman, 1993. How meteorologists go about predicting the weather.

What's for Lunch?
The Menu May Not Be Real

Menus	TEACH	These Conventions *Unconventionally*
Fiction and Nonfiction Menus		Genre: Menu writing Spelling: Common food words Using fiction and nonfiction
Extensions: Writing to Entertain		Using humor in writing Audience response

Today's menu is:

Figure 2.14

Katherine's menu.

> A hotdog with ketchup or mustard
> French fries, chicken nuggets and pizza.
> For drinks and dessert, they are giving out free
> root beer floats and a piece of wedding cake.

Sounds improbable, but that is what Katherine wrote in her menu report to the class. Surely this cannot be the case. Let's ask Mariah (Figure 2.15):

Today's menu is:

Figure 2.15

Mariah's menu.

> A pizza with pie crust and jello sauce.
> and coconut cheese, and fruit, and pepperoni,
> and gummy peppers and Jello punch to drink.

What is going on here? Are these selections from the world's most unusual school cafeteria? No, they are make-believe lunch menus written by children to read on a classroom news broadcast or to include in a classroom newspaper. They are examples of how "What's for Lunch?" an ordinary question every school day, can be given an imaginative twist to make a humor-filled combination of news writing and theater-like performances that entertains and amuses audiences of children and adults.

Fiction and Nonfiction Menus

Menu writing began accidentally one day ten years ago when Sharon told a youngster that he could read that day's lunch menu at a class meeting held every morning before lunch and known as "The Before Noon News." When he appeared less than enthusiastic, she asked if he and his friend would like to try a new idea. One boy would write the real menu, the other would compose a make-believe menu that sounded real, and together they would try to fool the rest of the class by reading both menus aloud and asking children to vote for the one they believed to be true.

The two eagerly began creating their selections, smiles of intrigue on their faces. With their menus began an ever-evolving form of writing for entertainment in the classroom that still continues today.

Every school year begins with a group of children writing multiple versions of the daily lunch menu to read to the class on "The Before Noon News." One menu is the day's actual cafeteria selections; the other versions range from fake but believable to wildly imaginary culinary items.

The menu writers decide together who will record the real menu and who will create the make-believe menus. The other children, the audience for the writing, vote for one of these menus after laughing and groaning about some of the over-the-top choices. Writing the menu quickly becomes a much-anticipated writing and reading event, a daily theater for performers and listeners.

Each year, the children spontaneously take menu writing in new directions—menus written by pairs, trios, quartets, and quintets; menus done as acrostic, two- and three-voice, or rhyming poems; menus acted out with puppets or with kids who perform their own written dialogue. Here are three examples:

Mariah and Gabrielle composed their menus after consulting a rhyming dictionary (Figure 2.16). Chris used descriptive language to construct an imaginative view of what will happen at lunch (Figure 2.17). A group of kids wrote and performed a five-part play that included actual menu items paired with wildly improbable food ingredients (Figure 2.18). False clues about the actual lunch menu were cleverly placed at the bottom of the page. Each child read her or his writing aloud, one after the other, followed by the real menu items (in bold print). The final writer combined all the items. The class then voted whether this seemingly embellished menu was the real bill of fare.

When kids see a genre or style in someone else's menu that elicits laughter from their classmates, they incorporate it into their menu writing. In this way, new variations are always emerging.

Sometimes children read poetry aloud as part of menu writing and performance. Arnold Adoff's *Chocolate Dreams* is one favorite collection of poems; another is *Laugh-Eteria: Poems and Drawings* by Douglas Florian. These poems interest kids in writing about food, eating, and family life, as Sarah did when she composed instructions for how to enjoy chocolate cake (Figure 2.19).

What accounts for the wide appeal of menu writing and performing among children?

- Many kids enjoy being onstage in front of an audience. Since menus are published daily to an audience who eagerly awaits them, they are a "Live at the

Our school lunch has banana punch and
knees with trees
and winter snows
and heavy clothes
and sun's rays
and lazy days
and the broom
and my room
and guess what,
there is a also an ape, a cape,
a drape, a grape,
a scrape, a shape,
and tape.

Our school lunch is like Captain Crunch.
If you eat a pear you will lose your hair.
If you eat a rose you will lose your nose
and toes.
If you jog you will turn into a frog.
If you itch your eye you will start to cry.
If you eat some Captain Crunch,
you will turn into someone's lunch.

Figure 2.16 *Mariah and Gabrielle's rhyming menus.*

Improv"–type theater for writers and listeners where the fun and enjoyment of the performance is the key experience.

- When structured as plays, poetry readings, riddles or performances for children and their friends, menus are a nonthreatening public-speaking format. Even shy youngsters feel they are in control of the situation, seeking center-stage opportunities to share their ideas.

- Menus, like poems, are short, compressed forms of writing. Every word counts. Kids learn through experience that brevity is important in creating humor for an audience.

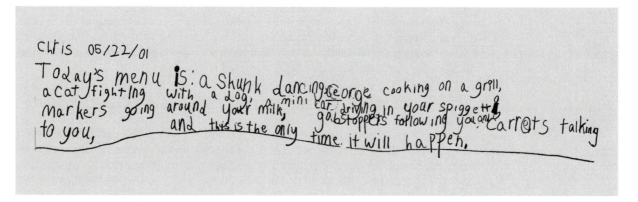

Figure 2.17 *Chris's menu. Translation:*

Today's menu is a skunk dancing, George cooking on a grill, a cat fighting with a dog, a mini-car driving in your spaghetti, markers going around your milk, gobstoppers following you, and carrots talking to you, and this is the only time it will happen.

Figure 2.18

Group menu.

First Child: Today's menu is tacos with whipped cream and wormberrys, hippos, frogs, tadpoles, pigs, and all animals, trees, leaves, and paper, sandcastles, balloons, rugs, and everyone. Who is doing this menu?

It's hamburgers.

Second Child: No! It's cheese with sprinkles on top. Hey also there is seven pancakes for everyone. Instead of water, there is strawberry juice and your milk is going to be frozen solid.

Dixie cups

Third Child: NO! It is strawberries, lettuce with marshmallows, cat tails, sharks and peanut butter.

French fries

Fourth Child: NO! It's not, it marshmallows, tomatoes, and

Fruit cups.

Fifth Child: NO! You're all wrong. It is apple crisp with trees growing out of it and markers. This paper and frogs and strawberries.

O.K.

It is hamburgers, French fries, Dixie cups and juice.

The End

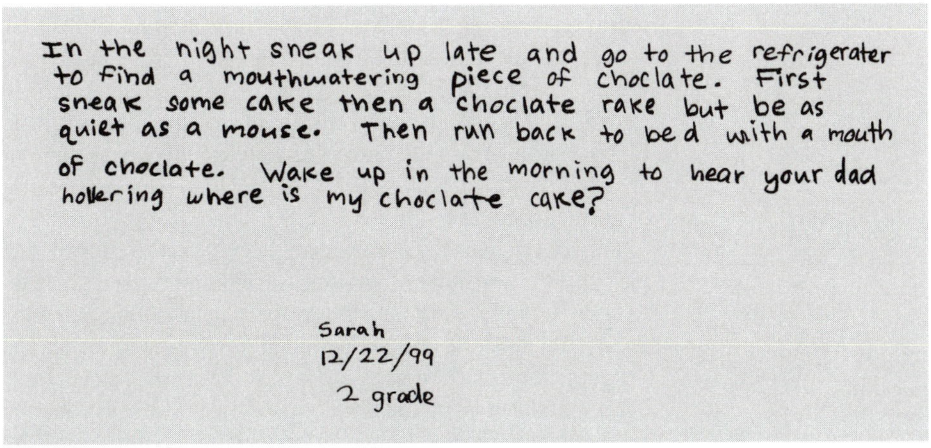

In the night sneak up late and go to the refrigerater to find a mouthwatering piece of choclate. First sneak some cake then a choclate rake but be as quiet as a mouse. Then run back to bed with a mouth of choclate. Wake up in the morning to hear your dad hollering where is my choclate cake?

Sarah
12/22/99
2 grade

Figure 2.19 *"How to Enjoy Chocolate Cake," by Sarah. Translation:*

In the night sneak up late and go to the refrigerator to find a mouthwatering piece of chocolate. First sneak some cake then a choclate rake but be as quiet as a mouse. Then run back to bed with a mouth of chocolate. Wake up in the morning to hear your dad hollering where is my chocolate cake?

Writing to Entertain

Sharon's remark after an amusing menu, "What a punch line!" occasioned a discussion of the meaning of this term. Creating and delivering a punch line thereafter became a popular position on the menu-writing team. Kids waited until last to read their menus, announcing to the other writers, "No, you have to read yours first. Mine's the punch line!" Another year, menus ending with "knock-knock" jokes were popular for adding humor to the writing.

Punch lines and jokes in make-believe menus introduce kids to how writing can entertain and amuse readers and listeners. A straightforwardly accurate presentation of "What's for lunch today?" informs, but an imaginative or improbable menu provides enjoyment and laughter. Creatively written menus that combine writing to entertain with theater-like performances become opportunities for young writers to learn how to express themselves in ways that capture and maintain an audience's attention.

As they write and perform menus, children receive lessons about how language affects an audience's response. Sometimes writers cause kids to say "oooo," "gross," "ugh," and "bleck," exactly what the writers were hoping for with their unappetizing lunch descriptions. Kids find that word choice is vital to the impact of writing.

Using humor in writing and performing menus shows young writers how writing to entertain involves deliberate attempts to make others laugh. Humor, however, is not always easy to achieve. What one person finds funny or playful, another may regard as offensive or insensitive. So some things are not usable in menus: people's names or anatomical terms.

Fiction and nonfiction menus require writers to consider how others will respond to their creations. If a menu is too "gross," an audience will be put off and will not enjoy the presentation. If a theatrical presentation is too wild or too hard to follow, the audience will not understand what is happening and will say so. Youngsters must write with a sense of their audience in mind. It is one thing to express one's ideas freely, creatively, and solely for personal enjoyment. Expressing one's ideas so that other children or adults will laugh and enjoy them requires re-evaluating what is being said to determine if both the author and the audience find the language funny.

The mirth and merriment of menus gives adults ways to talk with children about humorous writing. When and why is something funny? We laugh at fictionalized versions of everyday life that feature improbable or ludicrous juxtapositions of the normal course of events. The old pie-in-the-face gag is funny precisely because pies are not normally thrown at people. The comparison-contrast of real life and fictional events makes the situation funny. For this reason, strangers to a culture may have difficulty figuring out when people are serious and when they are just having fun. They lack a sense of perspective on the range of normal conduct in the setting.

Sheep Out to Eat by Nancy Shaw offers a way to connect menus with a wonderful example of how to use humor in writing. Five hungry sheep arrive at a local restaurant for lunch. As soon as the food arrives, disaster befalls the diners. They slurp and burp their soup, use sugar, salt, mustard, and pepper on all the wrong items, and in a fit of sneezing caused by the pepper, break the dishes and wreck the room. To everyone's relief, they eventually discover that the grass on the lawn outside the building is what they really wanted to eat. Here is an example of how humor arises from everything ordinary and normal being turned upside down by the sorry but wacky sheep.

Composing make-believe, made-up menus is a way to practice writing for entertainment. Ideally, they create a lighthearted, sometimes satirical, reverse-mirror view of people and events. They let readers see things through a new light. To be effective, such menus must combine elements of the usual and the unusual, as in a blend of story, poetry, weather reports, or geographical terms as Ian's menu does (Figure 2.20).

Figure 2.20

Ian's "It Is Everything" menu. Translation:

Today's menu is Europe, trucks, birds, Florida, lower California, Philippines, Japan, frogs, wolf, The rainbow, The FBI, Nobody Owns the Sky, cups, water, and lights. OH YAY. IT IS EVERYTHING!

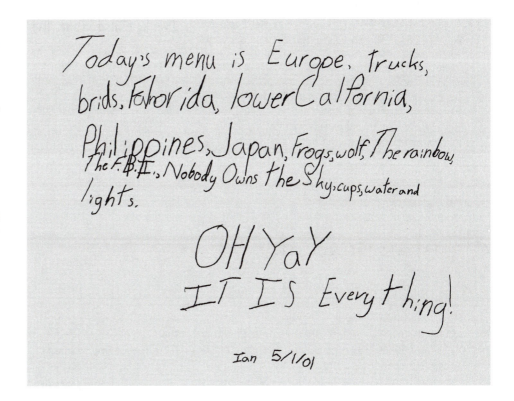

Children are knowledgeable about humor. They enjoy mimicking voices or body language of adults or their siblings. Many imitate the actions of a favorite TV character or sports figure. Cartoons, comic books, and children's shows also use parody as a key element in the storylines. Kids enjoy the humor of *Rugrats* or many of the shows on *Nick at Night* because normal elements of their own experiences are treated in such unusual, and thus funny, ways.

For writers, it is important to recognize the role prior knowledge plays in determining how much a piece of writing is funny. To write humorously about a baseball game requires insider information; otherwise calling an easy fly ball a "jar of peas" instead of a "can of corn" will confuse, not amuse, readers. In the same way, trying to write in a humorous way about a new computer game will be less effective if the readers have not played the game. Kids need to consider the background knowledge of members of the audience for the humor to succeed. As they make their humor connect to the understandings their readers bring to the text, they learn another way to make writing creative and entertaining.

Young Writers' Bookshelf for Menus

Something's Happening on Calasbash Street: A Story with Thirteen Recipes. Judith Ross Enderle and Stephanie Gordon. Illustrated by Donna Imgemanson. Chronicle Books, 2000. People from many different cultures choose foods for their evening meals.

Mouse Mess. Linnea Riley. Blue Sky Press, 1997. A mouse in search of a snack creates chaos in the kitchen.

The Runaway Tortilla. Eric A. Kimmel. Illustrated by Randy Cecil. Winslow Press, 2000. An irreverent tortilla creates a laugh-out-loud retelling of the *Gingerbread Man* story.

Cloudy with a Chance of Meatballs. Judi Barrett. Drawn by Ron Barrett. Scott Foresman, 1982. *Pickles to Pittsburg* (1997) is the sequel. Strange and wondrous happenings in the town of Chewandswallow involve all sorts of food.

What's on the Menu? Poems about Food, selected by Bobbye S. Goldstein. Illustrated by Chris L. Demarest. Puffin Books, 1995. Poems about food by Eve Merriam, Arnold Adoff, John Ciardi, and Aileen Fisher are among those featured in this delightful anthology.

Yummy! Eating through a Day. Selected by Lee Bennett Hopkins.

Illustrated by Renee Flower. Simon & Schuster Books for Young Readers, 2000. An amusing anthology of poems about food and eating. See also *Munching: Poems about Eating*. Selected by Lee Bennett Hopkins. Illustrations by Nelle Davis. Little, Brown, 1985.

A Cheese and Tomato Spider. Nick Sharratt. Barron's, 1998. Flip pages divided in half let kids create multiple combinations of colorful, surprising, uproariously funny foods.

1,000 Silly Sandwiches. Alan Benjamin. Pictures by Sal Murdocca. Simon & Schuster, 1995. Lift the flaps and all sorts of preposterous sandwich combinations appear on a giant grinder roll.

Books Cited in the Text

Sheep Out to Eat. Nancy Shaw. Illustrations by Margot Apple. Houghton Mifflin, 1992.
Laugh-Eteria: Poems and Drawings. Douglas Florian. Puffin Books, 2000.
Chocolate Dreams. Arnold Adoff. Lothrop Lee & Shepard, 1989 (out of print).

CHAPTER SUMMARY

Chapter Two, "Communications," explains different ways that writers share ideas and information with personal and public audiences. Writing is sometimes directed to one other person or a small group of friends and relatives; sometimes it is intended for a large number of readers. As children understand this distinction, they vary their written communications to address particular audiences.

Letters, notes, cards, and e-mails are mostly personal communications because the audience is limited to a small number of intended readers. Signs, weather reports, and menus are written for wider, public audiences.

As children use these writing genres to communicate with others, they learn conventions that are part of the elementary school curriculum. Letters have a head-ing, greeting, body, closing, and signature to help ensure that the correspondence reaches its intended reader. Signs present information in many different ways, both to inform readers and to persuade them to do what the sign says. Weather reports relay information in a short report format that lets kids practice combining accurate facts with interest-grabbing writing. Menus present information in seemingly straightforward ways, but kids can mix fact and fiction in a game called "Is it the REAL Menu?" Newspapers and news broadcasts give children ways to publish news from their own lives and from the world while teaching the importance of revising and editing what has been written before it is shared with readers and listeners.

CHAPTER THREE

Poems

Former poet laureate Joseph Brodsky once observed that in cultural matters, supply generates demand. When people gain broad access to a form of art, music, or language, they learn about its creative potentials and they want to make it part of their lives. The Beatles transformed music and culture in the 1960s and 1970s. In the past twenty years, rap and hip-hop rhythms—poetry in lyrics—have spread through society. In each case, the more listeners heard, the more they wanted to hear.

The same is true for children. When they start reading, listening to, and writing poetry, the wonder and magic of the language captivates them and they demand more. As psychologist Howard Gardner (77) has noted, poetry offers individuals, young and old, "a sensitivity to the different functions of language—its potential to excite, convince, stimulate, convey information, or simply to please."

Amazingly, children's daily conversations and observations are filled with the ingredients of poetry—inventive language, interesting experiences, lyrical moments, puzzling occurrences, fascinating characters, unexpected developments, wonderful surprises. Listen closely to children's talk and you will hear the poetry of their language, spontaneously filled with enthusiasm and verve.

Poetry is a limitless resource for children and adults to explore together, mainly because it is everywhere. A red geranium along a path in a garden is poetry, its vibrant color a vivid contrast to the green and brown of the foliage around it. An old hand-blown bottle is poetry, its irregular shapes and contours suggesting a hidden history to describe in verse. Song lyrics, commercial messages, and newspaper headlines are poetry, conveying everyday events in succinct melodies and phrases. Poets build poetry from such sources, observing life through a unique lens. Poets make ordinary events extraordinary through language, describing feelings and perceptions in ways that touch readers and listeners memorably.

Poetry's imaginative wordplay opens a doorway to literacy access and success for children—especially for kids who encounter difficulty reading and writing. Lengthy stories and chapter books can be daunting from the first paragraph to the last. A poem, with blank spaces breaking up the print, seems easier to read, start to finish. Writing a story of more than a few lines may appear to be an arduous task for a reluctant writer. By comparison, composing a short poem is a manageable, even an inviting way for kids to express ideas and feelings.

Awakening children's poetic imaginations involves hearing, reading, and writing poetry regularly. Kids learn from daily interactions with poets, young and old, published and unpublished, in books, on CD-ROM, online, or in person. As kids read poets and poems, they learn

- how language conveys images and feelings through poetry;
- concepts, vocabulary, and forms associated with poetry as a genre of writing;
- that they are poets right now as they communicate their imaginative perceptions through word choices they consider poetic.

Demonstrating how easy it is to stimulate children's love of poetry is the goal of Chapter Three: "Poems," for lovers of poems become lovers of words, images, surprise, humor, and thought. Poetry bestows excitement, satisfaction, emotion, and a glimpse of life through someone else's words. Poetry powers the desire to read and write prose and verse. Poetry's choices are so wide, so diverse, and so inspiring that infusing poetic language into children's daily activities can become the glue that builds relationships, improves moods, inspires conversations, and connects generations. Supply does indeed generate demand when kids like what is supplied.

The WOWs in this chapter begin with strategies for listening to and reading poetry and then present ideas for writing poetry using the different forms of acrostic, concrete, and voice poems.

- **WOW 8: Making Moments for Poetry Every Day** suggests that learning about the imaginative power of poetic language begins when children read and listen to poetry on a regular basis. "Extensions: Viewing Poetry as Poets Do" summarizes how several adult poets define poetry's essential elements: everyday experiences, intense feelings, compelling imagery, uncommon presentation, and unique viewpoint.

- **WOW 9: What's Hiding in Acrostic Poetry?** expands a kid-engaging form of poetry into a language play that kids enjoy doing over and over. An "Ever-Expanding Universe of Acrostic Wordplay" explains a host of acrostic poetry ideas that intrigue kids. "Extensions: A Treasure Chest of Spelling" discusses how acrostics assist youngsters to use the standard spelling of the words in their poems.

- **WOW 10: Concrete Poetry: Sketching and Sculpting Words into Pictures** introduces the creative possibilities of sketching and sculpting with words. Poems emerge from ways that writers arrange words to create unique visual pictures and displays. "Extensions: Picture Poems Lead Children to Spelling" shows how picture poems engage youngsters' creativity as they practice spelling.

- **WOW 11: Voices of Poetry** demonstrates how everyday conversations, both real and imaginary, can be the basis for imaginatively entertaining poems. Voice poetry can feature the singular voice of the poet, the different voices of two or more individuals (speaking in echoes or duets), or even the imagined voice of inanimate objects, animals, or other living things. "Extensions: Visual Spacing and Punctuation" considers how visual spacing and punctuation aid reading voice poems.

WOW 8

Making Moments for Poetry Every Day

Poetry Moments	TEACH	These Conventions *Unconventionally*
Magic Poetry Pot and Mystery Treasure Box		Introducing poetry
Reading Poetry Aloud • Poetry on CD-ROM		Read aloud strategies • Pitch, tempo, volume, tone
Reading Different Poets • Poetry Anthologies • Reading Individual Poets • Poetry by Kids		Anthologies and collections of poetry Publishing kids' poetry
Extensions: Viewing Poetry as Poets Do		Characteristics of poetry • Everyday experience • Intense feelings • Compelling images • Uncommon presentation • Unique viewpoint

Albert Cullum's 1967 book, *Push Back the Desks*, stresses inspiring children's learning by exciting their sense of wonder, humor, and curiosity. To animate poetry in a way that makes children want to hear and read poems often, he created a ritual called "Magic Poetry Pot." Before performing poetry, he darkened the classroom, placed a cast iron pot in the middle of the floor, lit a stick of incense to put inside the pot, and invited everyone to sit in a circle on the floor for a theater-like language experience.

Within the mood of mystery and drama, Cullum's recitations rose hair on the backs of necks and made kids laugh delightedly. Performance tools of timing, facial expressions, and voicing created his dramatic effects. Cullum and his students did not converse about the meaning of the poem's images or the meter and the form; every effort was directed toward enjoying these out-of-the-usual moments with poetry. Children, too, could bring their favorite poems to perform for Magic Poetry Pot. Once children were intrigued with poetry, Cullum would discuss vocabulary, tempo, rhyme, structure, and poets' styles at other times of the school day as part of language and writing lessons. In this way, Magic Poetry Pot attracted and sustained kids' affection for poetry all year long.

Adapting Cullum's method, Ruth purchased a small ionizer that oozed cool steam from its sides when submerged in water to create the illusion of a mystery treasure box transmitting poetry. To construct a surprising effect, she hid the ionizer inside a shoebox covered in plain black paper. In the shoebox was a plastic container with water to hold the ionizer. Its electric cord extended through a small hole cut in the cardboard. Ruth placed the black box near an outlet so she could quickly and inconspicuously plug it in whenever she wanted.

Her disguise of the ionizer kept everything dry and mysterious. The shoebox top was neither too loose nor too tight, allowing the cool vapor to escape uniformly around all four sides. The illusion of clouds emerging from under the lid was irresistibly attention-getting. When the treasure box's top was opened, a cloud of vapor rose skyward to reveal a poem taped to the lid.

The first time the children saw this happen, they stood transfixed with wonder. How had the box arrived in their room? What was the white smoke coming out of it? Why was a poem in the box? Who wrote it? Had anybody seen or heard anything that might be a clue to this mighty mystery?

No one but Ruth could explain how the poetry or the box had arrived in the classroom (and she was not hinting at its origins). The handwriting on a plastic overhead transparency was unfamiliar, giving no clue to the astonished kids. Seeing the poem projected onto a screen in front of everyone (via overhead projector) added even more excitement to the mystery! Ruth wrote her own poems on overhead transparencies in permanent marker. She copied poems from books onto transparencies at the copy machine. The plastic, being impervious to moisture, was the perfect vehicle for publishing the mystery poems.

Thereafter throughout the year whenever steam appeared—the signal that poetry was awaiting their discovery—children exclaimed: "It's happening again!" "There must be a message!" "Let's read it!" "Hurry Up!" These occasions became some of the most anticipated in the school week.

After the first few times that the mystery box produced vapor and poetry, kids began speaking to Ruth privately to give her poetry, jokes, riddles, or news that they had written, hoping it would appear in the box. She copied or typed their writing in book spelling, made an overhead, and taped it to the box lid. The children could either remain anonymous or read their writing aloud. In most cases, writers remained anonymous.

Whether poetry is introduced by a cast iron pot wafting incense into the air, an electric ionizer billowing waves of cool steam out its sides, or another equally surprising method, the desired outcome is accomplished. Out-of-the-ordinary activities propel children's excitement toward reading, performing, and writing poetry. Poetry connecting with audience anticipation, exhilaration, fascination, and participation produces an explosion of interest. Albert Cullum's fourth through sixth graders, Sharon's first, second, and third graders, and Ruth's kindergartners and first graders were thrilled by the mystery and the drama. They responded by writing, performing, and reading poetry for their own enjoyment and for their classmates' delight.

Reading Poetry Aloud

Poetry is meant to be heard. Its rhythms and rhymes, repetitions and rests, meters and cadences are as important to communicating its art as are the literal meanings of the words. Poetry closely resembles music and song whose notes and orchestrations must be heard to fully appreciate the composer's intent. But unlike music where the composer indicates instructions to the musicians, a reader must interpret the poet's words, building a memorable response to the language.

Though poetry appeals to its audiences for different reasons, its presentation invites reading aloud dramatically, humorously, expressively, passionately, convincingly, and excitedly. Octogenarian artist, poet, and performer Ashley Bryan regards poems as theatre pieces awaiting a voice and readers as conductors of a personal orchestra of voices and sounds of their own making. Bryan performs poetry to thrill and still, provoke giggles and gasps, produce edge-of-the-seat tension and shaking-with-laughter relief. Through varying voice, tempo, rhythm, and volume, Bryan maximizes a poem's potential to make listeners want to hear it again.

Read aloud performers Monty and Laurie Haas (1999) draw from their experiences as professional children's book readers and their years in broadcasting to teach adults how to create characters, to establish moods, and to reproduce the attraction of old radio story enactments by varying their speaking voices. With practice, anyone can develop a wide range of vocal qualities that will enliven poetic readings to kids:

- *Pitch*, from a low deep range to a high breathy range, creates illusions of size and power.
- *Tempo* changes mood—slowing down builds tension or creates suspense, speeding up generates excitement, fear, or the unexpected.
- *Volume* creates suspense or calm with whispering or hushed tones and tension or surprise with shouts.
- *Tone* adds meaning, revealing serious, ironic, joking, threatening, teasing, or lighthearted intent.

Demonstrations of how to vary pitch, tempo, volume, and tone appear constantly on TV, radio, the stage, or in the movies. Actors employ all of these tools to convincingly create the range of moods we call entertainment. Adults can practice these techniques to improve their poetry reading skills just as actors improve their performing skills. Children, renowned mimics, enjoy using these techniques to perform their own poetry and to experience the thrill of entertaining an audience with written and spoken language.

Poetry on CD-ROM

Poetry on CD-ROM lets kids see and hear poems performed aloud in a vivid interactive environment. Jack Prelutsky's *The New Kid on the Block* from Broderbund's *Living Books* series features the poet reading his poems. As he reads "When Tilly Ate the Chili," the poet's voice rises and falls, flows and chokes as the hot sauce reaches her throat. On the screen, the animated chili explodes from the heat. Kids will reread such memorable text to hear words and phrases again and again. Other excellent CD-ROM poetry programs include:

- *A Pizza the Size of the Sun*. Jack Prelutsky. Random House, 1999.
- *A Child's Garden of Songs: The Poetry of Robert Louis Stevenson*. Music for Little People, 1999.
- Dr. Seuss's *Green Eggs and Ham*, The Learning Company. Dr. Seuss's stories in poetic verse maintain a steady rhythm using rhyming couplets.

Children's songs and rhymes display poetry inserted into melody. Lyrics attract children to examine how songwriters use words to convey meaning and evoke emotion.

Reading Different Poets

Reading different poets introduces children to

- forms of poetry and styles of poets
- multiple ways a topic can be explored poetically

- the work of an individual poet
- the ways other children write poetry

Poetry Anthologies

Anthologies collect the work of many poets in one book where the different styles show poetry in action through

- single-verse poems
- longer poems with multiple stanzas
- rhymed and unrhymed lines
- use of repetition, similes, metaphors, and other figures of speech
- different poetic forms such as ballads, sonnets, voice poems, shape poems, and free verse

After children read for enjoyment, they can discuss the conventions of the form. In "Things," from her collection *Honey, I Love*, Eloise Greenfield contrasts the fleeting enjoyment of spending her weekly allowance on candy with the lasting joy of writing verses to keep forever. Her rhyme and rhythm catch the reader's ear and her use of distinct blocks of text on the page visually demonstrates the role of "stanzas" in poetry. Each stanza, like a paragraph, focuses on a specific topic.

A collection of poems exists for almost every topic that kids find fascinating, engrossing, and wonder-inspiring. Children's interests point them toward specific poetry collections. Lee Bennett Hopkins, Myra Cohn Livingston, and other poets have assembled collections on kid-riveting topics from growing up to reading books to learning mathematics.

Poetry organized by topic not only lets kids explore a topic of interest, but invites them to write poems about their special interests. *Sol a Sol*, a collection of bilingual poems written and selected by Lori Marie Carlson, celebrates one family's activities *de sol a sol* (from sunup to sundown) in English and Spanish. *My America: A Poetry Atlas of the United States* by Lee Bennett Hopkins describes states of the Northeast, Southeast, Great Lakes, Plains, Mountain, Southwest, and Pacific Coast plus the nation's Capitol in verse—an inspiring way to explore geography and social studies topics.

Reading Individual Poets

Reading a favorite poet is like inviting a special friend over to visit and have fun together. Adults and children can choose a poet and read her or his poems, a few at a time, for a week or longer, to increase familiarity with the lines, the language, and the poet as a person. Children may be inspired to write their own poems in a similar style, as Brianna and Quitze did after hearing selections from Arnold Adoff's *Chocolate Dreams* (Figure 3.1).

Poetry by Kids

Poetry composed by kids is another way to sustain children's interest in poetry. *Salting the Ocean: 100 Poems by Young Poets* edited by Naomi Shihab Nye with pictures by Ashley Bryan is one excellent anthology. Online, poetry by kids can be found at "Poetry Pals: The K–12 Student Poetry Publishing Project" at www.geocities.com/EnchantedForest/5165/index1.html and at Scholastic's "Poetry Writing with Jack Prelutsky, Karla Kuskin, and Jean Marzollo" at http://teacher.scholastic.com/writewit/poetry/index.htm.

(A)

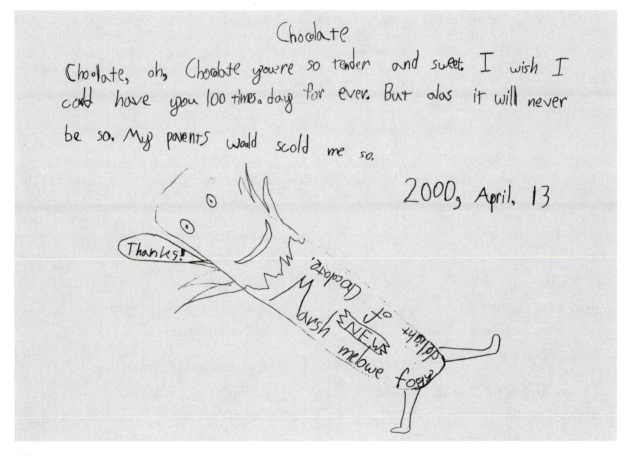

(B)

Figure 3.1 *"Chocolate" poems by Brianna and Quitze. Translations:*

(A) **Chocolate** by Brianna. Swimming in chocolate lakes, climbing on chocolate mountain, baking chocolate cakes, living the life of chocolate.

(B) **Chocolate** by Quitze. Chocolate, oh, chocolate, you're so tender and sweet. I wish I could have you 100 times a day for ever. But alas it will never be so. My parents would scold me so.

Viewing Poetry as Poets Do

Explaining to children what poetry is and how it differs from prose is not simple. Clearly, it is more than metaphor, simile and rhyme. But, to say that poetry is wonderfully descriptive language is incomplete. Description appears in all forms of fiction stories and nonfiction writing as well. In defining poetry's essential characteristics, Lee Bennett Hopkins, Ken Macrorie, David M. Johnson, Herbert Kohl, and Barbara Juster Esbensen emphasize the following features:

- Everyday experience
- Intense feeling
- Compelling image
- Uncommon presentation
- Unique viewpoint

These qualities suggest explanations for what poetry is. Examining each one imparts ideas for composing language poetically. In the selections that follow, we pair each adult poet's description of poetry with poems written by kids that convey the same qualities. Children presenting their feelings, images, and viewpoints poetically offer models for other kids as they portray their own experiences in verse.

Everyday Experience

"A poem is an experience," declares Lee Bennett Hopkins (8), "something that has happened to a person, something that may seem very obvious, an everyday occurrence that has been set down in a minimum number of words and lines as it has never been set down

---

Train Town
by Taylor
(who drew a picture of train tracks
to accompany his poem after
visiting Roanoke, Virginia)

Do you know what I think Roanoke is?
Train Town!
Can you hear the whistles in Train
Town?
Choo Choo Choo Choo
There is something coming down the track.

The Weather
By Elijah
(who wrote the weather report
for a day in October)

Today's weather is a feather.
Yesterday's was mostly hay.
Tomorrow's is raining sorrows.
Next week we're expecting cheeks.

Figure 3.2 *Two children's "everyday experience" poems.*

Figure 3.3

Mariah's poem.

Homework for Me
by Mariah

I love to do homework when Ms. Edwards gives it to us.
Loving homework is very weird and also from your teacher.
Orange homework. Yellow homework. It does not matter.
Violin homework. Piano homework. Reading homework. I don't care.
Even TV homework. I fill boxes of homework for me.
Right homework. Left homework. What a way to go.
Eating homework. Spelling homework. Let me say it again.
A box of homework for me. One or two and maybe three.
Do you know how much homework I want?

before." While poets use different forms and styles, "all write about everyday happenings from their own points of view about their environments." Ultimately, says Hopkins (19), "poetry should make us 'see, hear, and feel something that prose cannot'." (See Figure 3.2.)

Intense Feelings

Poetry "uses all the strategies of prose but more fully and intensely," states Ken Macrorie (217). Macrorie notes that epic poet John Milton saw poetry as more "simple, sensuous, and passionate" than prose. Simple in that poetry is "nothing fancy. No parading of the writer's vocabulary, no insisting with adjectives and adverbs" (218). Sensuous in that poems "appeal to the senses. Their objects and actions are not abstracted but presented concretely"

The Poem of the Orange Fairy
by Sarah

When the orange fairy comes out tonight her magic dust will make it light and wake up all the silver bells which give children orange peels.

The Poem of the Lilac Fairy
by Sarah

When the lilac fairy comes out tonight her lilac wand will become so bright that all the children will hide in fright and that's what will happen tonight.

Figure 3.4   *Sarah's poems.*

Figure 3.5

Mariah's "Winter/Spring/Planet" poem.

Winter, oh winter, is going by-by
    and spring is saying hi-hi. I am
    sad winter
Is going away, far away for the year.
Now I like the seasons, I like them a lot
Tardy spring, tardy winter, tardy fall
    and tardy summer.
Electric lights go on and off
Rabbits come out and say, Hi!!

Spring is here! Spring is here!
    Spring's the best time of the year.
Pouncing here, pouncing there
Ringing, springing, Spring is here!
I love old spring, the great old spring.
November spring, can it be true?
Green grass growing — it's spring!!!

People think there are nine planets
    but there are
Lots more. Scientists
Are finding lots more planets — 10, 11, 12, or 13 —
No one knows how much.
Eating peanuts on each planet
Tasting each kind there is.

(219). Passion is generated because "good poetry carries surprise" in the way it conveys feelings, emotions, intensity, or tranquillity (220). (See Figure 3.3.)

Compelling Imagery

"The image is the heart of poetry," says David M. Johnson (30). In his view, the creative process itself involves fashioning images that provide a "medium for participating in the world: seeing, hearing, smelling, touching, tasting. Images allow us to envision the world, hear its voices, smell roasting corn and cotton candy at the state fair" (28).

In Johnson's view, "song and story are twin poles of poetry" (17). Song comes from the spontaneous lyricism of poetic language. Story emerges from how poetry expresses the

If I had wings . . . .
By Jacob

If I had wings, I would soar through the air and be free.
I would choose if I would like to go to school or not.
I could sleep on a cloud instead of a bed.
Or maybe I could sleep in thin air.
Ha! But that's impossible.
You could only do that if you impossibly grow wings
Because that would be amazing.

Figure 3.6 *Jacob's poem.*

intensely memorable moments of daily life. Together, song and story make us pause and consider human experience and our own small connections to the whole. Creatively, the poet's images link people and experience, yet the stories of poems are not made-up, make-believe fictions, but extensions and reflections of personal experiences. Poetry, says Johnson, offers "imaginative narrative, but *not* imaginary narrative" (17). (See Figure 3.4.)

Uncommon Presentation

"Poetry is a form of song," concludes Herbert Kohl (4), "a boundary art between music and conversation." Kohl's love of poetry began in junior high school where he discovered "a world beyond my own world in images and phrases that both moved me and made me aware of the imaginative possibilities of language" (2). To appreciate poetry, Kohl urges an unhurried approach, "letting the images sit in your mind, hearing the rhythm of the poetry and the voice of the poet" (27) (see Figure 3.5).

Unique Viewpoint

Poetry illuminates "old familiar things as though we'd never seen them before," says Barbara Juster Esbensen (9). When her five-year-old son rushed in from the garden to declare there was a "celebration of bees" outside, Esbensen heard poetry in his words. Eight-year-old Edwin expressed a unique image one spring morning while studying the arrival of the vernal equinox. Coming in from outside, he declared: "In the early morning weird shadows walk to their places."

To compose poetry, explains Esbensen (10), no special rules or stylized language is needed. Instead, young poets choose words "to be accurate, to say what they really mean, and to say it as economically as possible." The goal is to "capture the feelings and impressions we call experience, the all but inaudible music we sense in ourselves." (See Figure 3.6.)

Reading or hearing poems by children and adults that emphasize, highlight, or display one of poetry's features, interest kids in composing poems that focus on that feature. This is a way for children to experiment with words and styles while presenting their own images and ideas poetically. In the writing, reading, and performing of poetry, kids develop affection for poetry and fascination with language.

Young Writers' Bookshelf for Poetry Moments

Poetry from A to Z: A Guide for Young Writers. Complied by Paul B. Janecczko. Antheneum, 1994. Kid-engaging poems, poetry writing ideas, and discussions with poets are included in this excellent introduction to poetry.

No More Homework! No More Tests! Edited by Bruce Lansky. Illustrated by Stephen Carpenter. Meadowbrook Press, 1997. A collection of poems about school.

Pass It On: African American Poetry for Children. Wade Hudson, ed. Illustrated by Floyd Cooper. Scholastic, 1993. Paul Laurence Dunbar, Countee Cullen, Langston Hughes, and Gwendolyn Brooks are among the poets featured in this collection.

Space between Our Footsteps: Poems and Paintings from the Middle East. Selected by Naomi Shihab Nye. Simon & Schuster Books for Young Readers, 1998. Over one hundred poems from Middle Eastern countries.

Americans' Favorite Poems: The Favorite Poem Project Anthology. Edited by Robert Pinsky and Maggie Dietz. W. W. Norton, 1999. Two hundred poems with comments by the readers who chose them.

A Jar of Tiny Stars: Poems by NCTE Award-Winning Poets. Bernice E. Cullinan, ed. Boyds Mills Press, 2000. An anthology featuring David McCord, Aileen Fisher, Karla Kushin, Myra Cohn Livingston, Eve Merriam, John Ciardi, Lilian Moore, Arnold Adoff, Valerie Webb, and Barbara Esbensen. David McCord has assembled twenty-five of his finest verses for children in *Every Time I Climb a Tree.*

Good Rhymes, Good Times. Lee Bennett Hopkins. Illustrated by Frane Lessac. HarperCollins, 2000. Also see *School Supplies* by Lee Bennett Hopkins (with illustrations by Renee Flower). Two of more than forty poetry collections for children by a leading anthologist.

For Laughing Out Loud: Poems to Tickle Your Funnybone. Compiled by Jack Prelutsky. Illustrated by Marjorie Priceman. Knopf, 1991. Many poets use forms of humor to describe all things funny.

Wonders: The Best Children's Poems of Effie Lee Newsome. Compiled by Rudine Sims Bishop. Illustrated by Louis Mailou Jones. Boyds Mills Press, 1999. A poetry collection by the first African American poet who wrote primarily for children.

Heart to Heart: New Poems Inspired by Twentieth-Century American Art. Edited by Jan Greenberg. Harry N. Abrams, 2001. Forty-three poems especially written for this book celebrate well-known works of contemporary art that are reproduced here in stunning color.

Books Cited in the Text

Salting the Ocean: 100 Poems by Young Poets. Edited by Naomi Shihab Nye with pictures by Ashley Bryan. Greenwillow Books, 2000.

My America: A Poetry Atlas of the United States by Lee Bennett Hopkins. Illustrated by Stephen Alcorn. Simon & Schuster Books for Young Readers, 2000.

Sol a Sol. Bilingual Poems written and selected by Lori Marie Carlson. Illustrated by Emily Lisker. Holt, 1998.

What's Hiding in Acrostic Poetry?

Acrostic Poems	TEACH	These Conventions *Unconventionally*
"Word Mystery Theater:" A Game of Suspense		Genre: Acrostic poetry Audience interest and involvement
An Ever-Expanding Universe of Acrostic Wordplay • Single Word Acrostics • Humor Acrostics • Detour Acrostics • Descriptive Language Acrostics • Story Acrostics • Acrostics across the Curriculum		Vocabulary building Different forms and styles of acrostics Exploring science, mathematics, and social studies
Extensions: A Treasure Chest of Spelling		Phonemic awareness Spelling knowledge Reading left to right Using the dictionary

Now I can call the roosters. Oh the stars! Our stars are gone. Very very slowly, maybe the sun will rise. Every minute everything gets bright. My my, it is pretty. I love it. Bells are ringing. Everyone get up! Rowdy noises fill the town.

Are these lines from a poem or sentences from a story? Were they written by an adult author or a young writer? Reading them, it is impossible to answer definitively. Reformating the text into a vertical stack and **bolding** the beginning letter of each line, a child-inviting style of poetry known as "acrostics" emerges from the position of the words (Figure 3.7).

Youngsters find that placing the letters of words vertically down the page and using each letter to propel the message and imagery of a poem is exhilarating rather than inhibiting. Here is a way to compose funny, beautiful, surprising, and thoughtful poetry without rhyming words, maintaining a rhythm, or creating stanzas.

The simplicity of the acrostic does not mean that simple poems emerge from it. Children's acrostics contain imaginative ideas and inventive language that delight young poets and older audiences alike. This unique style, combining the wordplay and mystery of hiding words, invites creativity and ingenuity. Young poets surprise readers and listeners with the expressive images they place in their acrostics and the apparent ease with which they compose them.

Despite kids and adults' enjoyment of writing them, acrostics are not as widely explored as they ought to be. Adults are unfamiliar with the potential of this poetry to express ideas, knowledge, and feelings possessed by young writers. Acrostics never limit creativity, they encourage children to think in uncommon ways, and thinking uncommonly is the beginning of composing poetry.

"Word Mystery Theater": A Game of Suspense

Children's acrostics initiate other kids' interest in writing these remarkable poems. After a child's poem is read aloud, we display the acrostic using an overhead projector and screen. In order to show the audience that there is a hidden word in the poem, we cover everything else but the word, written vertically down the side of the page, and we say: "See how Katherine has hidden 'November' in her poem." Then we read the poem aloud again, remarking that this poem is one of hundreds that could be composed using the letters of this word.

Reading a poem aloud without revealing the word hidden inside is how we begin acrostic poetry. We want the audience to hear the words, appreciate the language, and savor the imagery first. Then we introduce "Word Mystery Theater" where the audience tries to discover the word(s) hidden inside the poem. Once acrostics are a familiar form to kids, they listen with two intents—to appreciate the poem and to try to identify the hidden words. Audience engagement in the suspense is so intense that children do not recognize it as literacy practice in a creative, game-like format.

Here is how "Word Mystery Theater" can be played, time after time:

- A child writes an acrostic poem hiding a word or a phrase.
- The word(s) hidden in the poem is known only to the poet, and possibly a friend or two, who promise secrecy.

Now I can call the roosters.

Oh the stars! Our stars are gone

Very very slowly, maybe the sun will rise.

Every minute everything gets bright.

My my, it is pretty. I love it.

Bells are ringing.

Everyone get up!

Rowdy noises fill the town.

Figure 3.7 *Katherine's "November" poem.*

- The poem is read aloud in an interesting voice and manner for everyone's appreciation of the language, images, and content.
- The poet informs the audience that this is an acrostic and they are about to play "Word Mystery Theater." A classmate is chosen to be the recorder at the chalkboard or easel in front of the group.
- The poem is then reread differently, not for audience appreciation, but for detective-like investigation to identify the word(s) hidden inside. The poet reads the each line aloud and stops, waiting while the recorder writes the first letter of the first word in the line. The whole class is watching to make sure that the scribe records the correct letter. Left to right, letter by letter, the hidden word(s) appears in front of the audience.
- Youngsters select the word(s) they want to hide—"summer vacation," "meteor," "tarantula." Occasionally, Sharon assigns a word or phrase to pairs or small groups so the class can be surprised by the different poems that result. If everyone in the class hides the same word, no two acrostics will be the same.

When the recorder does not write the correct beginning letter for the first word in a line—the child may not know what letter makes a particular sound or how to write it correctly—other children are quick to offer hints and suggestions. If the recorder does not hear the first word, the poet rereads the line. This is one of the important features of the game—a child need not know all of the letters to be a recorder. Class involvement and assistance allow everyone to participate. This is why acrostics interest kindergartners, too, as they learn the sound/symbol correspondence of letters.

Hiding and uncovering words in acrostic poems engages youngsters' interest with language in new and different ways. First, they have reasons to spell words in standard spelling, a point we shall discuss in more depth later in this section. Second, children are in command of the writing process, making decisions about words to use horizontally and vertically in the poem. They encounter acrostic poetry writing as a language-rich experience where words convey meanings and images.

Finally, acrostic poetry acquaints young writers with the connection that exists between a writer and her or his audience. Playing "Word Mystery Theater," the poet observes how other children respond. Do they figure out the hidden word immediately or does it take awhile to solve the puzzle? The writer becomes as involved as the readers in this process of concealing, investigating, and discovering. What evolves from repeated observations of audience response is a thunderclap of awareness for many youngsters—they discover that word choices matter. As authors, they possess real power; how they compose their poem has a huge and immediate impact on their audience. Other kids are amused, delighted, and excited by these extraordinary poems, which is why "Word Mystery Theater" sustains its appeal throughout the year.

An Ever-Expanding Universe of Acrostic Wordplay

There are unlimited ways to construct acrostics. Seeing a new form or variation motivates kids to try it. What follows is the beginning of "An Ever-Expanding Encyclopedia of Acrostics." Expecting that you and your young writers will compose new forms and variations of acrostic poems, we urge you to add your ideas to the encyclopedia's collection.

Single Word Acrostics

Many youngsters, particularly beginning readers, start writing short acrostics that use either one word or few words per line, as Chelsea did when she composed a poem about a time of day that was important to her (Figure 3.8).

Figure 3.8

*Chelsea's "Daylight"
poem.*

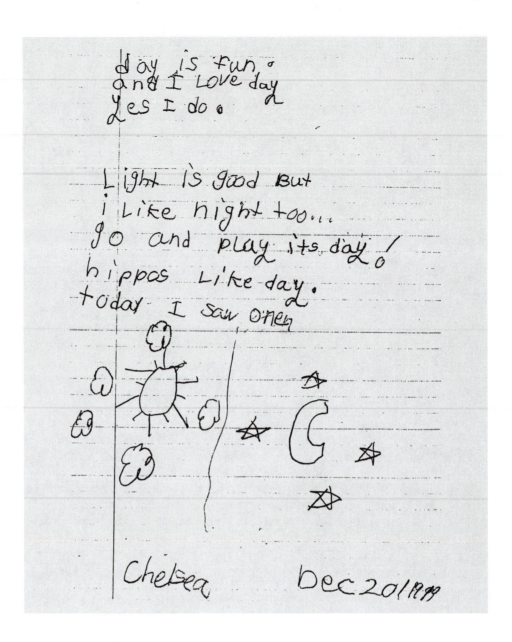

Humor Acrostics

Children purposefully encode a word or convey a message in their poem in a playful manner that is intended to make people laugh. Kids enjoy discovering unusual phrases or word surprises that come from their imaginations as they use the letters of the words to inspire their lines, as in the examples (Figure 3.9) by Izzy ("Peanut"), Elijah ("Christmas") and E. J. ("I Love You").

Detour Acrostics

When kids deliberately attempt to fool listeners into thinking a poem is about one subject when it is about an entirely different topic, they are structuring a detour for the audience. Quitze had a detour in mind with his word, "tarantula" (Figure 3.10). His poem describes the leaves changing color, leading most readers to assume he has hidden a word about fall or seasonal change. Instead, he has purposely misdirected his audience's attention, adding clever surprise to the "Word Mystery Theater" game.

Figure 3.9

Humor acrostics by Izzy, Elijah, and E. J.

Izzy 11/9/01

Peas are green
even in the pods.
At
night they are
usually peas but
tonight they are
monsters!

Christmas

Caterpillars
Hear tapes
Rewind
In
Summer. They also
Take your
Maple syrup
After
Sundown

I Love You

If you stand by me I might kiss you,
Love you and hug you and
Oooh I might marry you.
Very soon, very soon,
Even right now.
You make me happy.
Oh, you are magnificent.
Uck, I changed my mind.

As the kids in the class puzzled over what his hidden word could be, Quitze's satisfaction was evident. He had successfully achieved what he wanted to do with his poem—stump the audience!

Descriptive Language Acrostics

Acrostics offer endless possibilities for using language imaginatively and descriptively. Here are two examples from the same second-grade poet (Figure 3.11). In the poem called

Figure 3.10

*Quitze's "Tarantula's"
poem.*

Today the leaves are turning different colors
And everything is beautiful.
Ready to see the leaves on the trees.
Animals like the leaves too.
Nobody does not like the Fall.
Tomorrow I am going to get some leaves.
Under the trees the leaves do fall.
Leaves in Fall are beautiful.
A leaf, I love leaves.

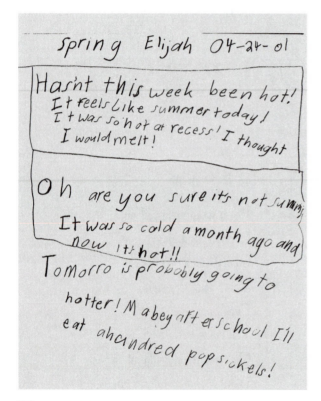 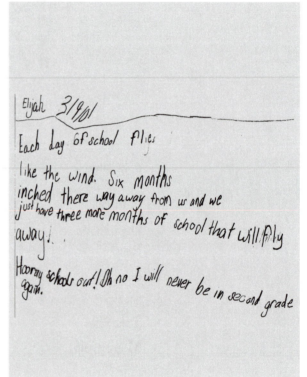

Figure 3.11   *Two acrostics by Elijah. Translation:*

Spring

By Elijah

Hasn't this week been hot! It feels like summer today! It was so hot at recess I thought I would melt.

Oh are you sure it's not summer. It was so cold a month ago and now it's hot!!

Tomorrow is probably going to be hotter! Maybe after school I'll eat a hundred popsickles!

Elijah

By Elijah

Each day of school flies

Like the wind. Six months

Inched their way away from us and we

just have three months of school that will fly

away.

Hooray school's out! Oh no, I will never be in second grade again.

"Spring," Elijah creates multiple sentences to accompany each letter of the word "hot." In a poem using the letters of his first name, Elijah comments descriptively on the passing of the school year.

Montana recalls her "Summer Vacation" in sentences that wrap around (continue from one line to the next) to make the description flow (Figure 3.12).

Story Acrostics

Kids tell stories, both true and make-believe in acrostics. "The Best Field Trip Ever" by Chantel and Khalea is a factual report of a class field trip, in which the two authors compose alternate lines (Figure 3.13).

Acrostics across the Curriculum

Acrostics give children a format for reflecting on important concepts and complex ideas in science, mathematics, and social studies using something other than an expository form of writing. Kids will express sophisticated ideas freely in an acrostic format, as Sharon discovered when she asked her first and second graders to write and send cards to the civil rights pioneer Rosa Parks on her seventy-fifth birthday. Six-year-old Kayla decided she was going to use verse to convey her message and began "Roses are red, violets are blue."

"That rhyme is so old, let's do something new," suggested Sharon as she wrote "Rosa Parks," vertically down the blackboard with "Rosa" and "Parks" in two columns, side-by-side—an acrostic form not yet tried by anyone in the class. A small group assembled as

Summer Vacation

By Montana

Summer is almost here
Until it is Fall again.
My
My
Everyone loves warm weather,
Really they do.
Very pretty rainbows shine up ahead.
A bumblebee's nest filled with honey.
Could it be true that summer is
Almost here?
Tomatoes are ripening
In my garden.
Oh what a joy
Never been such a pleasure.

Figure 3.12 *Montana's "Summer Vacation" poem.*

The Best Field Trip Ever

By Chantel & Khalea

Today we had a great field trip.

Have you ever been to Hastings before?

Eek yes.

Bertucci's is fun to go and eat at.

Everytime we went outside on the field trip it was raining.

Some people got soaked.

Today only 13/18 came.*

Five and one is six and that's how many books Ms.

Edwards got the class.

I liked when Ms. Edwards got the class Smarties.

Liking Smarties is good.

Do you know Khalea and Sarah can play?

The violin was

Really good but it was a machine.

I liked to pretend that I was really good at the violin.

Playing the violin is hard for some people.

Everybody wanted to play the violin but Ms. Edwards said "No." The

Violin had batteries in it.

Everybody walked to Bertucci's. The

Rain was dropping hard.

*18/18 represents the whole class of eighteen students

Figure 3.13 *Story acrostics by Chantel and Khalea.*

Kayla and Sharon looked at this new format for a moment before making suggestions for the text.

"Kayla, you could begin with 'Rosa Parks'," Sharon said excitedly as she pointed to *R* for Rosa and next to it *P* for Parks.

"On a," one of other the children continued, looking at the *o* and the *a*.

"Seat," said Bob as he read the *s* in Rosa.

"Bye everybody," said Kayla, leaving to finish writing the acrostic by herself (Figure 3.14). After completing a first draft, Kayla postponed eating her lunch to create a final version, adding a drawing of Rosa Parks standing beside a bus, and decorating the page with red and yellow wallpaper samples.

Figure 3.14

Kayla's poem to Rosa Parks. Translation:

Rosa Parks
on a
seat riding
an unkind
sity [city] bus.
Happy Birthday.
From Kayla.

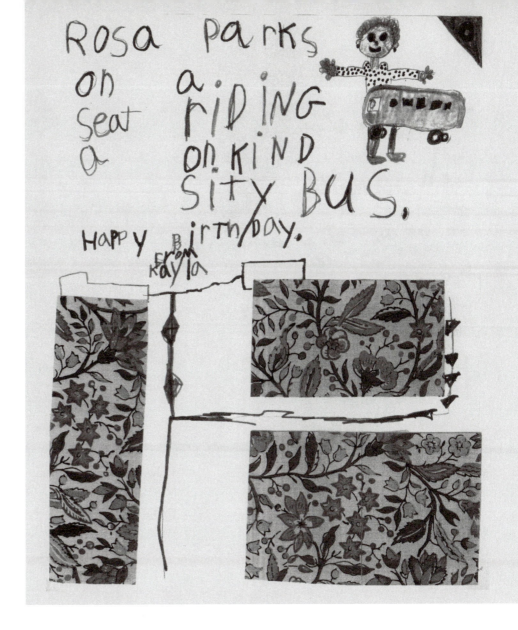

Kayla's acrostic poem was one of those unexpected and unplanned classroom moments that teach adults so much about how children learn to express their ideas using poetry. Although the class had been listening to many forms of poetry read aloud, and the children had written acrostic poems several times, Sharon never anticipated that a young writer could communicate her thoughts about history and discrimination so powerfully using an acrostic structure.

Acrostics can report science facts and information or responses in a personal form. Two examples from a study of earth changes by second graders demonstrate this. The first, written by Ben in November, announces the Leonid Meteor Shower. The second, by Garrett, reflects on a March snowfall (Figure 3.15).

At the end of his poem, Ben added this expression of voice that personalizes his report for his audience: "Meteors can be as small as gravel or as big as Texas! I find that amazing. How about you?"

In mathematics, acrostic poetry connects ideas from one language, that of numbers, with another language, that of words. Kids can use this frame for explaining math activities, concepts, or definitions, as Chris has done in his poem about measuring the seasons (Figure 3.16).

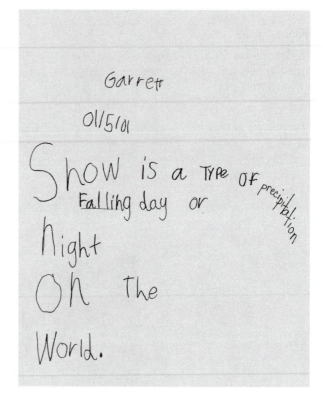

Figure 3.15 *Children's science acrostics by Ben and Garrett. Translation:*

Meteors are burning rocks
Eek something hit me!
To be a meteor you have to be on fire.
Everybody loves shooting stars.
Oh something hit me.
Rah a giant meteor.

Snow is a type of precipitation falling day or
Night
On the
World.

Figure 3.16

Chris's math acrostic.

May is a season that has Memorial Day in it.

Easter is in April.

April is the month before May and there are two more months left until

Summer!!!! But . . . . . this month is

Unusual.

Really it is unusual to be in the

Eigthies.*

[*the temperature for a week in May was unusually high]

A Treasure Chest of Spelling

Acrostics focus children's attention on exploring words, their meanings, and their spellings. They are an entryway to learning more about letter sound relationships, left to right reading progression, and using dictionaries and other word resources.

Spelling Knowledge

To enjoy playing "Word Mystery Theater," words must be written in "book" or "dictionary spelling." When Caroline hid the name "Mighty Joe" in a poem, but spelled mighty as "mimty," the class became confused and frustrated trying to read it. This was a powerful demonstration of readers depending on standard spelling to convey a message. When words are spelled in a child's spelling, other readers cannot easily decipher what is being communicated or enjoy the anticipation and excitement of discovering the hidden mystery terms.

As they begin playing the acrostic mystery game, young children do not focus attention on spelling first. What matters to them are the game-like features of this poetry—the hidden words, the opportunity to mystify an audience, the excitement of discovering what others have written. Yet identifying sounds and their corresponding letter symbols is inherent to the acrostic format. To figure out the spelling of a hidden word, children first ask themselves, "What letter(s) makes that sound?" Then they inquire "How do these letters blend together?" As more letters are revealed, they concentrate on identifying words: "What words begin with these letters?" The audience expresses its satisfaction at identifying a hidden word before it fully appears.

As words emerge, kids and adults have opportunities to discuss letter sounds as clues for word spellings. For example, with "circle," a child recording the letters might ask, "Which letter do I write, *s* or *c*?" presenting a teachable moment for the class. If the recorder does not ask the question, another child usually remarks, "It is a *c*, not an *s* in that word." Seeing the dictionary spelling of hidden words shows kids that book spelling in English may be close to or astonishingly different from the way words sound. This initiates discussion about how similar sounds may come from different letters, which is one reason for learning a lot about spelling.

Acrostics give adults and children the opportunity to analyze many phonemic features of letter sounds and spelling patterns:

- Spelling of words that sound the same may look different (*weight/wait*).
- Similar sounds may have multiple possible spellings (*caught/ought/hot*).
- Endings change spellings for plurals (*baby/babies; day/days*).
- Adding *ed* is tricky because words like *jumped*, *stepped*, or *walked* have an ending sound like *t* not *ed*.
- Adding *ing* requires most words with one vowel to double their final consonant (*running*) but not when followed by two consonants (as with *camping*, *golfing*, or *sorting*).
- Identifying odd-spelling patterns that make sound chunks—*ight* as in *light* and *might*; *tion* and *sion* in *action* or *commission*.
- Recognizing small words inside larger words—*if, is, up, on, at*—or sound combinations inside larger words—*ing, un, ar, er, ly*.
- Teaming two vowels may produce different sounds (*bear, fear, weather*) or *ou*, as in (*soup, should, out*).

- Examining silent letters in English spellings in words like *knee, piece, cake, sword,* and *people*.
- Blending consonants (*st, str, bl, pr, br, fr*) or constructing consonant digraphs with two letters to make one sound (*sh, ch, wh, th*).

In the process of identifying the standard spelling of words for their poems, readers and writers analyze multiple phonemic components within a word. The word *friend*, hidden in a poem, includes a silent letter (*i*), a small word inside a bigger word (*end*), and a consonant blend (*fr*)—all important knowledge for spelling.

In kindergarten and first grade as children begin to spell, write, and read, names hiding in acrostics demonstrate letter sound correspondence while attracting attention to and inviting interest in literacy development. Children like to see their names emerge on the chalkboard and everyone tries to identify the name in the fewest letters possible. A teacher might compose an acrostic name poem to read aloud each day at meeting time to initiate activities with spelling, phonics, reading, and writing. It is unnecessary to tell a group or a class that a child's name is hidden in a poem once they have seen a poem reveal a name.

Reading from Left to Right

Young readers and writers profit from daily practice visually scanning text from left to right. Consistent directionality of reading and writing is a convention best learned by interacting with and creating text over and over again. Publishing acrostics on chalkboards or write-on, wipe-off boards, one letter at a time, lets kids practice scanning the word(s) being revealed left to right.

Many youngsters do not know that while English reads left to right, Hebrew and Arabic reads right to left, Chinese and Japanese reads top to bottom. Kids are surprised to learn that when printing first occurred, people read right to left and at the end of the line, read back left to right.

Using the Dictionary

Identifying the standard spelling of words hidden in acrostic poems invites an explanation of the use of dictionaries—so people living in different parts of the country and the world can communicate more easily in common spellings. Needing to do the same thing—correctly spell the words they are hiding so that their classmates can read them—raises children's interest in seeking out resources to assist them. Kids turn to dictionaries, pictionaries, electronic spellers, or other resources to find the spelling of favorite words (from "tiger" to "tyrannosaurus rex"). Dictionaries also give kids access to many word choices, familiarize them with alphabetization, and demonstrate the usefulness of knowing words' definitions and spellings.

The New Oxford Picture Dictionary: English/Spanish is an excellent resource for early readers or ESL (English as a second language) learners. *The MacMillan Dictionary for Children* is used by second, third, and fourth graders. *The American Heritage Children's Dictionary* and the *Simon and Schuster New Millennium Dictionary* on CD-ROM are attractive and interactive with animation, games, and voice-over pronunciations of words.

Electronic spellers with a speaking voice that reads the words are another resource for finding book spellings of words kids want to use in poems. Franklin Electronic Resources (www.franklin.com) has excellent hand-held dictionaries and spellers, including one with English and Spanish language voice capacities.

Young Writers' Bookshelf for Acrostic Poetry

Spring: An Alphabet Acrostic. Steven Schnur. Illustrated by Leslie Evans. Clarion Books, 1999. Short acrostics and bright color illustrations paint word pictures of the spring season. Also *Summer* (2001) and *Autumn* (1997) by the same author.

Animal Acrostics. David Mark Hummon. Illustrated by Michael S. Maydak. Dawn Publications, 1999. Animals and their habitats are described in acrostic poetry.

Scooter. Vera Williams. HarperTrophy, 2001. Wonderfully elaborate acrostic word pictures begin each chapter of this story about the adjustments that a young girl must make when her family moves to New York City.

Concrete Poetry: Sketching and Sculpting Words into Pictures

Concrete Poems	TEACH	These Conventions *Unconventionally*
Designing Picture Poems • Words Fill a Picture • Words Outline a Picture • Words Shape a Picture		Genre: Concrete poetry building vocabulary Spelling practice Left to right progression
Poetic Letters and Word Sketching • Poetic Letters • Word Sketching		Letter sound associations Letter formation Upper and lowercase letters Encoding and decoding
Sculpting Three-Dimensional (3-D) *Picture Poems*		Word recognition
Extensions: Picture Poems Lead Children *to Spelling*		Spelling knowledge Spelling picture poems Phonemic patterns Homophones

Concrete Poetry? Why would anyone write poetry in concrete? Won't writing on paper accomplish the same result? Concrete poetry is not about etching words in cement. It is about painting pictures with words. Words become tools—the pencils, pens, and paints—that make visual images, as the following young poets show in their poems (Figure 3.17).

Quitze's black-handled, gold-domed bell releases its *RRRRRRRING* in long peals. Khalea and Jamie's dolphins leap from a blue ocean on an intensely bright day as rays of sunshine stream down from a golden sun. Birds and clouds fly by an island and a palm tree.

Welcome to the eye-pleasing, out-of-the-ordinary realm of "concrete" or "picture" poetry. Once made or viewed, these poems possess a permanence of unique image different from that of words or pictures alone. As concrete mixes water and sand to make a stronger substance, so concrete poetry combines words with images to produce memorable pictures.

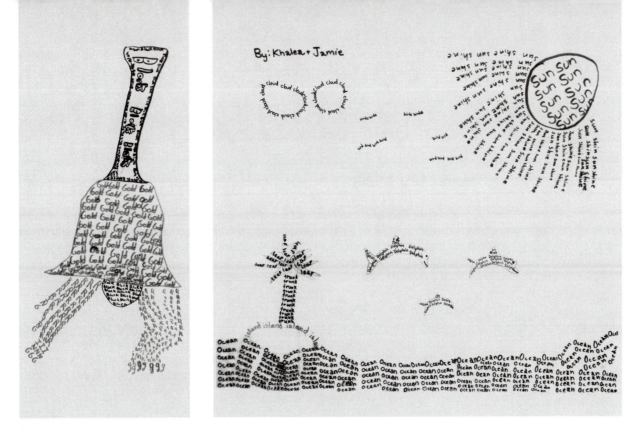

Figure 3.17 *Picture poems by Quitze, Khalea, and Jamie.*

Picture poems assemble words for graphic design to make different hues and textures, colors, and shapes. In concrete poetry, notes Ron Padgett (53), "typeface, symbol, shape, spatial relationships between letters, words, and lines" are the essential ingredients in the writing. Arranging picture poems offers endless opportunities for children to easily, entertainingly, and energetically increase their knowledge of vocabulary and spelling.

Designing Picture Poems

Concrete or picture poems start with abandoning the idea that poetry must be a linear, left to right progression across the page, instead adopting the idea that words, lines, and letters can go in many directions—horizontally, vertically, diagonally, or in geometric patterns. "Box" may appear conventionally as **BOX** or poetically as:

```
BOXBOXBOXB        BOXBOXBOXBOX
O        O        BOXBOXBOXBOXBOXBOX
X        X        BOXBOXBOXBOX
B        B        BOXBOXBOXBOXBOXBOX
O        O        BOXBOXBOXBOX
XBOXBOXBOX        BOXBOXBOXBOXBOXBOX
                  BOXBOXBOXBOX
```

```
BBBBBBBBBBBBBBBBBBBBBBBBBB
OOOOOOOOOOOOOOOOOOOOOOOO
XXXXXXXXXXXXXXXXXXXXXXXX
```

In picture poems, not only do words move in unusual ways, but paper also becomes a movable medium. Turn it sideways, upside down, and even fold or cut it. The shapes, sizes, curves, and patterns of the letters become tools for design, transforming writing surfaces into endless varieties of unique linguistic and artistic images. This process of thoughtful design is child-directed, intellectually stimulating, and imaginatively exciting. Here are three styles kids have employed in their picture poem designs:

Words Fill a Picture

A poet draws an object and fills it with words related to the object. The word *ball* written many times might fill in a circle. *Black*, *white*, *red*, and *soccer* appear inside the patterns of a soccer ball. Ola's "Rocket Plane" (Figure 3.18) displays an aircraft filled with drawings of rocks and the spellings of the word "plane."

Words Outline a Picture

A poet uses names of persons, places, or things to outline the shape of an object. In Elijah's snowy day poem, words form the clouds, snowflakes, blue sky and the sun's rays as well as the sled, snow, grass, leaves, and rock lying on the ground (Figure 3.19). Words adorn the outline of the tree, house, road, door, and window.

Words Shape a Picture

A poet uses words to create pictorial images that "dramatize their meaning by the way they look" (Padgett 52). A "waterfall" might be crafted with some of the letters making a pool

Figure 3.18

Ola's "Rocket Plane."

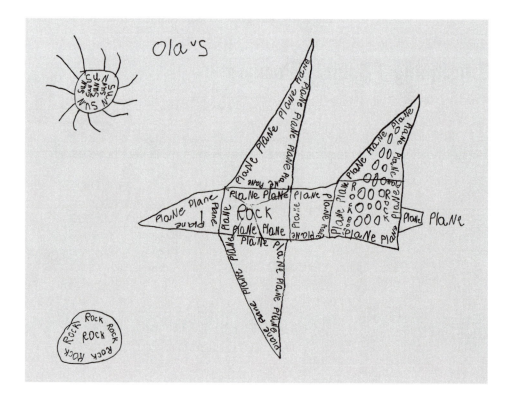

Figure 3.19

Elijah's "Snow Day."

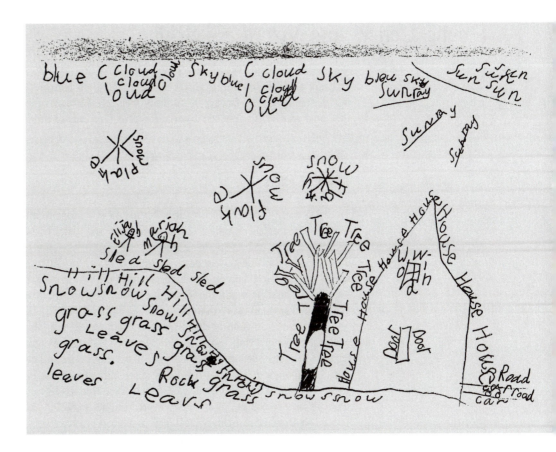

while others fall down the page as if water were flowing over a dam. Leah uses the idea of shaping words into a picture in her "Candy" poem where a make-believe lunch menu is artfully swirled into a licorice whip (Figure 3.20).

In a unique use of words to form a shape, Ruth invited her kindergartners to create picture poems using the correct spellings of their first and last names. "Everyone has names they must learn how to spell," Ruth told the students. "If you were going to put your name in a picture poem, what would the poem look like?" The children discussed what a poem made entirely of their own names might look like before everyone began writing. They decided that since they were using their names, the pictures they created should be of themselves.

Lily shaped a two-foot-tall self-portrait of herself walking with only her last name outlining her head, arms, legs, and torso. Another child wrote his last name many times over, correctly for the first time all year, to fill in his outline of himself. Other children used their names to create details—ears, hair, buttons, caps, and even shadows!

Mixing and maneuvering words is how young poets use filling-in, outlining, and shaping spaces to create elaborate word picture poems. Ben's poem shows a boat on a yellow surfboard riding waves of brown and blue water with an accompanying poetic description: "My boat is surfing on the twilight water."

Because these poems are visual art, children especially enjoy crafting their pictures on large sheets of paper—the bigger the paper, the more expansive the outcome—and the better the poems look for display on classroom or corridor bulletin boards. Large writing surfaces encourage wide-angle views with many objects in the scene, giving young poets freedom to experiment with color, font, and presentation.

To give kids ideas for designing picture poetry, we show examples of adult poems on an overhead projector. *Seeing Things* by Robert Froman, *Splish Splash* and *Flicker Flash* by Joan Bransfield Graham, and *Doodle Dandies* by J. Patrick Lewis contain dozens of dazzling examples of concrete poetry that stretch everyone's creativity. We also display children's picture poems on the overhead or in their original large-paper versions.

Poetic Letters and Word Sketching

"Poetic Letters" and "Word Sketching" are Ruth's innovative methods for focusing kindergartners' attention on letters and words to excite their learning about decoding and encoding written language. Engaging students' artistic eyes opens their language ears and invites first and second graders, ESL students, and children of any age to feel successful with words.

Poetic Letters

The idea that the letters of the alphabet are poetic arose in an October study about how writers use graphic design to capture readers' interest. "Look at this!" Ruth said to the kindergartners. "When Kaylee comes to the end of the line her pencil takes a turn and writes down the side of the page. Leigh writes in tiny letters when he can't fit all of his words into a space. Travon bends his words in different ways to make them look interesting. On his sign he made the letters look like they are shouting 'Shh...!!' to surprise you. You looked at them more than once."

Writers are constantly deciding how their words will best communicate to someone walking by a sign, glancing at a newspaper, or leafing through a book. What makes readers stop to notice: Beauty of the letters? Surprise of shape and color? Variations of font? The class began to study letters—typefaces, sizes, capitalizations, and styles—on posters, signs, and notices from the school office. Kids observed that letters appeared to be "**SHOUTING**," sending *quiet* messages, or asking to be read in a 𝓕𝓐𝓝𝓒𝓨 𝓥𝓞𝓘𝓒𝓔.

Interest widened from what began as a short study of poetic letters to an examination of how authors create reader interest through the layout designs of their books. Kids' questions propelled their investigations over two months:

Figure 3.20

Leah's "Candy" poem. Translation:

Today's menu is everlasting gobstoppers, pixy sticks, candy corns, ice cream floats, Reese's Pieces, rock candy, candy bracelets and watches and a present and inside there is candy.

- In alphabet books, how is each letter featured on a page?
- Why do some words only start with a capital while others have all capital letters?
- Why do some words form circles or other shapes instead of appearing straight across the page like most other words do?

Children's inquiries and Ruth's guidance promoted an enthusiastic search through many different alphabet books, convincing the class that poetry is evident in the presentation of words. Letters can be poetic—attention-riveting, visually engaging, and thought-provoking—and writers can add these qualities to words in a text. To make letters poetic means imparting visual uniqueness to their shapes, sizes, sounds, and positions in words. The letter *s* in Massachusetts, for example, becomes poetically interesting by changing its capitalization, size, or font to highlight its repeating shape and sound:

MaSSachuSettS

After studying how adults design poetic letters in alphabet books, newspapers, and picture books, the children were ready to try their ideas for making letters dramatic, comic, or surprising parts of words. They decided to design a class alphabet to hang on the wall, and some children continued the exploration by composing their own alphabet books.

Fiona transformed the *o* in *owl* into one of its eyes. Ian elongated a curving *s*, making it into a playground "slide" with a child enjoying its slippery ride. Sarah's *s* sat atop a cone, mimicking the shape of two scoops of bubble gum-flavored ice cream with the caption: "Sarah likes ice cream." Later in the year, Sharon's second graders designed poetic letters for their April calendars, surprising each other with their ideas (Figure 3.21).

Imagining letters and words as shapes, pictures, and flexible forms enabled the children to understand some creative characteristics of graphic design. Words can take on personalities that evoke moods, qualities, and textures, giving new life to common terms. To the trained adult eye, these techniques are known as the layout of a page—the visual effect that writers and publishers try to achieve as they transmit their messages. In kid-friendly terms, the way words are arranged on the page can be one of the most interesting parts of the writing. The placement of words on the page is an essential feature of picture poems.

Like most children, the kindergartners imagined writing as putting words on paper in a compositional style, left to right, letters on a line, with correct spelling, capitalization, and punctuation. Seeing how the same letters carry different messages and how the look of the letters command attention was a mind-flexing experience for them. "And it is also possible," explained Ruth, "to manipulate words in many interesting ways."

Word Sketching

Word sketching—the crafting of words into shapes—is illumined by a description of how five-year-old Destin created a picture poem of a dog. First, Destin wrote "dog," by himself in book spelling (a proud moment for this young writer displaying his knowledge of words). He did not know how to expand his idea, so Ruth demonstrated how he could arrange the letters *d-o-g* on the paper, forming them into an image, just as if he were holding the word in his hand and molding it like a piece of clay. The letters and the word could stretch across paper—up, down, and sideways—to form a visual image of a dog. Ruth helped him by guiding the pencil as he held it, demonstrating that it could perform like a brush stroking the letters onto the paper. The result was more inventive than just writing the word. Having never seen or tried anything like this before, he was astonished by what he might do with the word "dog" to create an image.

As they created his poem, Destin and Ruth engaged in the following conversation:

Ruth: "Now that you know how to spell the word dog, there are lots of ways to use that word in a poem. Look how you can turn the paper and write *d-o-g* again. This time you can form it into the shape of a dog's body." (Ruth demonstrates how turning the paper helps him to curve the word.)

Ruth: "I moved the paper to help shape these letters into the dog's body. Here you try." (Ruth hands him the pencil.) "We can work as a team. You write *d-o-g* and I'll move the paper."

(Destin uses the pencil to write the letters *d-o-g* on the page as Ruth turns the page in a circular motion. The letters follow the turn of the paper creating the shape of a dog's body.)

Word sketching enables letters to move, turn, shrink, grow, stretch, or tightly converge. The novelty of this process propelled Destin's imagination and his vocabulary. Responding to Ruth's conversation, he wondered about other words he might use to describe his dog: "head," "legs," and "ear." One word led to another in an expanding discovery of vocabulary to use in the poem.

Ruth: "What else do dogs have?"

Destin: "Legs."

Ruth: "You can do the same thing with the word leg that we did with dog."

(Ruth begins to sketch the letters *l-e-g* vertically down the page contouring the shape of a leg from them. Destin follows this model making the other legs.)

Destin: "Let's do a head. How do you spell it?" (Together they sound out and write: "hed.")

Ruth: "Those are three of the letters that you need. We need a silent '*a*' for book spelling. (Ruth writes *h-e-a-d* on a piece of scrap paper." Destin begins to curve *h-e-a-d* into a circle. He and Ruth spell more words to add more parts to his dog—tail, eyes, and mouth.)

Ruth: "Look at that! You are writing poetry!"

Destin: "Can I try it again?" (He leaps up to get paper for his next poem, "Rock.")

Figure 3.21

Allie's April.

Word sketching is a particularly useful technique for inspiring writers and readers who feel uneasy or anxious about their knowledge of book spellings, letter formation, or ideas for writing:

- The repeated movements of paper and pencil along with Ruth's conversation about the possibilities of design and craft reinforced Destin's sense of himself as a creative artist and poet. He gained confidence in his ability to express his ideas on paper. Structuring or designing picture poems is essentially recognizing that paper is a canvas for creative thinking and words are the design tools—paint, pencils and pens—for sketching.

- Destin wrote "dog" more than thirty times to shape the body and limbs of his canine, seeing "dog" as a word that can be written left to right as a group of letters or shaped into a figure that resembles the animal itself. In this way, Destin achieved ownership of the word—he knows its meaning, its book spelling, and its relationship to other words he paired with it. By the time he had finished the poem, he had written at least twenty other conventionally spelled words and then inquired if he could write more. Conventional spelling was learned through creative use, a distinct advantage of word sketching.

- Sketching words pictorially stretches their meanings for young writers. Words become stronger and more interesting than when they sit statically on a page or a wall. Fashioned and applied to a paper canvas, words become tangible, lifelike. Children can imagine a picture poem as a short movie, springing to life before their eyes. By crafting words into shapes, Destin and his classmates forged an emotional and artistic connection to the words in their poems.

Sculpting Three-Dimensional (3-D) Picture Poems

Three-dimensional picture poems are a mathematical application of the techniques in poetic letters and word sketching. Ruth invented and introduced this idea by telling the children that a sculptor is an artist who molds and arranges materials in different shapes and sizes—like kindergartners do when they mold clay or play-dough. Then she invited the children to sculpt something with Crayola Sculpty, but because it was expensive material, a measured amount was all each one could have. The kids deliberated about their choices of what to make before beginning to shape their clay. Fiona chose to make a toy model-size boat. Walter designed a model bed. Paige sculpted a bird's nest. No two children chose to make the same object.

Later in the week when each sculpture was complete, Ruth asked the children to choose one word that was important to or that described their sculpture. Each child typed her or his word into the computer multiple times, printed them in a small-size font, cut them apart, and pasted the words onto their models, thus creating picture poems in three dimensions.

Then a remarkable development occurred, a mind-opening experience like that of the "dog poem" sketched with words. Fiona, busily constructing and labeling her ship declared, "I need to know what part of my boat is the stern." To the library she went, accompanied by a teacher's aide, to research the various parts of a ship so she could add "stern" to her sculpture. Fiona learned that a boat has many parts and can be described in detail with more words.

Fiona's discovery of boat words inspired her classmates to consider adding other words to their poems. Ruth informed the class that in picture poems—2-D or 3-D—kids are not confined to one or two words. Endless supplies of words are available for their use. Walter, gazing at his model of a bed, inquired: "Do I put a cover on it?" "Do I put something under the covers?" After consulting with other kindergartners, Walter chose "pillow," "person," "bottom," "blanket," "clock" (on the wall), "mirror," "glass," and "edge" (of the bed) to type and add to his sculpture. Walter's inspiration for these selections arose from multiple conversations he had with children and adults.

While sculpting three-dimensional picture poems, children are practicing word recognition, vocabulary building, and spelling:

- Kids have authentic reasons for learning new words; they want to expand the details of and the interest in their picture poem sculptures.

- Associating words with art inspires kids to refer to many resources for spelling information and precise language. Kids locate words in dictionaries and thesauruses, type them into the computer in conventional spelling, then shrink or enlarge them, curve or straighten them, bold or color them to fashion the design of their sculptures.

- Kids read an array of interesting books to collect words for their poems. Alphabet books, books of words about specific topics or themes, word play books, and children's magazines are available and popular. Dictionaries and *I Spy* books are inviting sources of words, and are available on compact disc.

EXTENSIONS

Picture Poems Lead Children to Spelling

Picture poems require conventional spelling because reading the words is fundamental to their design. Kids understand that misspellings do a disservice to their poems and to their audiences. Words spelled unconventionally distract readers' appreciation of the poem's image and meaning.

Picture poetry encourages children's efforts to learn conventional spelling through repetition, personal interest, and unique artistic effort.

- *Repetition:* Writing words over and over again strengthens children's memories of how words are spelled. While practice does not guarantee perfection, it does improve performance. Like a basketball player practicing free throws, a young writer develops greater consistency from the repeated writing of words. Hall of Fame basketball player Larry Bird knew he would complete his free throws during a game because he had mentally and physically practiced them so often that they were second nature to him. Young children gain a similar sense of confidence about how words are spelled after writing them many times in a picture poem. Importantly, the value of repetition depends on words being spelled correctly from the beginning, as they need to be in picture poems—otherwise children practice nonstandard spellings that are hard to unlearn.

- *Personal Interest:* Choosing and arranging words, designing color combinations, and forming sizes and shapes of letters invigorates children's interest in conventional spelling. Children recall the spellings of personally important words. They add such new words to their vocabularies and recite the spellings of complicated words to the surprise of adults. Picture poetry is a unique genre for expanding children's knowledge of interesting and fascinating words.

- *Unique Artistic Effort:* Visual representation—each youngster's perspective— connects pictures to words and spellings. The word *grass* might appear as a lawn mowed straight across or as stalks wiggling in a gentle wind. Sketching, shaping, or sculpting *g-r-a-s-s* unites a sensory experience with a visual product in a child's mind.

grass grass grass grass grass grass   **g g g g g**

                                                    r r r r r

                                                    a a a a a

                                                    s s s s s

                                                    s s s s s

Picture poetry's three ways of connecting children and words is very different from practicing spelling lists or rewriting the conventional spelling of a misspelled word ten times. Fashioning a picture poem stimulates a creative process where words convey an image or a scene imagined by the author. As children place words on paper, their association with and knowledge of the words deepens, strengthening the memory of standard spellings through emotional and cognitive paths. Words become more tangible: they acquire concreteness for the writer who knows the definitions and how the letters look artistically, sequenced in conventional spelling.

Picture poems present opportunities for children and adults to engage in thoughtful conversations about how words are used in everyday situations. As topics of discussion, words acquire importance and individuality. They are "personal choices" and "powerful tools" that enable writers to communicate with other people. Talking about words helps children acquire expansive personal vocabularies, curiosity about definitions, and interest in remembering conventional spellings.

Here is an opportunity for children to put together their own personal dictionaries filled with words from their picture poems—important words, interesting words, words that they know how to spell. Their enlarging dictionaries indicate increasing word knowledge. Recalling conventional spelling imparts "ownership" of words and the confidence to say, "I know how to read and spell . . ."

Spelling Picture Poems

Spelling practice can develop into a "Spelling Picture Poem." Shaping words into pictures links phonemic awareness, language study, and practice of difficult-to-remember words with picture poetry construction. Sources of words for spelling picture poems include

- *Spelling Lists:* The weekly spelling lists assigned in classrooms can become picture poems—even if the words are unconnected by a phonemic pattern or a topic of study. As children visually represent words from the spelling list, they build a sense of familiarity, meaning, and context for each term.

- *Phonemic Patterns:* Words with the same phonemic patterns can form spelling picture poems. *Girl, first, bird, third, stir, stirred, stirring, squirt, squirted,* and *birthday* with *ir,* or *lake, cake, make, bake, shake,* and *rake* with *ake* are examples of word lists. Kids may include all of the words from a list in a poem, connect several of the words in a funny way, or make separate small poems for each word.

- *Kids' Own Words:* Words that kids find personally interesting are easily incorporated into poems. The words can be special nouns (*soccer, ocean, dolphin, snake*), words for decorating a space or composing an object (*tree, sky, water, rain, blue, gold, black, red*), or terms that they think will add interest to their poems (*clock, foot, mirror, stern, port*). Kids' own words may be combined with words from an assigned spelling or phonemic pattern list to add creative choice to poem writing.

- *Homophones:* words that sound alike but have different spellings and meanings are challenging choices for poetry creations: *to, too, two; buy, by, bye; where, wear, ware; their, they're, there; pain, pane.*

- *Words from Other Cultures and Languages:* Our English language includes words from other cultures and places that cannot be pronounced as they spelled. The spelling and pronunciation are the same as in the original language: *pasta* and *pizza* (Italian), *tortilla* and *salsa* (Spanish), *croissant*, *depot*, *ballet*, and *chandelier* (French).

Here are three open-ended spelling picture poem formats to try once words are chosen:

- *Single Word Spelling Picture Poems* use one word as the basis for the poem, letting young poets express the word in many different shapes and forms, as in the examples below by Candise and Lauren (Figure 3.22).
- *Collage Spelling Picture Poems* compile a group of words into several small poems that form a picture. *Rain, snow, puddles, ice, condensation, evaporation,* and *precipitation* are words with a weather theme in common. They can be used in a weather picture poem by a group of students who design and take turns writing all of the words in the picture. This way everyone writes each of the words a few times.
- *Story Spelling Picture Poems* have a story to accompany the picture in the poem. The list of *ir* words, *girl, first, bird, third, stir, stirred, stirring, squirt, squirted,* and *birthday* lends itself to a brief story as well as to a picture poem. Some or all of the words may be included in the poem and the story. This works well in a classroom where kids can illustrate and compose a poem and story individually, in pairs, or as groups.

Figure 3.22 *Single word picture poems by Candise and Lauren.*

Young Writers' Bookshelf for Concrete Poetry

Seeing Things: A Book of Poems. Robert Froman. Crowell, 1974. Poems shaped from words; "On The Beach" features the giant letters of W-A-V-E crashing against a beach of sand with grey rocks, pebbles, and starfish.

Splish Splash. Joan Bransfield Graham. Illustrated by Steve Scott. Ticknor & Fields, 1994. Picture poems about the many shapes of water. In "Babbling Brook," the words bounce gently across the page as would the water in a mountain stream. Words flow swiftly from top to bottom of the page in "River" and rise quickly from a pot on a stove in "Steam." *Flicker Flash* by Joan Bransfield Graham and illustrated by Nancy Davis (Houghton Mifflin, 1999) features picture poems celebrating light.

Doodle Dandies: Poems that Take Shape. J. Patrick Lewis. Images by Lisa Desimini. Atheneum Books for Young Readers, 1998. Photographs enliven the illustrations of these poems.

Wake Up House! Rooms Full of Poems. Dee Lillegard. Illustrated by Don Carter. Alfred A. Knopf, 2000. Short poems about three-dimensional household objects.

If at First You Do Not See. Ruth Brown. Holt, 1989. Writing on all sides of the page accompanies pictures to convey how ordinary things look differently when viewed right side up or upside down.

Mortimer. Robert Munsch. Art by Michael Martchenko. Annick Press, 1985. Key words in the text are displayed using an imaginative, all-over-the-page visual design.

Candy Corn: Poems. James Stevenson. Greenwillow Books, 1999. Noted poet, picture book author, and illustrator pens short, descriptive verse in many different fonts, sizes, and colors that invite reading aloud. See also *Popcorn* (1998) and *Sweet Corn* (1995).

A Poke in the I: A Collection of Concrete Poems. Paul B. Janeczko. Illustrated by Christopher Raschka. Candlewick Press, 2001. Thirty poems by visual poets who use letters, words, typeface, and space on the page to create expressive images; these are accompanied by dazzling illustrations.

Winter Eyes. Douglas Florian. Greenwillow Books, 1999. Some of the poems take on the shapes, sizes, and behaviors of wintertime.

Your Ant Is a Which. Bernice Kohn Hunt. Harcourt Brace Jovanovich, 1976. The pairing of familiar homophones in poetry create mind-bending images for language play. (Out of print.)

Software Cited in the Text

I Spy series on CD-ROM from Scholastic, including *I Spy School Days* and *I Spy Treasure Hunt*.

Voices of Poetry

Voice Poetry	TEACH	These Conventions *Unconventionally*
Good Conversations Make Good Poems		Genre: voice poems
Voices Continue the Conversation • Creating Fictional Characters • Telling a Story • Expressing Points of View		Fictional characters Telling a story Humor Point of view
Duets and Echoes in Poems		Language play
Extensions: Visual Spacing and Punctuation in Voice Poems		Use of periods, commas, and other punctuation marks

"Who's on First?" by comedians Bud Abbott and Lou Costello is a distinctive piece of American humor, instantly recognized by baseball and non-baseball fans alike. Shown daily at the National Baseball Hall of Fame in Cooperstown, New York, their rendition of zany misunderstanding delights listeners who relish the wordplay in this comedy routine.

The dialogue opens with Costello, an aspiring baseball player, questioning Abbott, a confident coach, about the team's opening game lineup. The running joke arises from confusion over the first baseman's name, "Who," and continues through the list of the other players on the team whose names include "What," "I Don't Know," "Today," and "Tomorrow." Costello, knowing none of the names, becomes increasingly exasperated as he asks what he thinks are perfectly sensible questions that always cycle back into nonsense: "Who" is on first, today's starting pitcher is named "Tomorrow," the catcher's name is "Today."

The humor of "Who's on First?" evolves from the language play created by the dynamic interaction of two characters in conversation. This form of writing is not new. The skits composed by old-time vaudeville and radio performers were full of double meaning wordplays that continue to delight, excite, and entertain young audiences as new generations discover them. Similarly, Shel Silverstein's poem, "The Meehoo With An Exactly What" shows kids how two questions—"Me Who?" and "Exactly What?"—create hilarious interactions between two characters where one understands the conversation and the other is completely confused.

"Voices of Poetry" explores how talk between children and adults becomes entertaining poetry. One form of voice poetry, "conversation poems" begin from everyday remarks among friends. Besides conversation poems, young writers can try poems that give a voice to fictional characters and inanimate objects. Finally, there is a special form orchestrated by Paul Fleischman called "Two Voice Poetry" where the words of a poem can be performed aloud with echoes and duets of voices.

Good Conversations Make Good Poems

How many times do you wish you could hear all the wonderful conversations that kids have when they get together? They say things in each other's company that they might not ordinarily say with an adult present. Sometimes inspiring, interesting, funny, or vividly descriptive, writing begins with speech.

Conversation poems are a unique way to compose poetry. Every adult has heard a child say, "I don't have anything to write!" or "I don't have any good ideas!" But, put that same youngster in a group of friends and she or he will talk everyone's ears off in wonderfully expressive language. We have seen this over and over again, always thinking to ourselves, "With so much to say that child can be a fantastic writer."

Transitioning from oral to written expression is extremely difficult for some young talker-extraordinaires. Conversation poems in the voices of different speakers are engaging ways for youngsters to share a story, a personal memory, or whatever else might be on their minds. These poems invite kids to use their strength—talk—because "from good conversations come good poems." Shy or quiet kids enjoy this format as well. The written dialogue is easier to recite in front of an audience than voicing ideas or opinions during group discussions. In the poem below by Khalea, Jamie, and Marianne, three voices discuss an egg that is hatching (Figure 3.23). The poem reads left to right across three rows.

Teamwork and cooperation are another part of the appeal of this type of creative self-expression. Children enjoy working together to build a poem that moves back and forth between two or more people. Conversation poems include everyday experiences as ready-made sources for dialogues or poetic exchanges between many speakers. Conversation poems between two, three, four or more voices are possible, which make them challenging for kids to construct and perform.

Voices Continue the Conversation

Any topic can become an interesting conversation poem as young writers expand the form to include the elements of fictional characters, storylines, and different points of view.

Creating Fictional Characters

Conversation poems let young writers explore one of the essential ingredients of writing—creating fictional characters. Story writers use language to give characters personality, style, and ways of being in the world, as in Brianna's poem "NO" about a second grader who tries to convince her four-year-old sister to cooperate, only to meet resistance at every turn. Brianna and Sharon worked together on the first draft, then Brianna completed the poem (Figure 3.24).

By giving a sense of uniqueness to fictional characters, kids are reminded that those same qualities make them unique—individuals whose ideas are different from everyone else's.

Khalea: "What is hatching?"

        Jamie: "A baby dinosaur!!"

                Marianne: "What kind?"

Khalea: "I think it is a
T. REX!!"

                Marianne: "I think it's new
species!"

        Jamie: "I think it is an
unusual animal."

Khalea: "Why do you think
that is an unusual animal?"

        Jamie: "Because. . . ."

                Marianne: "I'm leaving!!!
And I've got a good
reason to."

Khalea: "Why?"

        Jamie: "I'm going too!!"

                Marianne: "The egg is
hatching into a dinosaur!
A T. REX"

Khalea: "I'm going too!!
Bye egg!"

        Jamie: "Bye dinosaur!"

Figure 3.23 *Three voice poems by Khalea, Jamie, and Marianne.*

Conversations among fictional characters are central to the poetry of Dr. Seuss. In *The Cat in the Hat*, the conversations personify cautious kids and a frisky, tricky cat. The inner monologues of "The Grinch" and "Horton" reveal each of their personalities to readers. We know them through the words they speak.

Telling a Story

Kids use conversation poems to narrate a story, giving them a different way to compose fiction. In the following poem by Chantel and Julia, the humor of the story is created not by misunderstanding, but by compromise and accommodation between a daughter and her mother (Figure 3.25).

Figure 3.24

OK. Are you ready to go?

NO.

You know you had so much fun yesterday, Are you ready to go?

NO.

Yesterday when we got to the pool you had a great time. Let's go.

NO.

I have a surprise for you. Let's go.

NO.

I'm not going to tell you where we are going, but it's really fun. Are you ready to go?

NO.

OK! Let's go, let's go, let's go!

NO.

OK. . . If you don't come with me so we can go I am going to kiss you.

NO NO NO!

Smooch! Smooch! Smooch! Smooch!

NOOOOOOOOOOO!

Mommy, can I have a baby cat?

Mom, don't be silly.

Hey, Mom, look what I bought.

Yes, do you have a credit card?

Fine, I will let you use my credit card.

What!!!! You brought an elephant home! It can't fit in the house. Besides, it eats too much.

Yes it does, but still elephants are my favorite. Oh, just let me have it please.

Maybe we can do something. Oh, I got a great idea. Put it in the garage!

O.K., I will feed it everyday.

And you will clean the poop.

Figure 3.25 *Chantel's and Julia's "Baby Cat" poem.*

Expressing Points of View

Point of view conversation poems ask young writers to give voice to objects and things that normally do not speak—trees, rocks, the computer, a doll, the moon, and so forth. Any inanimate object can talk through this poetry; the fun comes from kids imagining what the objects would say if they could express themselves conversationally.

In the following poems, second graders construct the conversations of three different objects—a calculator, an umbrella, and a school bus. Each poet uses language to reveal thoughts from the object's point of view. Children see how writers make readers care about characters or everyday objects by giving them a unique voice with distinctive things to say (Figure 3.26).

Figure 3.26

Three point of view poems by Patrick, Emily, and Sean.

Calculator poem

I am calculator

I have a sore stomach from everybody messing with me.

I had enough!!

Ahhhhhh! Splat. I broke.

Call the fix-it man.

Umbrella poem

I know I am helpful when it is raining.

But when it is very windy

all I do is blow away.

So I think it is smarter to not have me open when it is very windy.

O.K.?

O.K.

Hey, by the way, be more careful with me.

All you do is throw me on the floor.

School Bus poem

I carry kids to and from school.

I carry kids on field trips, too.

I'm yellow with a long black stripe with white letters.

What am I????

I'm a school bus!!!

Sometimes kids will paint me and make me look like the countryside

And they will give me a new name, the Ecobus

I am a grain of sand. I have been in this little container since this guy scooped me up off the ground and tried to suffocate me, but, ha ha, I don't need to breathe! Well before I got trapped in here I blew around Saudi Arabia for thousands of years. Whew. What a ride! You wouldn't believe how much fun that is! Oh well! I guess in another thousand years I will have just as much fun. Or maybe not. Ow! I wish it wasn't so cramped in here! I want to go home!

Figure 3.27 *Erin's "Sand in a Bottle" point of view poem.*

Assembling a treasure box full of interesting, unusual, kid-attracting objects—a teddy bear, a ball, a piece of beautiful cloth, small plastic animals, tiny model cars and trucks, and assorted other items—is a great way to get kids started writing point of view conversation poems. Pulling the objects from the box one at a time, we ask children to imagine what each is thinking. "What is its life like?" "What would it say if it could talk?" We urge kids to hear the voice and become the object. Erin, a fourth grader, composed the following conversation poem from the point of view of a grain of sand enclosed in a small bottle (Figure 3.27).

In another variation of this idea, children's artistic creations become objects whose point of view is expressed in writing. In art class, students made clay pouches to display on a wall or desk. Each child gave her or his pouch a unique design and glaze before baking so each looked different. Sharon then asked the children to write what the pouch might say if it were able to speak. Allie wrote the following poem (Figure 3.28).

Figure 3.28

Allie's "Pouch" point of view poem. Translation:

I think Allie will put cards in me to send to other people. I bet I'd shine in the sunlight like the stars shining in the moonlight. I think she will put me on her desk to sleep like a statue.

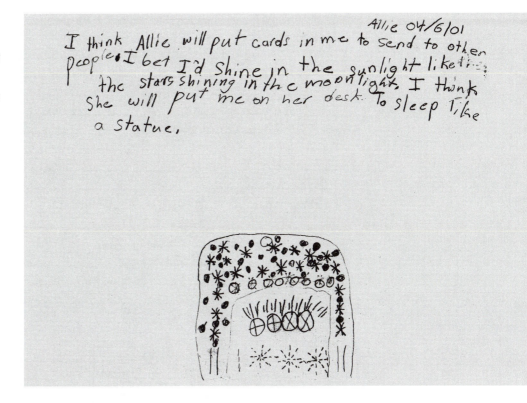

A collection of magazines with interesting photos offers kids choices of objects that become voice poetry greeting cards. When opened, the voice of the photo has a written message inside for the person receiving the card.

Duets and Echoes in Poems

So far we have looked at how poems with voices can be drawn from the conversations of real or fictional people as well as inanimate objects. An entertainingly different form of voice poetry emerges from arrangements of words on a page signaling ways to read verses aloud as *duets* and *echoes*. These poems unite a cadence of voices in a theater-like experience of language; the audience hears lyricism and song in the words orchestrated by different voices.

Leah structured her "School Week" poem (Figure 3.29) as she had seen Paul Fleischman do in *Joyful Noise*, his celebrated collection of poetry where all verses are conversations between insects. Fleischman uses two columns to delineate two voices—voice one on the left and voice two on the right. The two voices are read as a duet when words appear on the same horizontal line in both columns just as the names of the days and other lines do in Leah's poem. The voices are solo whenever the words appear by themselves in their own column.

Voices in duet usually necessitate a rehearsal by readers before a performance. When rehearsing is not possible, an alternative method is for one voice to speak after the other,

Figure 3.29

Leah's "School Week" poem.

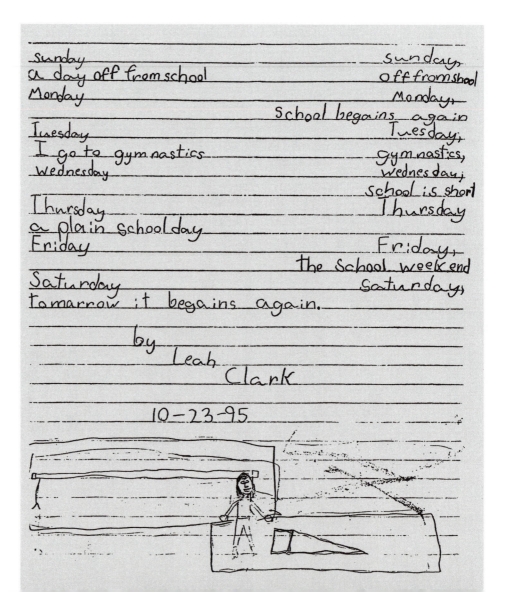

creating an echo instead of a duet. Both methods offer dramatic and different read-aloud options.

In Fleischman's poem "House Crickets," the word "cricket" reverberates between the two voices when read as an echo and sounds like a group of crickets communicating back and forth when read as a chorus. Leah achieved a similar effect by placing the days of the week in both columns to be voiced simultaneously or as an echo. Pairs, trios, or foursomes of writers can compose duet or echo poems with each youngster contributing separate parts to the whole. *Big Talk: Poems in Four Voices*, the latest of Fleischman's collections of poems, offers wonderfully creative ways to build poems with many voices.

Duets and echoes are irresistible to kids. The song-like quality of the voicing catches their ear and attention. These poems quickly become wonderfully open-ended forms of expressive writing. Kids in Sharon's class have taken voice poems in many new directions, composing two, three, and four-voice lunch menus, weather reports, and stories—performing them with verve and glee.

EXTENSIONS

Visual Spacing and Punctuation in Voice Poems

Visual spacing of words on a page as well as punctuation of sentences and phrases play essential roles in poems with voices. Look at the following poem by Christina and Jane (Figure 3.30).

Now imagine the same poem without commas, periods, capital letters, or words for different speakers arranged on separate lines. Without these conventions, following the interaction of the voices and identifying the words of the speakers would be confusing. Communicating a clear meaning is the reason to examine how visual spacing and punctuation serve as traffic signs used by writers to direct readers through a poem.

We ready voice poems for publication by looking first at the visual spacing of the words. Here are strategies to try:

- Adult poets employ columns to distinguish one voice from another. This is useful for kids to try. On large sheets of paper, each writer has the left or right side of

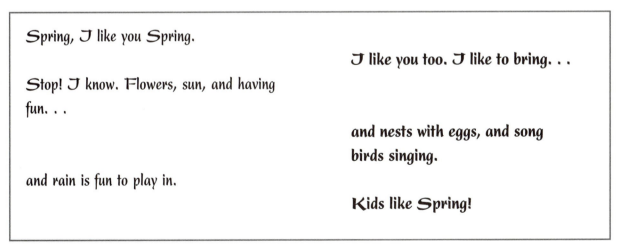

Figure 3.30   *Christina's and Jane's "Spring" poem.*

the page for their voice. A third voice could use the middle of the page. Kids may need to re-copy their poems to achieve more clearly spaced text, or they can cut and paste the original onto another sheet of paper.

- Different colored pens or markers denote different voices in their poems. Composing a poem over several days, kids identify which voice is saying what by the colors of the words.

- When poems are printed on a word processor, different-sized fonts offer a visually dramatic way to distinguish between the voices.

- Separating voices into columns or printing in different colors are two ways that help readers to read the poems correctly, but punctuation is needed to show the intentions or motives of the speakers. The voices belong to individuals with their own personalities and unique ways of communicating their ideas. These individuals speak in different tones of voice, depending on whether they are stating information, asking questions, or asserting a viewpoint. Before publishing it is important to consider placement of periods, question marks, and exclamation points that slow down or speed up the text.

YOUNG WRITERS' BOOKSHELF FOR POEMS WITH VOICES

Joyful Noise: Poems in Two Voices. Paul Fleischman. Harper & Row, 1988. Poems by insects are wonderful resources for making conversations poetic or for studying such science topics as bugs, change, and growth and development. Also by Paul Fleischman: *I Am Phoenix: Poems for Two Voices* (1989) and *Big Talk: Poems in Four Voices* (2000).

A Mouse Told His Mother. Bethany Roberts. Illustrated by Mary-jane Begin. Little, Brown, 1997.

I Am the Dog, I Am the Cat. Donald Hall. Pictures by Barry Moser. Dial Books, 1994. A dog and a cat in their own words tell us who they are and what they like to do.

My Name is Jorge on Both Sides of the River: Poems in English and Spanish. Jane Medina. Illustrated by Fabricio Vandenbroeck. Boyds Mills Press, 1999.

Voices in the Park. Anthony Browne. DK Publishing, 1998. Four strangers who meet in a park describe the same events from their own points of view.

Mouse Views: What the Class Pet Saw. Bruce McMillan. Holiday House, 1993. Colorful photographic puzzles of common school objects as seen from the point of view of a mouse.

CHAPTER SUMMARY

Chapter Three, "Poems," immerses children in poetry and its imaginative power by reading, performing, and writing poems regularly. They learn how poetry presents everyday experience with intense feeling, compelling image, uncommon presentation, and unique viewpoint. These essential elements then evolve in children's poems in surprisingly delightful ways. Open-ended and engaging poetry styles such as acrostics, picture poems, and voice poems give children countless opportunities to write poetry. Since children use these forms in many unique ways, poetry writing does not become boring or repetitive. Kids anticipate opportunities to express their ideas in poetic form while practicing standard spelling and correct punctuation.

CHAPTER FOUR

Stories

Stories, notes educator Herbert Kohl (115), allow youngsters to "become intimate with their imaginations and explore what they might like to be as well as understand who they are." The stories children tell and write are "windows into their uniqueness." They promote self-expression, self-confidence, and self-understanding. A reluctance to write, however, can undermine or block children's experiences with the worlds of story.

The WOWs in Chapter Four, "Stories," start from the belief that kids are story-writers, right now, because they are already eager storytellers and attentive story listeners, readers, and viewers. The key is for adults to connect various story-writing forms and strategies to children's experiences and interests. The WOWS in this chapter explore how writers manage the interplay between realms of fiction and nonfiction. For most children, the boundaries between what is real and what is imaginary are permeable and constantly changing. As writers, children benefit when adults discuss matters of fact and fiction and guide them in making decisions about how to use reality and imagination in their writing.

Story writing pushes the boundaries of children's thinking about themselves as writers. Most children do not think of the events of their lives as stories or that they are telling and enjoying stories all the time. As they connect fiction stories and personal experiences, children think about who they are and who they might like to become.

- **WOW 12: From Oral to Written Tales** introduces story writing through the child-familiar venue of storytelling. Children are frequent tellers of stories and "A Story Frame" developed by storyteller Eshu Bumpus provides a framework to shape oral tales into written stories that feature characters, setting, storyline (or plot), and problem/resolution (or tension). "Extensions: Writing Stories Together" discusses how adults can be effective writing partners with young writers.

- **WOW 13: Words for Pictures and Performances** presents ideas for promoting children's story writing. Wordless picture books invite children to compose words to accompany the illustrations. In this way, a unique partnership is formed between young story-writer and adult book illustrator, each of whom tells the story his or her own way. "Performing the Words" is an interactive classroom activity where groups of kids build written stories from live performances of an original tale. "Extensions: Play Me a Story" discusses how children can perform their own pretend play theatrical productions. Creating written scripts for the characters in their plays broadens children's knowledge of stories presented through dialogue.

- **WOW 14: New Versions of Old Tales** invites humor-filled story writing from children's knowledge of fairy tales, folktales, and nursery rhymes. Orally and in print, kids create their own versions of well-known tales by changing some of the essential ingredients of stories. Writers might place an old tale in a modern setting, add previously unknown characters, reverse the expected ending, or even tell the story from the point of view of a different narrator. Constructing versions is an excellent way to introduce kids to folktales from many world cultures, expanding multicultural learning. "Extensions: Who is Telling the Tale?" introduces the convention of "point of view."

- **WOW 15: Fiction/Nonfiction Story Writing** explores how writers combine elements of facts (the world of reality) and fiction (the world of make-believe) in their stories. "Is It Real or Make-Believe?" is a game in which young writers try to stump their audience by writing stories that may or may not be true. The game shows how story construction and language use affect how readers respond to a piece of fiction writing. "Extensions: Fictionalized Facts and Factualized Fictions" offers suggestions for discussing how writers blend reality and make-believe in their stories.

WOW
12

From Oral to Written Tales

Story Crafting Strategies	TEACH	These Conventions *Unconventionally*
Crafting Stories • Telling Stories Orally • Story Mapping		A story writing frame and story mapping
Exploring the Ingredients of Stories • Characters • Settings • Plot • Tension/Problem Resolution		Characters Setting Plot Problem or tension Dialogue
Extensions: Writing Stories Together		Writing partnerships Strategies for writing with kids Story leads

"Detective Charles and His Wife Charlene" is the title of eight-year-old Emily's first mystery story (Figure 4.1). The story opens as follows:

> On a dark night the criminal came into the Sheriff's office and took out the 300 million dollar watch. As the criminal's hand reached into the safe, he had this big gold ring on with a sapphire in the middle and it twinkled.
>
> The next day, Detective Charles and his wife Charlene came into the office of the Sheriff. He was almost broken down in tears, he was sad that his watch was missing.
>
> cont'd.

Detective Charles was busy looking for his pen to write everything down. But poor Charlene just sighed and said, "Dear, your pencil's on your ear."

"Well, I knew that," replied Detective Charles, "I was just going to see if you were sharp enough to see."

Then the Sheriff said, "Can we get back to my 300 million dollar watch? "

And Detective Charles says, "Okay, what's up?"

"Well yesterday," the Sheriff says, "I was sitting in my office when I heard something outside. I went outside to check on it and when I came back the safe was open. Nothing was gone but my watch."

Figure 4.1 *Opening to Emily's mystery story.*

Interested, intrigued, ready to hear more? We certainly were. Emily's opening scene successfully incorporates many of the essential ingredients that a story-writer needs in a good story. There are memorable characters, including bumbling Detective Charles and his astute wife Charlene. "She does all the work," explained Emily, "but he gets all the credit." There is an organizing event or problem—the mystery of the missing watch—and there is a setting or place where the action is happening—the office of the sheriff. Unwritten, however, are answers to "What happens next?" Emily never completed her story to give it the narrative plot needed to move her characters from opening to conclusion while resolving the mystery along the way.

Why didn't Emily continue the tale of the two detectives and the watch? Perhaps she became bored with the idea or perhaps she was satisfied with what she had already written. Maybe she felt unsure how to continue organizing her ideas within a basic story structure. Because Emily was an avid reader, she intuitively knew what creates a story, but from a writer's standpoint, she would have benefited from explorations with adults about the craft of story writing.

Young writers like Emily abound. They love stories and are ready to compose them, but they often create less-than-complete story structures. Some have a neat idea for the plot, but no resolution for the story. Others have a setting but not the characters to populate the world they are imagining. Still others create beginnings without endings, endings without beginnings, or imaginative scenes that set up but do not resolve some compelling problem or tension.

These fractions of a whole story are not incomplete or insufficient ideas; they are the beginnings—the foundations—on which young writers can build the rest of their stories. Like "phrases" and "bridges" in music that must be arranged to compose a song, "plot," "setting," "characters," and "tension" must be combined to form a story. In this chapter, we explore the craft of story writing, offering techniques and strategies for young writers to form their ideas into stories. Understanding stories lets children expand their knowledge of fiction into an explicit framework for composing original tales.

Crafting Stories

A story, explains poet and writer Ralph Fletcher (56), "requires the intersection of three spheres: plot, setting, and characters." These elements are interconnected like the circles of a Venn diagram, each one having both an independent and an overlapping relationship to the whole. In his view, a story is all of the elements together, not one without the others. "Character drives plot . . . which gets sculpted by the setting . . . which in its turn, is affected by the characters." First among equals are the characters who "contain the crucial human link, that element of human destiny, for the reader to identify with."

Building on the image of interconnected circles, Fletcher (101) adds six more elements to the mixture of story ingredients. Good stories have an engaging opening or lead, the "right" ending, "unforgettable language," a "playfulness with time," and a compelling subject or theme. Most essentially, the characters in the story must encounter a problem, a complication, a situation out-of-the-ordinary that must be resolved before the story is completed. Fletcher prefers the word "tension," adding that for adult story readers "this is such a fundamental expectation that while we read we are always on edge, slightly tense, awaiting the first signs of calamity." It is when "something happens" that things really become interesting and readers want to discover how the problem is overcome or resolved.

One way for young writers to begin exploring the craft of story writing is to use a frame to plan how a story might flow from the first page to the last. Storyteller Eshu Bumpus suggests the following structure, one he uses to guide the oral stories he invites his audiences to create with him.

A Story Writing Frame

1. Character goes out into the world.	2. Character meets a problem.
3. Problem is resolved nonviolently or cooperatively.	4. Story is finished and character returns home (to where the heart is).

Like Ralph Fletcher, Eshu begins to craft a story by identifying the character(s). In the first frame (Box 1), the character(s) initiates the plot by journeying into the world where a problem, dilemma, or predicament is encountered (Box 2) and then resolved (Box 3). Ultimately, the adventure is finished and the character(s) returns home "where the heart is" (Box 4).

The four sections of the frame are the top of a box that then lifts off to reveal a vast array of possibilities beneath the lid. For example, characters do not always go out into the world; sometimes the world comes to them. Similarly, resolutions come in many forms which are not always simple, but for purposes of the game are always nonviolent and cooperative.

The words "home" and "heart" are not always meant literally, although many children's stories finish with characters returning to the security of family and friends. Home and heart are also metaphorical, suggesting how a character's state of mind and personal feelings have been shaped by the adventures of the story. A lesson learned or an insight gained changes the character who is now ready for what will happen next (although that may be the subject of another story).

Kids readily connect to the story frame because they understand how to use it to guide their choices. It encourages them to wrestle with the kinds of decisions and choices that adult writers make in composing a story. Plot, setting, characters, and problem/resolution emerge imaginatively as young writers follow the frame, weaving the elements of stories together in the telling of a tale.

The frame conveys a sense of dynamic movement. In a good story, things are never static. People and situations change, resulting in adventure, suspense, laughter, sadness, and a spectrum of other emotions. We envision the frame as a broad outline that lets young writers assess their own writing to see if they have all the elements of a memorable story. The frame unifies the elements of story writing whether the topic is rooted in personal experience or in imaginative fantasy.

For adults, the story frame is a flexible tool to be used in more than one way when exploring story writing with children. Here are two examples: One uses Eshu's oral storytelling method; the other uses the story frame for story mapping.

Telling Stories Orally

Eshu conducts his oral stories sitting in a circle with the children, asking leading questions and playing the role of a guide. The story that emerges dazzles listeners because of the children's imaginative contributions to its crafting. Every question Eshu asks has "Infinity answers!" said one amazed second grader.

An oral tale using Eshu's method might begin as follows:

> With a thinking expression on her or his face, an adult turns to one of the children and says, "Tell us the name of a character and whether he is an animal or a person in a sentence that begins, 'Once upon a time.'"
>
> The child responds, "Big Hopping Mike was a kangaroo."
>
> The adult adds, "Once upon a time" and the child rephrases the opening as "Once upon a time there was a kangaroo named Big Hopping Mike."
>
> The adult gazes at a second child, "Tell us who Big Hopping Mike lives with in a sentence that begins, 'Big Hopping Mike lives with . . .'"
>
> The second child responds, "Big Hopping Mike lives with Longtail Ted, a lizard."
>
> "Hmmm," says the adult focusing on a third child, "Where do they live? Tell us in a sentence."
>
> "They live in an underground cave and they climb up and down a ladder to get in and out," replies this youngster.
>
> With characters and setting now chosen, the adult interjects the problem on which the story will turn by asking a fourth child, "What is it that Big Hopping Mike warns Longtail Ted not to touch while he is out?"

In this way, stories emerge from an adult storyteller's questions and children's answers, flowing seamlessly back and forth through the frame. The adult follows the lead of the children, pursuing the characters and storylines they invent, always including their imaginative words into the tale. While the posing of questions guides the story, the children's answers become the sentences that describe the developing plot.

When children participate in building oral tales, the ingredients of stories and the story frame become an authentic part of conversations between adults and kids. Eshu, for example, always refers to the people who populate the story as "characters" so children learn the term within the context of their own ideas. All the key conventions adults need to teach become parts of oral stories, giving children multiple ways to hear the terms and understand their meanings. More information about Eshu's methods and materials is available at his website www.folktales.net.

Story Mapping

Aaron, when teaching first grade, applied Eshu's story frame to map or diagram children's favorite stories, showing how children's book authors use these essential elements of a story-writer's craft. While reading volumes of Mary Pope Osborne's *Magic Tree House* adventures, Aaron's class charted each book into the structure of the story frame. They constructed the following template as a starting point:

The Character(s) of the Story

Eight-year-old Jack and his seven-year-old sister, Annie, who live in Frog Creek, Pennsylvania.

Character(s) Meets a Problem

Annie and Jack find a tree house in the woods. When they climb into it, the tree house spins them back in time to the location of a picture they are looking at in a book. There they encounter a mystery to solve, which is complicated by the historical figures they meet.

Problem Is Resolved

Unknown to the two siblings, a dinosaur, a knight, or some other character assists their search for the needed clue and their escape from danger while solving the mystery.

Character(s) Return Home

Just in the nick of time, they climb into the tree house, and it spins them home and back to the present time without anyone noticing they have been gone.

Figure 4.2 shows seven-year-old Allie's story map of *Jerome the Babysitter* by Eileen Christelow.

Exploring the Ingredients of Stories

Eshu's story frame identifies the essential ingredients of a good story and presents a coherent structure within which young writers can freely explore and innovate as they write. Rather than labeling the parts of a story as beginning, middle, and end—terms that are vague and unhelpful to story crafting—kids focus on the actual story-writing conventions of characters, setting, plot, and tension/problem resolution. As each of these ingredients plays its role, they produce a whole story together.

Characters

Characters are the figures who populate and bring every story to life. Authors have infinite choices in creating characters for their stories. They decide if the person is tall or short, slender or heavy-set, brown or beige, female or male, younger or older, talkative or reticent, sympathetic or unsympathetic. A character can be at the center of the action (the protagonist or antagonist) or on the periphery of the tale (a minor figure). A character can come, go, or undergo a dramatic personality transformation, all by decision of the author.

Fiction story-writers strive to create memorable characters; otherwise, readers have little reason to care about the plot. Here is an important lesson for young writers—readers

Character(s)	Character(s) Meets a Problem
Jerome, the babysitter, his sister, her friend, and a family of mischievous kids.	Jerome's sister accepts a babysitting job for him with a family of kids who are troublemakers. She knows how troublesome the kids can be but she does not share that knowledge with Jerome.
Problem is Somehow Resolved After tricking Jerome more than once, the kids are watching a scary story. Jerome disguises himself, scares the kids, and tells them to go to bed.	**Character(s) Return Home** He has the final laugh when he gets home because he gives his sister a heart-shaped box with frogs in it.

Figure 4.2   *Allie's analysis of "Jerome and the Babysitter."*

want to identify with or at least understand the characters: They do not have to like them. Lord Voldemort in the Harry Potter books is a thoroughly disreputable character. The degree of his evil power, balanced against Harry's ability to neutralize it, is always in question. Readers care whether Harry ultimately defeats his nemesis.

In fiction, the characters can be people, animals, other living creatures, or even new life forms. Even inanimate objects have their own stories to tell. Kids can experiment with the characters they create, testing audience reaction to what words and actions will interest readers in their characters.

Settings

Settings are places or locations of a story—small towns, bustling cities, high mountains, barren deserts, the high seas, the frozen Arctic, lush tropics, the heart of the jungle, the vast reaches of distant space. Sometimes the setting is one that readers recognize instantly because of its local familiarity, while at other times, the place is an imaginative creation that transports the reader far beyond everyday life into another realm of existence.

Like adult writers, children have many creative choices of setting. They can locate their story in one spot or move the characters around to different places. Like an artist painting a picture, their words portray the setting as calm, inviting, benign or turbulent, unsettled, frightening. Description and dialogue convey the mental pictures that create a feeling of witnessing the action first-hand.

Plot

Plot is the journey that writers give readers. Writers choose where to go, when to start, what stops to make along the way, and where to finish the trip. Every story requires a plot or storyline that goes somewhere to give readers a reason to read on. Plot construction happens easily as youngsters follow the elements of the story frame.

Some stories are constructed with a main storyline plus one or more subplots. Such stories within a story enlarge the creative possibilities of story writing by introducing more characters and more issues or tensions to be resolved. Adult writers regularly insert the twists and turns of plots and subplots so that readers can enjoy a longer, more complex excursion that includes surprise destinations.

Writers, as they map the plot, use elements of time to add interest and help the story arrive at its destination. Some stories cover only a short amount of time (minutes, hours, days); others extend to greater length (months, years, decades, centuries). A story can go backward in time (like *The Magic Tree House* series), spring forward into the future (as in *Star Trek* or *Star Wars*), or occur and encompass yesterday, today, and tomorrow. Time can be creatively measured in worlds where normal rules do not apply (as in *Alice in Wonderland*).

Tension/Problem Resolution

Characters and setting coalesce into a good story only when there is a central problem or tension that must be resolved by the end of the tale. This produces the plot. Problem or tension refers to the issue or question around which a story turns. A mystery revolves around discovering who committed the crime. An adventure features harrowing escapes and daring feats as the heroes race against time to save the day. Historical fiction uses events from the past as key elements in the changing lives of the characters. Family stories recount the interactions and struggles of different generations.

Writers use the central problem to make readers care about the characters, to enliven the sense of place, and to give energy and direction to the plot. Sometimes, the problem is one readers have faced in their own lives so they easily relate to the experiences of the characters in the story. At other times, the problem is far removed from readers' daily lives, but is still intriguing enough to gain and sustain interest. Either way, readers must care enough about the problem facing the characters to want to read on to discover how it will be resolved.

Running out of milk and having to replenish it at the store is not a problem that sustains curiosity or ignites passion till the author puts the store on the other side of a neighborhood ruled by a bully—a character we have all known in some way. Add a timid youngster with a five-dollar bill sent to buy the milk for his mother, an encounter on the street, and now problem, setting, and character require a resolution. The audience's curiosity involves them, and in spite of what may appear to be a foregone conclusion, they want to know if their prediction or their hoped-for outcome happens.

EXTENSIONS

Writing Stories Together

"*O*nce upon a time in the Lost Kingdom there was a dragon named Cyberdragon who helped people," begins seven-year-old Alex's story, "The Amazing Adventures of Cyberdragon." The action takes place in "Alex's Kingdom," the floor of a playroom adjacent to the family's kitchen that is filled with a large Lego castle surrounded by a village of people, animals, houses, and dinosaurs. To Alex, the room is an elaborately conceived universe of imaginative play where wondrous events occur every day.

In conversation, Alex is eager to explain at length what is happening with his toys and blocks. The plastic trees sprout forth "magic fire" and the room of his kingdom is protected by an "invisible force field." He giggles with delight when adults try to enter the room only to be "stopped" by the powerful energy rays emanating from his imagination. But to our suggestion that he write the story about his magical and majestic city, he emphatically replied, "No!"

Like many youngsters, Alex's confidence about telling stories does not transfer to writing them. Unsure about the conventions—word choice, spelling, and punctuation—he is reluctant to risk making mistakes in print. Unaware of the reasons for writing—enjoying his ideas, remembering his actions, celebrating his accomplishments—he equates writing with confronting his weaknesses, not with declaring his strengths. Unwilling to take time away from what he finds enjoyable and easy, he assumes that writing will only diminish his imaginative play time.

Orally, Alex's ideas flow forth, spiraling through levels of complexity and invention, encased in interesting vocabulary. But when he writes, the process of self-expression is much different. His thoughts race faster than his capacity to record them on paper and questions about the mechanics of writing multiply with each sentence. His solution for escaping these uncomfortable feelings is to decline to write while remaining eager to verbally communicate his ideas. For Alex to become as confident a writer as he is as a talker, he needs adult collaboration and encouragement to capture his words in print.

"I'll put your story on paper," said Sharon. Liking and trusting her, Alex agreed. They gathered colored pencils and paper and returned to the kitchen table to write and draw. While Alex illustrated, Sharon wrote his dictation underneath each picture. Once they had completed the first group of words and pictures, Sharon passed the pencil to Alex so he could write two words of the text before continuing his illustrations. They continued in this manner, sharing the writing, till the story was finished (Figure 4.3). Alex proudly declared himself the author, identifying Sharon as the "Printer" of his words.

Writing with an adult can free children from the constraints of worry and focus them on thinking imaginatively about their stories. "The Adventures of Cyberdragon" emerged from a story-crafting team that inspired Alex's confidence to write as well as tell his story. All kinds of tales flow forth from these partnerships, surprising younger writers who do not realize that marvelous adventures and exciting dramas are inside their minds waiting for opportunities to emerge in conversations or on paper or computer screen.

Writing Partnerships

Story-writing partnerships work one-on-one; in a small group or with an entire class; on paper, chalkboard, computer, or videotape; with or without items such as Lego creations, puppets, costumes, or other props. Whether the writing tool is a pad and a pencil or a video camera, the purpose of a story crafting partnership is for younger and older writers to compose together, each partner conveying some of the elements of the story.

Writing partnerships require a delicate balancing act on the part of adults. It is important that a child experience leadership in the creative process—brainstorming ideas, writing and drawing scenes, revising and editing the text, and deciding when the story is ready to be published. But to support the process of children putting ideas on paper adults must provide direction to the writing. Sometimes a child's feeling of accomplishment evolves from the partnership of an adult willing to subtly structure choices, offer alternatives, and demonstrate how interesting language play is to an author.

The adult role, therefore, means sometimes leading, sometimes following, and sometimes getting out of the way. The necessary balance comes from knowing which one of the three to do when. The adult must express enjoyment, exercise patience, make helpful sug-

Figure 4.3 *Original of "The Amazing Adventures of Cyberdragon" by Alex. Translation:*

Once upon a time in the Lost Kingdom there was a dragon named Cyberdragon who helped people.

Cyberdragon:	"Hi."
Knight:	"Can you help me?"
Cyberdragon:	"Sure! What should I help you with?"
Knight:	"I've lost my horse."

And with tricorder in hand they set off.

[A rope extends from the computer across the page to lasso the horse and return him to the Knight.]

Cyberdragon:	"Here he comes!"
Knight:	"Thank you."
Cyberdragon:	"Don't mention it."

Colorer/Author/Illustrator: Alex

Printer: Sharon

gestions at appropriate moments, compliment and reward efforts, and avoid taking total control because the goal is to make the child feel comfortable as a story creator while maintaining the momentum that gets words and illustrations on paper. Adults may suggest voice, characters, plot ideas, and vocabulary and the child chooses whether to use any of these suggestions. The reason this teamwork is important is because with repeated successful experiences, a child builds the necessary skills for collaborative story writing with other children and for creating stories independently.

The techniques adults use depends on each child's confidence as a writer. Youngsters less eager to write, who continually request spellings, or comment "I don't know how to write that," or "I don't want to write" benefit when an adult scribes all or many of the words, offers suggestions for opening the story, creates dialogue, and adds description and details to the plot line. More confident writers easily compose an entire story, passing the pencil or keyboard back and forth, sustaining the balance of conversing about the plot, the characters, the dialogue and description, and using two creative imaginations to enhance the story creation.

Working together to involve children in story crafting is important because many youngsters do not know how to write stories independently. A partnership with an adult makes every child a story creator. At the same time, the adult is practicing and modeling the very skills the child needs to develop as a story writer—considering and choosing words and sentences, creating leads, inserting characters, developing storylines, and formulating and resolving the problem around which the story is based. As child and adult hone their writing skills together, both learn from the process. And since the adult has to make creative contributions too, ownership of the story is shared between older and younger writers.

Following are strategies for story writing. They are successful methods for children who enter classrooms not having heard many stories, unfamiliar with a wide variety of words, and unaccustomed to thinking about fiction.

Scribe and Describe the Child's Story

Scribing and describing the child's ideas are excellent ways for adults to craft stories with kids. Each represents a different role for the adult, as shown in the following box. As a scribe (Box 1), the adult records the words as the child dictates the story; as a describer (Box 4), the adult confers with the child to add interesting and clarifying information to the tale. In between (Boxes 3 and 4) are ways for adults to combine the scribing and describing roles.

Story-Crafting Roles for Adults

1	2	3	4
Adult scribes all or most of the words.	Adult scribes many of the words while the child writes some of the words.	Adult and child share the writing, each contributing details and some of the text of the story.	Children write most of the story with the adult suggesting clarifying details and description.

Adults must gauge how much to write or draw each time they partner with a youngster so as not to be always responsible for scribing. For youngsters just beginning to craft stories, having them write one or two words per story or one or two words they know how to read and spell is sufficient. These stories begin with the adult taking dictation, handing the pencil or keyboard to the child, and then taking it back to continue scribing. More proficient writers can easily create sentences, paragraphs, or entire scenes before handing the pencil or keyboard back to the adult.

An Improbable or Novel Opening

An improbable or novel opening gets children excited about inventing more information for the setting, characters, problem, and plot. Well-known local icons, symbols or events can open a story. Bob created a beginning using the giant-sized polar bear balloon standing on the roof of a soda company's downtown headquarters in Worcester, Massachusetts. To begin "sharing the pencil" with kids at a school-sponsored evening writing party for families, he wrote:

A giant polar bear lived atop the soda company building. One day, he was gone! "Oh, no!" said the manager. "Where is our bear? Where has he gone?"

Bob then walked around the room reading what he had written and asking different children to speculate about the whereabouts of the bear. They replied:

"He went to buy another bear for the company."
"He went to the North Pole to take a vacation and meet Santa Claus."
"You are talking about a cola soda company. He went to another one. He was tired of sitting up there. He could take turns with another giant bear."

Next, Bob invited a group of first graders to continue the plot, and together they composed the following adventure (Figure 4.4):

The manager had everyone search for the polar bear, but nobody could seem to find him. So they went to the Arctic Ocean and searched there, but he was not there, so they said, "Where could he be?" Then they went to the houses to see if he went to somebody's house. At one house they heard a big sound, so they went into the house and they had people go all over it and in one room the bear was sleeping on a bed. And it broke. Then they brought the polar bear back to the store and tied him extra tight so he would not get away again. The End.

Figure 4.4 *Group story.*

Create Choices for Leads to Stories

One day in class, after completing an extraordinary drawing of a man's face on a huge sheet of paper, the artist proudly declared that he had drawn a magician. As he received compliments galore from kids and adults, his teacher Sharon suggested he use this illustration in a story. Immediately his joy and confidence vanished, replaced by fear and frustration. He had no idea of what to write for his amazing drawing. There was no story in his head about the stranger he had carefully designed and drawn. He had been drawing, not writing. Imagining a story to go with the picture was more than he had intended to do.

Sharon quietly stated that authors have many choices of story beginnings, all of which they carefully consider, as he had carefully considered choices of eyes, hair, mustache, and hat before drawing these to create the magician's face. Folding an equally large sheet of paper into fourths to hang on an easel next to his picture, she explained that sometimes authors open a story with someone talking.

Then she read aloud as she wrote in the first quarter-page, "Where is that rabbit?" asked the magician. "The show is about to start!" In the second quarter she wrote and read, "What is happening? Is that rabbit trying my tricks? He's disappeared again!" Now the boy was smiling, reading the words himself, and considering which choice he liked better.

But with two quarter-pages still empty, Sharon explained that authors may open stories with description, as he might like to do. In the third square she wrote, "The magician's rabbit has disappeared, right as the show is about to begin, and the magician has no idea where to find it." The boy's face had become thoughtful, committed to seeing what would appear in the fourth square. Sharon wrote, "The hat was empty, the rabbit was gone, and the magician was upset. What would he do with just a hat and no rabbit?"

She and he read the four options together. Sharon asked if he liked any of them or if he wanted to see four others. The boy chose his favorite to begin the story. His decision opened the process of creating in words something that had become equally as interesting to him as his illustration. If he had not liked any of the openers, he and Sharon would have crafted others together. The goal was for him to be relaxed, confident, and ready to compose a story in partnership with her.

After choosing the opening, he and Sharon discussed what the rabbit looked like, where it was, and how the magician might find it. Sharon wrote some of the words, the child wrote some of the words, and both of them made suggestions about plot, dialogue, description, and resolution. The rest of the class watched and read the story as it progressed daily over the week, with revisions and new choices, until side by side, the story and the illustration were completed. The child was doubly impressed with what he had accomplished. His facial expression was a blend of pride and astonishment seeing his first large drawing, his first fictional story creation, hearing endless compliments from his classmates, and feeling immense satisfaction from seeing his ideas on paper.

Not knowing how to open a story or create a problem for the characters causes consternation and disheartenment to youngsters who are not confident story writers. Offering interesting beginnings for their consideration invites them to participate in story crafting with an adult. These are behaviors that authors employ in their decisions about writing and this is one technique that ignites and energizes youngsters' efforts to be part of a story crafting team.

Recognize Story Beginnings Appearing in Children's Conversations

Kids themselves will often provide their own story beginnings, as did Fiona one day when she arrived at school wearing different-colored knee-high socks.

"Oh, look how interesting," said Ruth enthusiastically, drawing attention to the unique personality and style of the wearer.

"Do you know why I did it?" asked Fiona confidently. "This is the leg of fire and this is the leg of ice."

Before long, Fiona wore different mittens, explaining to Ruth and the class which hand had "the mitten of the sun" and "the mitten of the rainbow."

Like Kente cloth of Asante peoples of Ghana and Togo where different woven color patterns communicate messages, Fiona's socks and mittens contained secret stories for the members of Ruth's class. It did not take long for the other children to begin imagining and writing stories about their own clothes.

The story-writing strategies of scribing and describing, finding an improbable opening, creating choices for leads, and recognizing story beginnings in conversations all require a conscious decision by a young author to trust her or his ideas in constructing a story. The willingness to explore ideas, to play with words, to give voice to a character is necessary for the imagination to speak. Every adult who facilitates the act of writing with a child also strengthens that child's ability to engage imagination, the source of ideas and confidence as a story writer.

Young Writers' Bookshelf for Story Crafting

The Three Pigs. David Wiesner. Clarion Books, 2001. The three pigs, huffed and puffed right off the pages of the book by the wolf, land in the middle of other fairy tales from where they try to find their way back home to their own story.

Doctor DeSoto. William Steig. Sunburst, 1990. A mouse who is a dentist must figure out how to care for a potentially deceitful fox.

The Storytellers. Ted Lewin. Lothrop, Lee & Shepard Books, 1998. An Arab storyteller in the streets of Fez, Morocco, recreates the tales and traditions of an ancient culture.

Lilly's Purple Plastic Purse. Kevin Henkes. Greenwillow Books, 1996. Lilly takes her wonderful purple purse to school to share and the misunderstanding that occurs teaches everyone a lesson.

Arthur Writes a Story. Marc Brown. Little, Brown, 1996. After receiving a creative story writing homework assignment, Arthur's imaginative ideas expand with many suggestions from family and friends.

Beware of the Storybook Wolves. Lauren Child. Arthur A. Levine Books, 2000. A little boy named Herb must deal with the complications when characters from "Goldilocks and the Three Wolves" and "Cinderella" spring to life after his book is left open.

CD-ROM

Mercer Mayer's *Just Grandma and Me* is an interactive story book from Broderbund. The book comes alive for young readers who can listen to the animated text in English, Spanish, French, or German and click on different parts of each page to discover what the characters will say or do.

Storybook Weaver by Broderbund lets kids create their own stories using words, pictures, and sounds.

Words for Pictures and Performances

Collaborative Stories	TEACH	These Conventions *Unconventionally*
Writing Words for Wordless Books • Dialogue and Description for Wordless Books		Genre: Wordless picture books Read the pictures Chapter books Picture books and comic books Story-building partnerships Dialogue and description
Excite the Story by Performing the Words • Strategies for Building and Performing Stories		Drafting Revising Audience Story elements
Extensions: Play Me a Story		Genre: Playwriting Dialogue Narration Revision

Innovative visual storytellers like David Wiesner, Mitsumasa Anno, Fernando Krahn, Peter Sis, Alexandra Day, Emily Arnold McCully, and Mercer Mayer do what most of us would never attempt. They tell engrossing, humorous, multi-layered stories through pictures without words. These tales are so surprising and entertaining that as the number of wordless picture books increases, so does the size of their audience. Virtually all topics—daily life, fantastic adventures, historical moments, science fiction—are presented through the visual imagery of stories without words.

Kids and adults of all ages can enjoy wordless picture books by doing three things simultaneously: reading the pictures, adding words from their own imaginations, and exploring how writers convey stories through dialogue and description. Together, these activities make wordless books a uniquely powerful learning experience for young children. The book's illustrations present the story, but readers construct their own interpretations of what they see on the pages. Without words, readers are free to compose a story to accompany the pictures, and every interpretation is right!

Most young children already possess the skill of putting words with pictures, readily supplying them to match advertising logos, product labels, symbols and signs, or television program previews. "Look, Sharon, look! Digimon's *next*!" declared four-year-old Alexander, pointing to a small picture in the lower corner of a TV screen showing characters in the upcoming show on that network. He needs no oral announcement or written text because the small image tells him the program schedule. He imagines the characters saying to him, "Keep watching, Alexander. We're coming next."

Alexander reads the picture announcement in the same way that people read words:

* He recognizes these cartoon characters as part of a much larger array of characters—each different yet all members of the same group (as he will learn in recognizing letter symbols).

* He recalls their names (as he will learn in recalling letter sounds).

* His prior experience informs him that whatever appears in the little box is next on today's schedule (as he will learn in placing letters in a particular order to spell words).

What children's television programmers know today is what audiences of silent films knew a hundred years ago—pictures are not wordless. Viewers use their imaginations to create dialogue and description to accompany each scene. Creators of pictograms did this thousands of years ago. By assigning meaning to symbols, people would understand the message as they read the pictures. Wordless picture books use the same process, letting readers describe the action of the story in their own words.

Even when some of the visual images and evocative references are not recognized by a reader, wordless picture books still succeed as a story because so much information in the pictures is widely understood. Herein lies the uniqueness of this genre in the book market. They are inclusive for readers, young and old, new to or fully immersed in the culture, fluent in English or speakers of other languages. In excellent wordless books, readers recognize enough clues to make the story interesting and pleasurable to read and reread.

Writing Words for Wordless Books

An examination of the different types of children's books highlights how writers use words and pictures to convey a story. Consider the differences between chapter books with many words but few illustrations, picture books and comic books with many illustrations and fewer words, and wordless books where the story is conveyed exclusively (or almost exclusively) through the pictures.

Chapter books impart a story or information through words and occasional illustrations. Kids must construct their own mental movies from the author's language. In the opening of *Wayside School is Falling Down*, Louis Sachar's madcap adventures about a most peculiar educational place, the custodian carries a large, heavy package containing a brand new computer—with full-color monitor and two disk drives—up thirty flights of stairs to Mrs. Jewls's classroom on the top floor of the building.

Once the children unpack the box and marvel at its contents, Mrs. Jewls promptly pushes the machine off the window sill to demonstrate the concept of gravity. Only at Wayside School would gravity be explained like this! The hilarity of the scene comes from the reader constructing a mental picture of the computer being lugged to the classroom, unpacked, marveled over, and then hurled from the window to smash onto the pavement below.

Picture books and comic books combine pictures with few or many words to relay a story. They are inviting because of their pictures, their language, their story, or any combination of these elements. Think of picture or comic books kids enjoy—*Cloudy with a Chance of Meatballs* by Judi Barrett, *The Very Hungry Caterpillar* by Eric Carle, *Tintin* by Herve—and notice how in each, readers can access the story through pictures, words, or combinations of both.

Wordless books are unique. The meaning of the story comes from how the reader interprets the visual images of the text. In *Anno's USA* by Mitsumasa Anno, a traveler rows into a California harbor and begins a journey west to east across the country, witnessing scenes from United States history. Some of what the traveler sees appears to be out of sequence chronologically: San Francisco's skyline is visible in the distance behind a seventeenth-century indigenous fishing village; a movie crew films wagon trains crossing Monument Valley, Utah; a city of skyscrapers appears on the page adjacent to colonial Philadelphia. By juxtaposing contemporary and historical time throughout the book, Anno suggests that the present is fashioned from the actions and decisions of people in the past.

In chapter books and picture books, the author chooses the words. In comics, the writer/illustrator determines how many words accompany the pictures. In wordless books, readers' imaginations must create the text. What all three genres share are the conventions of communicating a story through dialogue and description. Books without words are a ready-made opportunity for kids to learn the roles of dialogue and description by writing or speaking them to a wordless text.

Dialogue and Description for Wordless Books

After listening to Quitze's read-aloud of David Wiesner's *Tuesday*, Ben marveled, "It's like he has all the words in his head!" Quitze did, and Ben did, too. He just did not know that he could express them for his own and for others' enjoyment.

All wordless books offer a story writing partnership between illustrator and reader. *Tuesday*, the tale of amazing happenings on a seemingly ordinary evening at twilight, is one of our favorites. A calm evening transforms into a tall tale when the frogs in a pond levitate, rise out of the water onto lily pads, and fly all over town, in and out of people's houses and yards. Images of the laws of common sense wonderfully disrupted keep children turning the pages in eager anticipation of what extraordinary event will occur next.

Sharon introduces this book to first, second, or third graders on the first Tuesday of every school year, reading the title and the author as if it were full of words. Opening to the first illustration divided into three picture panels, she inquires, "Who would like to read this page?"

"How do you read the pictures?" the kids wonder aloud if they have never before composed words for a picture book.

"I'll show you my way," replies Sharon, creating frog dialogue first, and then description of the event. Choosing a volunteer to create another version of the dialogue and description opens the activity to everyone. The eagerness to read pictures intensifies with each child's composition of dialogue and description. With one or two children creating words for each page, the entire class takes a turn reading the first half of the book. Then, with copies of *Tuesday* in hand, groups of two or three spread throughout the room to finish reading, composing versions of the story.

Before everyone disbands, Sharon says "Oh, this is my favorite page! Look what is happening here," adding to the excitement already present.

In character voices, she provides dialogue for the frogs, "Look how small the house appears from way up here, Fred!"

"I wouldn't have believed it, unless I saw it with my own eyes, Lily!"

In narrative language she describes the scene, *"The yards, the houses, the trees, everything that appeared large from a frog's pond-level view now seemed to shrink in size, growing smaller before their eyes as the frogs gazed down from a bird's height in the sky."* After modeling dialogue in character voices and description in narrative language a second time, she invites children to do the same. And they do!

It is the very absence of written text that makes a three-way story writing partnership between book author, child reader, and teacher, parent, or caregiver. In this partnership:

- Author/illustrator presents a story visually.
- Child reader imagines dialogue and description for the pictures.
- Adult and children create dialogue and description together, modeling use of character voices and enjoying the story.

When adults and children read pictures, the adult is not automatically assumed to be the better reader. Adults and children are on equal footing as they compose dialogue and description together. Since both are creating a "right" version of the action, they are equal co-contributors to the process, conversing about the details in the illustrations, wondering about what is going to happen next, and imagining conversations between the characters. Here are strategies for writing a text for wordless books with kids:

- After reading a story with a class or a small group, prepare two or three of the book's illustrations on overheads to demonstrate how readers might describe what is happening and what characters might be saying. With washable pens, readers write conversations in speech bubbles on the overhead transparencies and descriptions at the top or bottom of the pages.
- After seeing the overhead transparency demonstration, kids write dialogue in speech bubbles and scene-by-scene descriptions on sticky notes to attach to the book's pages.
- Record on audiotape a child's version of the story to replay with the book or to write a transcription.
- Copy the book's pages, with space at the top or bottom of each page for writing dialogue and description. Distribute the copies to groups for their writing.
- Scan the book's pages into a computer for writers to type onto directly or to record their text into the computer.
- Videotape a child or group of children reading the text of a wordless book, showing closeups of the book illustrations, as *Reading Rainbow* does with its read-alouds.

Excite the Story by Performing the Words

THE CASTLE

An elephant stood at the door.
The King said, "Go away."
The Queen said, "Who are you talking to?"
An alligator walked up to the door.
He opened the door and bit the king on the neck.

Nineteen kindergartners composed this first scene of their collaborative story. The plot, characters, and scenes emerged as children orally contributed ideas and dictated lines for Ruth to record on chart paper in front of them. As their words appeared in print before their eyes, the class read their story aloud, eliciting many giggles and much quoting of words they found funny. As the discussion lengthened, however, the readings multiplied, laughter diminished, creativity flagged, and attention waned.

Ruth, observing the behaviors, saw that she had achieved what she was hoping for—audience boredom. In a sprightly voice she said, "It appears that we have a story finished. Great! Let's read it together."

"Ohhhh, who wants to hear *that* story again?" moaned Steven, stretching his body flat onto the floor in a pose of total disengagement, "This is such a *boring* story!"

"Say that again, Steven and be sure everyone hears you," said Ruth. "I feel the same way you do!"

You might wonder why any adult would happily bore a group of students if the goal is to inspire them to think. "Why is this story so boring?" asked Ruth. "Perhaps, if we act out what is happening in it, we might see why it is not interesting."

Live performance immediately re-energized attention. Then it revealed something amazing to the children. Acting out the lines of the story, kids saw how each other's interpretation of the same words produced different mental pictures in their minds. No two of their personal movies matched.

Performing the line "An alligator walked up to the door," one child slithered to the castle on her stomach. Another sedately sauntered on two legs, arms barely moving at her sides. A third stomped across the room, arms swinging wildly, head bobbing, voice growling. With three contrasting versions to consider, the class conversed about which of the alligators they wanted to feature in their story. They chose the third for its boisterous and flamboyant entertainment.

Seeing the words enacted provided the realization that their writing on paper lacked the excitement and suspense of the live presentation. The children concluded that if readers of their story were not viewing a performance, the words describing the action had to more effectively convey what the authors wished the audience to envision. To create a story as engaging and affecting as watching live playacting, these authors decided to revise their first draft to include detail and description.

Ruth's goal was achieved, as her young writers began to portray with words what they were creating through live action drama. She directed the group's attention to writing by inquiring, "What do you want your audience to see the alligator doing?" Then she modeled walking sedately, slithering on the floor, and stomping, bobbing, and growling to the door. The children unanimously reaffirmed the choice of the version with the most rousing action because it made them laugh.

"Your words have to make a picture of what is happening. You have to say in words what you want the audience to see, hear, smell, taste, and feel," Ruth told the class. Thus began a process of revising the story. Acting stimulated ideas, and ideas stimulated actions. Writing decisions evolved as the movies in kids' minds were played out for class viewing. Three questions focused and helped determine class preferences and decisions:

- How do we best portray these characters to produce the most entertainment?
- What might another audience find most entertaining?
- How can we create on paper the images we see in front of us? What words best describe what is happening?

Each day's work on the story combined acting and discussing, choosing precise language, and evaluating what would maximize entertainment value. By not hurrying decisions or discussions, Ruth imbued everyone with the notion that artists and writers think about their ideas while they do other things—enjoy recess, ride home on the school bus, talk with families and friends, drop off to sleep. Having time to hatch ideas, to mull over choices, to decide what to do are important parts of writing.

As each day's half- to three-quarter-hour work on the story evolved, small group interactions replaced whole group brainstorming. While part of the class drafted description and dialogue, small groups did other jobs. One child designed a mask for the elephant. Two kids developed ways for the king's head to roll off his body. Three kids painted a door to the castle. At the end of each day's session, the class assembled to see what everyone had accomplished and written.

The actors added facial expressions, hand gestures, and sound effects to their story enactment. Peter, the owl, hooted his way to the front door, grimacing with impatience while waiting to be noticed by the King. Queen Paige's voice inflections portrayed her feeling of apprehension when King Travon's laugh turned sinister. Leigh, the alligator, announced his entrance with loud, chomping noises.

Ruth focused the students' attention on revising by discussing each decision in terms of its impact on potential readers. She asked the children to

- View, then compare and contrast the different ideas children had in their imagination about how to portray the action in words.
- Construct description concretely, anticipating what mental images the words would convey to audiences who had been invited to hear the story and then view a live-action performance of it.
- Focus on a collaborative effort to create the most interesting story.

The following is a condensed version of the process of discussing the options and making decisions for "The Castle." Conversations between Ruth and the students are italicized and the story revisions are in bold print.

The class assembles to write a story about a castle, dictating to Ruth who scribes their words.

Ruth: *"What is the title?"*

The class decides: **"The Castle."**

Brey: *"Let's turn off the lights while we read it* [so it's a scary story]*."*

Ruth: *"But how do we know that the castle is scary? There are no words that say that here."*

After a short discussion, the class decides to call the story: **"The Scary Dark Castle."**

The lights go off. A piece of cardboard is used as a makeshift castle door.

The class chooses an elephant as the first character to stand at the castle door.

Peter: *Hoots* [as he portrays the elephant at the door].

The audience suggests that a hooting elephant looks and sounds mean.

A vote results in a no hoot decision.

The children write: **An elephant stood at the door.**

A discussion of what the elephant should look like occurs next. Luke wants to create a mask made of gray paper and covered with spots for the elephant to wear.

Ruth: *"How would you describe the mask in words?"*

The children converse and decide: **A bright gray elephant with blue polka dots stood at the door.**

Kaylee, the King, positioned inside the castle, opens the door to the castle, and speaks. A discussion regarding the details of the King's dialogue ensues.

The children write: **The King said "Go away!"**

Kaylee authoritatively yells the King's dialogue, spurring a discussion of appropriate punctuation and whether or not an exclamation point should be added.

Travon delivers the King's line in a sinister voice.

A vote is taken is favor of an exclamation point.

The class agrees: **The King opens the door. The King yells "Go away!" in a scary voice.**

Following the King's strange behavior, Paige portrays the Queen's terror at the King's sudden fierce personality. Her face becomes twisted, she bends at the knees and her voice shakes: The Queen said, *"Who did you say that to?"* The class, impressed by her interpretation, tries to capture the emotion in words.

"Who did you say that to?" the Queen asks in a wobbly voice.

The class introduces a new character, an alligator. As the alligator walks up to the door, Peter, the child playing the elephant, begins to exit the scene.

Ruth: *"Where is the elephant going? Do you want the elephant to leave the reader's mind?"*

No decision is made on whether to keep the reader's attention on the elephant, so Peter stands quietly waiting to be brought back into the story.

The class decides some time has passed and indicates this in words: **The next day, there was an alligator at the door.**

A suggestion is made that the alligator open the door of the castle so it is visible to the King and Queen.

The class writes: **The next day, there was an alligator at the door. He opened the door.**

Leigh: *"How would an alligator open a door?"*

Fiona demonstrates using her teeth to open the door.

The class writes: **The next day, there was an alligator at the door. He opened the door with his teeth.**

A discussion ensues about attaching a paper towel to the door so the alligator has a sanitary place to bite. As they try this out, the paper towel comes off in the alligator's mouth.

The children like this and add the action to the story: **The next day, there was an alligator at the door. He opened the door. He opened the door with his teeth and bit a piece of it off.**

Writing and performing the first chapter of "The Castle" engrossed kindergarten writers and actors for three weeks. Even after the writing and acting had ended, the kids continued discussing what might occur next, behaving as authors of an unfinished story. Kids' questions ("What's going to happen to the alligator now that it has misbehaved?" or "What will the Queen do now that she has lost her husband?") led to thoughtful conversations about characters, plot, setting, and tension/resolution.

Strategies for Building and Performing Stories

"Acting the Words" is a successful strategy for composing young children's collaborative stories because it engages them in an age-appropriate, mind-focusing experience of whole group learning. Everyone is important from the beginning to the end of the process.

- Scribing the children's oral dictation on large paper makes the evolving tale immediately visible to everyone. Its permanence on paper invites authors to reread, consider, revise, or approve the text.
- Large paper allows viewing drafts simultaneously, the original next to the revised. (Ruth scribed the original text in one color, and used a different color each day to record ensuing revisions.) Kids see the step-by-step process of story redrafting by viewing the different colors.
- As each working copy becomes cluttered, a clean copy of the latest draft is written (in one color), producing a new version for further revising.

- All of the drafts are saved and posted so students see the evolution of a story as different ideas are combined or re-envisioned. They can refer to the previous drafts to suggest actions by the characters or to add new scenes to the story.
- Giving everyone opportunities to perform the story as actors stimulates the collective creative flow of ideas. Each child offers ways of enacting the characters that produce new insights and suggestions for variation of the story. Their live dramatizations support children's eagerness to add vital plot-enhancing details and to assume the roles of "word testers and choosers," witnessing how words affect an audience's engagement in and enjoyment of the story.
- Asking clarifying questions from a reader's point of view provides insights about how to bridge the audio and visual effects of the live action performance and convey these images in written text. The children understand the need to make a movie in a reader's mind and that they revise their text to improve the theater of the mind for the reader. They evaluate the effectiveness of their written dialogue and description to recreate the story's live rendition.
- Using the terms "characters," "setting," "plot," "tension," "dialogue," and "details" in the context of generating and revising a collaborative story makes them understandable to young writers. These terms become the tools for kids' independent story writing thereafter.

EXTENSIONS

Play Me a Story

Siobhan wrote "The Little Girl, the Two Parrots and the Lion King" (Figure 4.5) so she and four friends could stage a puppet play for her second-grade class. The cast (three girls and a boy) knelt behind a cardboard divider, and while Siobhan narrated her story, the actors improvised the dialogue for the characters. The audience was thoroughly engrossed and applauded vigorously when the performance ended. Inspired by the excitement and enjoyment of performing, other kids started writing plays to stage for the class.

Young children love watching, performing, and writing plays, either individually or with other kids. A play is a story or a tale brought to life by actors who speak and move on a theater stage set or in television, movies, and videos. When children actively participate in writing and performing a play, they become "players as well as listeners in the world of stories" (Cooper 72). Play performances stimulate learning about how language conveys ideas in old tales and new stories.

By the time they enter kindergarten, children are already immersed in the world of plays—even if they have never written or acted one. They use the elements of a play when they "pretend play" with dolls, action figures, puppets, invisible friends, real friends, Legos, or wooden blocks. Pretend play is based on past experiences told new with people, places, and events re-created through action, dialogue, and setting.

Pretend play is not associated with staging a play, where kids act in costumes or speak through a puppet, but both of these experiences arise from the interweaving of the same story elements: characters, plot, setting, problem, resolution, and dialogue. The differences are that pretend play is spontaneous, performed solely on that occasion for children's own enjoyment without any intent of public viewing. Staged plays are rehearsed, dialogue is memorized, and the performance occurs in front of an audience.

Children's impromptu pretend play is an opportunity to convert the fun and enjoyment of playmaking into an exploration of playwriting as a genre of written language.

The Little Girl, the Two Parrots and the Lion King
By
Siobhan

Once there was a little girl and she owned two parrots. She had a happy life. In the jungle there was a lion and he said he was king! One day when he was taking his nap, a little mouse came along and crawled up his back and it tickled. He woke up. He grabbed the mouse. But the little girl heard him roar and ran to the rescue! "Let go of him," she yelled and the lion king ran away and never came back and the girl adopted the mouse and they all lived happily ever after. THE END

Figure 4.5 *Siobhan's play.*

When a child writes a script or an adult scribes the lines, pretend play appears on paper as a written story that may be performed repeatedly. Adults can support children's playmaking and playwriting in multiple ways:

- *Performing Old Tales.* Well-known tales like "The Three Bears" or "Cinderella" easily become a play. The children already know the storyline and the characters so it is easy for them to act out the story, adding dialogue and making plot changes if they wish. When children "play the story" they are placed firmly in an imaginative frame of mind. They experience the thrill of performing, the power of transforming a story, and the cooperativeness of acting in a group instead of reading alone.

- *Writing It Down/Playing It Back.* Taking dictation for young writers so they see their ideas on paper lets them recognize how the elements of a story are fitting together to make a whole play. The presence of the adult acting as the reader—pointing out missing story elements, suggesting possible language, asking questions to explore possibilities fully—is a powerful stimulus for children's creative thinking. Their changes, rewrites, and decisions are in view on paper, assisting their evolving ideas about story construction.

- *Combining Story Ingredients to Make a Play.* Children and adults can use any of the essential story ingredients as the beginning point for a successful play. A memorable character, for example, can be stimulus for imagining the rest of the story: Where does the character live? What is the character doing right now? Who is the character talking to? What problem is the character facing? Once those questions are raised, a story structure begins to form. But a play may also emerge from choosing a setting, a problem, or a plot line.

- *Staging a Puppet Show.* Puppet shows offer an especially inviting way for kids to perform their plays. Kids enjoy using props and dialogue to create setting, characters, and plot. Giving a voice to inanimate objects has its own inherent creative power that arises from all the different ways to make the puppet characters come alive through word choice and voicing. Adults can support kids creating, writing, and performing puppet shows by scribing the text, playing a character, being a narrator, or enjoying the performance as an audience member.

When kids develop plays from new, well-known, or much-loved tales, they hear and use words differently. They incorporate "book language and story form" into their descriptions and dialogue (Cooper 72). They include the wonderful language of their favorite authors in their own narration and speech. Children's authors compose poetic descriptions and exciting dialogue to convey the personalities of characters and the nature of settings. Kids want to achieve the same emotion and engagement in their plays. As children use the words and phrases of adult authors in plays, this new vocabulary appears in their conversations and written communications.

Focusing on Dialogue

Dialogue is the device that conveys the story of a play. Children may construct plays as Siobhan did writing the plot and letting the characters invent the dialogue, or they may write the dialogue for the characters to speak as written, as in the following selection from "Little Bear and the Three Mermaids." After reading E. H. Minarik's *Little Bear* books, four second graders wrote a play with the assistance of a student teacher who was their scribe and typist.

In the play, Little Bear and his good friend Duck go to the sea for a day's adventure. Upon arrival, they enter the water where they meet Crystal, Rainbow, and Sarah, three mermaids who live in the sea. In the second scene, Little Bear sees something floating in the water, swims over for a closer look, and discovers it is mermaid hair. To clearly distinguish action from dialogue, these young writers used quotation marks to indicate who was speaking and what was being said (Figure 4.6).

Sarah: "Oh my, there is a bear underwater!"

Crystal and Rainbow: "Quick, let's swim to the castle!"

Sarah: "Hey, wait for me!"

Little Bear: "Wait, I'm not bad, come back and play with me."

ACTION: Little Bear swims after the mermaids.

Little Bear: "Oh, no, I've lost them."

ACTION: Little Bear turns around and starts swimming back to Duck.

Crystal: "Hey, wait, come back. We're sorry."

Little Bear: "I thought you didn't want to play with me."

Rainbow: "We were shy because we didn't know if you were a good bear or a bad bear, but now you seem like a good bear."

Little Bear: "That's right, I'm a good bear, and I have a good friend named Duck. Would you like to meet him?"

Crystal: "We'll think about it. We need to have a private talk. Can you go find Duck and make sure he won't scare us?"

Figure 4.6   *A selection from "Little Bear and the Three Mermaids."*

Acting out a familiar tale, writing an original play, or creating a puppet show highlight the elements of stories. The plot serves as the skeleton for the play, providing a problem and a resolution that create an understandable story for the audience. The setting is a location for the action; the performers are the characters. As children write plays, they discover the importance of a *narrator*, the person who tells the story. A narrator provides information to the audience not spoken by the characters.

Without all of the story's ingredients, performances turn into everyone doing something disconnected. Before a classroom play is performed, a small test audience previews the dialogue and storyline to see if the performance will be understandable to viewers—just as playwrights revise their plays to promote audience enjoyment of the performance.

Young Writers' Bookshelf for Wordless Books and Story Building

Wordless Picture Books

Sector 7. David Wiesner. Houghton Mifflin, 1999. A young boy on a class field trip is transported from the top of the Empire State Building to a top-secret factory where clouds are made. Also by David Wiesner, *June 29, 1999*. Clarion Books, 1992.

Dinosaur! Peter Sís. Greenwillow Books, 2000. A little boy's bath with a rubber toy turns into a fun-filled romp with live dinosaurs: Stegosaurus, Tyrannosaurus, Apatosaurus, Triceratops, and others.

Rosie's Walk. Pat Hutchins. Scholastic, 1987. Rosie the Hen never sees the fox that follows her across the barnyard where each of his attempts to capture her results in near misses and a final fox mess-up.

The Silver Pony: A Story in Pictures. Lynd Ward. Houghton Mifflin, 1973. Eighty pictures tell the story of a young boy and a winged horse who escape a midwestern farm and learn about the lives of people in faraway places.

The Mysteries of Harris Burdick. Chris Van Allsburg. Houghton Mifflin, 1984. Visually riveting black-and-white illustrations and brief captions present disturbing enigmas and conundrums that invite children to construct explanations.

The Snowman. Raymond Briggs. Random House, 1987. The warm indoor world of a young boy and the cold outdoor world of a snowman that he made connect and produce a series of adventures in 100 illustrations.

Pancakes for Breakfast. Tomie dePaola. Voyager Books, 1990. After dreaming of pancakes for breakfast, a woman collects the necessary ingredients only to find her pets have made their favorite breakfast, too.

Will's Mammoth. Rafe Martin. Illustrated by Stephen Gammell. Putnam, 1989. A young boy and a wooly mammoth play in the snow and go on exciting adventures together back into prehistoric times.

A Day, a Dog. Gabrielle Vincent. Front Street, 2000. A lost dog faces loneliness, causes a terrible car crash, but ultimately finds friendship in this powerful story told exclusively through spartan black-and-white sketches.

Time Flies. Eric Rohmann. Crown, 1994. A bird flying inside a natural history museum encounters dinosaurs who may be alive.

The Red String. Margot Blair. Drawings by Greg Colson. J. Paul Getty Museum and Children's Literacy Press, 1996. A red string unites many worlds of creativity when it becomes a piece of a story wherever it goes.

Playwriting

Hear, Hear Mr. Shakespeare. Story, Illustrations and Selections from Shakespeare's Plays. Bruce Koscielniak. Houghton Mifflin, 1998.

Books Cited in the Text

Anno's USA. Mitsumasa Anno. Putnam, 1989 (out of print).
Tuesday. David Wiesner. Houghton Mifflin, 1997.

New Versions of Old Tales

Versions	TEACH	These Conventions *Unconventionally*
The Interrupting Story Game		Genre: Fairy tales and folktales
		Retelling tales using humor, irony, or contradiction
		Changing elements of stories orally (characters, setting, dialogue, description, plot, problem, and resolution)
Everything Old Is New Again		Featuring multicultural versions
• Feature Multicultural Tellings		Creating a parallel tale
• Compare Old and New Versions of Stories		
• Create Parallel Tales		
• Choose Stories that Stretch Children's Thinking		
• Stories from Language Play		
Extensions: Who Is Telling the Tale?		Points of view

In the original "The Three Little Pigs," unsuspecting pigs encounter a determined wolf who threatens to huff and puff and blow their houses down. Well, you know the story. Or maybe not.

In Jon Scieszka's *The True Story of the Three Little Pigs by A. Wolf*, the narrator—Mr. Alexander T. Wolf—claims he had nothing but the best of intentions when he went to borrow sugar for a birthday cake he was baking for his grandmother. Regrettably, a bad cold caused his earth-shaking sneeze that blew down the first little pig's house. To protect public health, he could not leave a dead pig lying in a pile of straw, so taking responsibility for cleaning up, he ate the pig for dinner. Although the pigs had never been very neighborly, what ensued thereafter was a big misunderstanding, and certainly not what the wolf intended to happen.

Eugene Triviza's *The Three Little Wolves and the Big Bad Pig* reverses the roles of the characters, creating a mean-spirited pig who destroys every dwelling three good-natured wolves build, even using dynamite to blow up a house constructed with iron bars, armor plates, and reinforced steel chains. On the advice of a friendly flamingo, the wolves make a house of flowers which so entrances the Big Bad Pig with its lovely scents that the four become friends who live together happily ever after.

Adult writers fashion new versions of timeless tales by spinning humor from "What if?" questions: "What if there were a fourth little pig who was the bright light of the family?" (as in *The Three Little Javelinas* by Susan Lowell). "What if Jack climbed the beanstalk to find a giant no longer powerful but weak, unhappy, and glad to see Jack?" (as in *Jim and the Beanstalk* by Raymond Briggs). Creating new characters, reinterpreting storylines, inventing dialogue, and changing the point of view of the narrator are tools for exploring unique imaginative possibilities with readers.

"New Versions of Old Tales" is a way for children to play "what if" with fiction stories and with daily realities. Kids revise well-known fairy tales and folktales with remarkable results. In their versions, they express inner wishes: weaker outmaneuver stronger; smaller triumph over bigger, poor gain wealth, unfair becomes equitable, and what is hoped for really happens.

As young writers change elements on which familiar tales are built, they look *unconventionally* at the conventions of story writing: creating characters, constructing plots, incorporating dialogue, defining problems to be resolved, adding imaginative or fantastic happenings, and employing unusual resolutions or endings. It is amusing to imagine what a story might be like if the following were to happen:

- *New setting* (Cinderella lives in a modern city or town.)
- *Different story angle* (The wolf is an innocent victim of circumstances.)
- *Role of previously unknown characters* (The three pigs receive assistance from their clever and more sophisticated sister.)

The allure of writing versions lies in altering long-established assumptions about how a story is supposed to be told. In a fourth grader's tale of "The Real Story of Sleepy Hollow," a headless horseman becomes a ballet dancer, a cool rapper, and a star baseball player for the New York Yankees. The horseman's many personalities contrast with the classic story in humorous ways. In the pages that follow, you will discover ways to make new versions of old tales a many-faceted WOW idea.

The Interrupting Story Game

"The Interrupting Story Game," taught to us by storyteller Eshu Bumpus, is an interactive oral language game for constructing new versions of familiar tales. It can be played with any number of children.

Eshu's rules for the "Interrupting Story Game" are simple: Don't raise hands just interrupt, one interruption per child, no violence or bathroom jokes, no use of someone's else name, and no changing someone else's change. In return, Eshu agrees to incorporate each element of change to characters, setting, problem, and resolution suggested by the audience into the plot of the story while maintaining the structure of the original tale as the frame for the new. These few rules structure the activity to support individual creativity and cooperative group story crafting. Kids easily grasp the idea and join in the fun.

"The Interrupting Story Game" works only if a story is familiar to the children so they can anticipate in advance changes they might make to the story. For this reason, everyone agrees ahead of time which tale they will change. An interrupting story might begin this way:

> "*If we choose 'Goldilocks and the Three Bears' as our old story,*" the adult explains, "*I might say: Once upon a time there were three bears*" and someone might interrupt to say "*porcupines.*"
>
> "*Oh yes,*" the adult agrees, "*Once upon a time there were three porcupines who lived together in a cozy little house.*"
>
> "*A really big boat,*" a child might say.
>
> So now our story begins: "*Once upon a time three porcupines lived together in a really big boat. One morning for breakfast the mother porcupine fixed a big pot of porridge,*" and another interruption might change "*porridge to pizza.*"
>
> The new story evolves from the old as everyone interrupts the storyteller once.

One interruption per child keeps individuals from dominating the construction of a new version. With each child changing one detail, everyone is eager to discover how the new version will compare with the original. To enjoy the story over and over again, we tape the oral telling, transcribe it, and then let kids illustrate the text.

Recrafting a familiar tale frees imagination and creates confidence. After seeing a class demonstration, youngsters working alone, in pairs, or in groups write new versions. Some youngsters retell an original story by making a few minor changes, perhaps to the setting or ending. Others add or subtract characters or build complexity into the story's central problem. Others put familiar characters in entirely new situations, transforming their personalities, adding dialogue, and resolving problems in a new way.

The excitement of orally contributing to a new version is a powerful catalyst for story writing, storytelling, and story changing by kids. Starting but not finishing an interrupting story invites children to imagine unique resolutions to the problems or dilemmas faced by the characters. New characters, scenes, and plots developed from the interruptions of the group inspire ideas for continuous writing over many days. The process grants kids the freedom to explore and create, and see what happens when they do.

Everything Old Is New Again

All types of old tales and rhymes are fair game for young revisionists: "Cinderella," "Jack and the Beanstalk," "Little Miss Muffett," "Goldilocks and the Three Bears," "The Ugly Duckling," "The Tortoise and the Hare," "Rumpelstiltskin," and "Little Red Riding Hood" as well as contemporary stories from television and the movies. Reading and discussing folktales from different cultures opens a multicultural perspective on the stories of different peoples and countries.

One key to successful version writing is everyone knowing the original stories, the characters, and the plots. Instead of familiarity breeding boredom, prior knowledge becomes the basis of fascinating, often wildly amusing retellings. Reading aloud or showing a filmed version of one or more tellings of old tales insures that everyone has the information necessary to compare and contrast a new version with an original. In this way, familiar tales are the beginnings of a wide array of available choices for rewriting new versions. Version writing can be supported in the following ways:

Feature Multicultural Tellings

Multicultural versions demonstrate that old tales are inclusive in themes and ideas, not exclusive to one originator. The Cinderella story is retold in more than 100 versions, most from different cultures and countries: Cinderella is based in Africa in *Mufaro's Beautiful Daughters* by John Steptoe, China in *Yeh-Shen, A Cinderella Story from China* by Ai-Ling Louie, Korea in *The Korean Cinderella* by Shirley Climo, Indonesia in *The Gift of the Crocodile* by Judy Sierra, Mexico in *Domitila* by Jewel Reinhart, the Caribbean in *Cendrillon* by D. D. San Souci, and from the American South in *Smoky Mountain Rose* by Alan Schroeder. Each version is an example of how authors from different cultural traditions craft the tale. The setting, dialogue, numbers of characters, identity of the magic benefactor, the remarkable outcome, and the resulting situation for the evildoers are determined by the cultural characteristics of the telling.

Multicultural books offer comparable stories from different cultural traditions and viewpoints, and unique opportunities for author study. Children learn how writers personalize struggles and achievements of different peoples in their stories.

Compare Old and New Versions of Stories

The plots and characters in old tales offer a vast source of ideas for new versions. "Jack and the Beanstalk," for example, is a tale of high adventure, mystery and suspense that puts a rich, powerful giant in competition with a much weaker, smaller, but clever child for treasures that rightly belong to the child's family.

Kate and the Beanstalk by Mary Pope Osborne and *Jim and the Beanstalk* by Raymond Briggs show how versions by two contemporary authors contrast with the tale's traditional rendition. In the first, the hero is a quick-witted, resourceful young girl who outsmarts the mean giant. The second account occurs in a modern city where a young boy aids a toothless, aged, infirm giant. The results are incredulous, harmonious, and unforgettable.

Create Parallel Tales

"Wishbone," shown on public television, cleverly pairs the telling of a contemporary story with the enactment of a classic original. The narrator is a terrier named Wishbone who is also the lead actor in the old tale. The contemporary story tells a tale with the same plot or theme of the original, but set in the lives of three kids, their families, and a dog belonging to one of them. Honesty, fairness, hard work, and problem solving are parts of the classic stories as well as their modern partners. Kids are intrigued by the idea of using an old tale to frame a modern story and then acting them out in tandem. This study of story line, cast in different historical times, captures kids' imaginations and focuses their writing strategies into more complex, sophisticated thinking.

Choose Stories that Stretch Children's Thinking

Children from African, Asian, or Latin American cultures may not be familiar with stories originating from European-American cultural traditions and children familiar with stories from European-American cultural traditions may not have heard stories originating from African, Asian, or Latin American cultures. Today tales from oral storytelling cultures are being written and published, offering opportunities for writing new versions. Knowing something about a culture, the region, its history, and characteristic architecture connect social studies with story-creating ingredients.

Kids can see how authors craft versions of a tale by incorporating elements of their lives and surrounding culture. In *The Three Little Javelinas*, Susan Lowell moves the story geographically and culturally to southern Arizona, adding Native American legends. In her version, the wise sister javelina helps her two brothers outsmart a hungry coyote by building a house with adobe bricks. When coyote comes down the stovepipe, a fire in the stove gives him an unusually warm reception.

Stories from Language Play

Creating new versions of old tales emerges from an oral language play that is a part of children's daily experiences. Rhymes, riddles, jokes, chants, nicknames, slang words, and songs are distinctive forms of language play used primarily within children's peer groups, as anthropologists Iona and Peter Opie (1959) found in Great Britain during the 1950s. Five thousand children from all sorts of backgrounds and communities—rural and urban, low-income and affluent—contributed to the Opies's collection of playground language that "circulates from child to child, usually outside the home, and beyond the influence of the family circle." These "verses are not intended for adult ears. In fact part of the fun is the thought, usually correct, that adults know nothing about them." Given their familiarity, popular stories and lyrics are easily revised and updated by kids, often irreverently, as demonstrated by much-sung alternate lyrics to the Happy Birthday song.

In their classic book, *The Lore and Language of Schoolchildren*, the Opies concluded that rhymes, jokes, songs, and other language play are an integral part of a children's "culture." Some versions of rhymes popular today and passed orally from generation to generation were sung by children 150 to 200 years ago.

EXTENSIONS

Who Is Telling the Tale?

New versions of old tales focus children's attention on point of view, an essential convention of story writing. Point of view refers to the perspective of the narrator of a story who expresses her or his own explanation, idea, belief, or argument about what is happening or what has happened. Sometimes, the narrator speaks in an unusual or unexpected voice, presenting a dramatically different account from anything heard before. At other times, the narrator appears to be a neutral, unbiased observer who is simply reporting events to readers.

Inviting children to consider the point of view of an author expands their talents as writers and storytellers in three ways.

Writing from One's Own Point of View as an Author

Young writers are able to do what adult authors do—write from their own viewpoint. Six different children will create six different retellings of the same tale. Indeed, since every teller is unique, an infinite number of possible stories arise from the original. They can retell a story from their own point of view by including whatever changes they want in the setting, storyline, characters, or basic problem or tension to be resolved.

> ### 1. The Little Red Hen
> Once upon a time there was a little red hen . . . "Wait a minute how come I'm always red. Why can't I be blue or green or pink? That's it. I quit."
>
> ### 2. The Three Bears
> Once upon a time there were three . . . "Hey! How come there's only three? Why can't we have four or five or six? That's it. We quit." The end.

Figure 4.7 *Varun's fairy tale openings.*

Writing from the Point of View of a Character Who Is Narrating a New Story

Writing from a different point of view is one way that adult authors build interest in a new version of a story. Readers discover the unknown personality and perspective of a narrator as the storyline unfolds through that individual's eyes. In *Cinderella's Rat*, Susan Meddaugh uses the familiar story of Cinderella only as the backdrop for the new, unknown story told from the point of view of a rat transformed into a majestic coach horse by the fairy god-mother's spell.

Children build interest in a new version by choosing a different point of view for their story. The chosen viewpoint can be that of any character. Even inanimate objects can be brought to life by letting them tell a story from a point of view. Endless tales can spin out of the original storyline.

Sometimes, shifting from the tale's usual voice and point of view to an unheard voice with a new point of view makes the story even more engaging to readers. After hearing selections from *The Stinky Cheese Man and Other Fairly Stupid Tales*, one first grader wrote the lead lines of his version entitled "Stupid Fairy Tales." Cranky characters voicing their opinions of what might happen if they were writing the story caused peals of laughter from the audience (Figure 4.7).

Writing from a Biased or Slanted Point of View

Writer Barry Lane has suggested that point of view is another term for "what is not being said." By this he means that most stories are told from one particular point of view that, intentionally or not, includes certain facts while leaving out other pertinent information. Such a viewpoint has a bias or a slant: One way to see this is to consider what the author is not telling the reader.

Young writers might construct versions not only from their own perspective, but from the viewpoint of specific characters who may have a special case to make, as in the following story by two fourth graders writing from the point of view of Cinderella's stepsisters (Figure 4.8). These young authors chose to make the stepsisters the heroines, omitting Cinderella's voice altogether.

Writing from different viewpoints is a way to examine why and how a point of view shows bias. Kids might try writing a version in which a main character is made to look as virtuous as possible, then as crafty as possible. Each version becomes a study in how language is used to tell stories and to persuade readers to think one way or another.

Figure 4.8
*Veronica and Erin's
version of* Cinderella.

Cinderella's Stepsisters Tell All!
A Really True Story
by
Veronica and Erin

We are writing to right a wrong. All these years, we have gotten the raw end of the deal. Everyone calls us the wicked stepsisters and Cinderella the fair-haired good girl. Well, it's a bad rap, a bum steer, a big lie, a distortion of the truth.

Cinderella was mean to us; everyone liked her best, and she got all the breaks. We had to do all the really hard work of running the house, paying the bills, and managing the family business, a local Taco Bell franchise. Our slogan: "Tacos are Greato!"

All we wanted her to do was some easy light house cleaning and laundry. What's so difficult about that while we were busy deciding how many beef burritos to make for the big Friday night dance crowd?

We wanted revenge.

So, one day she came into our room and told us that with some money she had saved she was going bungie jumping. She said when she came back she wanted her bed made. We first protested, but then we got an idea and agreed. While she was gone we snuck into her room and loosened the poles on her canopy bed. Then she came back and giggling we told her to take a nap to gain energy for a dance that night, since she was going with a very cute prince.

She fell asleep and we took that canopy down and put it on top of her so she couldn't get out. Pretty soon she woke up and started screaming, but the covers muffled her cries and she was stuck. Then we happily got ready for the big dance ahead of us. When her date came, we told him sadly that she decided that she was too good for him. He was sad, but said he didn't like her that much and said he would take us instead.

So he took us on a flying camel and we rode to the dance the most original way. After dancing all night he said he was glad she didn't come, and took us home. She decided to take over the housework, cooking, and paying the bills. Now we are all even and happy, but *we* are now the ones who go to the dances on Friday night.

YOUNG WRITERS' BOOKSHELF FOR VERSIONS

Squids Will Be Squids: Fresh Morals, Beastly Fables. Jon Scieszka & Lane Smith. Viking, 1998. Outlandish modern-day fables with humorous endings that spoof morals. Also by Jon Scieszka: *The Frog Prince, Continued*. Jon Scieszka. Paintings by Steve Johnson. Viking, 1991; and *The Stinky Cheese Man and Other Fairly Stupid Tales*. Scholastic, 1992 (cited in the text).

Little Lit: Folktale and Fairy Tale Funnies. Edited by Art Spiegelman and Francoise Mouly. HarperCollins, 2000. Fractured fairy tales in a comic format designed by seventeen well-known illustrators. Also *Little Lit, Book 2: Strange Stories for Strange Kids*, Raw Junior, 2001.

Henny-Penny. Retold and illustrated by Jane Wattenberg. Scholastic, 2000. The story of the hen who thought the sky was falling is reborn in all new vibrant photo illustrations and rip-roaring language play with puns, action verbs, and unusual adjectives set against a backdrop of travel icons around the world.

Doctor Coyote: A Native American Aesop's Fables. Retold by John Bierhorst. Pictures by Wendy Watson. Macmillan, 1987. Scott Foresman. Mesoamerican and European cultures blend in tales featuring the animal tricksters, Coyote and Puma. The Aztec peoples began adapting Aesop's tales in the 1550s from Spanish texts.

A Handful of Beans: Six Fairy Tales Retold. Jeanne Steig. Pictures by William Steig. Michael di Capua Books, 1998. New versions of "Rumpelstiltskin," "Beauty and the Beast," "Hansel and Gretel," "Little Red Riding Hood," "The Frog Prince," and "Jack and the Beanstalk."

The Bravest Ever Bear. Allan Ahlberg. Illustrated by Paul Howard. Candlewick Press, 2000. When Baby Bear reads an ending to a version of "The Three Bears" that he dislikes, he writes his own story; then one of his characters writes the next story and so it goes, characters creating new stories.

New Versions of "The Three Little Pigs"

The True Story of the Three Little Pigs! by A. Wolf. Jon Scieszka. Scholastic, 1989 (cited in the text).

The Three Little Wolves and the Big Bad Pig. Eugene Trivizas. Illustrated by Helen Oxenbury. Scholastic, 1993 (cited in the text).

The Three Little Javelinas. Susan Lowell. Illustrated by Jim Harris. Northland, 1996 (cited in the text).

Ziggy Piggy and the Three Little Pigs. Frank Asch. Kids Can Press, 1998. Ziggy is the fourth and carefree pig in this version; without preparation or worry Ziggy goes to the beach and saves the pigs.

The Three Pigs. David Wiesner. Clarion Books, 2001.

New Versions of "Cinderella" (cited in the text)

The Korean Cinderella. Shirley Climo. Illustrated by Ruth Heller. HarperCollins, 1993. Also see *The Egyptian Cinderella* by the same author and illustrator.

Mufaro's Beautiful Daughters: An African Tale. John Steptoe. Lothrop, Lee & Shepard, 1987.

Yeh-Shen: A Cinderella Story from China. Ai-Ling Louie. Illustrated by Ed Young. Putnam, 1982.

Domitila: A Cinderella Tale from the Mexican Tradition. Jewell Reinhart Coburn. Illustrated by Connie McLennan. Schen's Books, 2000.

Cendrillon: A Caribbean Cinderella. D. D. San Souci, R. D. San Souci, and C. C. Perrault. Simon & Schuster, 1998. The story as told by a Caribbean fairy godmother.

Smoky Mountain Rose: An Appalachian Cinderella. Alan Schroeder. Illustrated by Brad Sneed. Puffin Books, 1997.

The Gift of the Crocodile: A Cinderella Story. Judy Sierra. Illustrated by Reynold Ruffins. Simon & Schuster Books for Young Readers, 2000. A Cinderella story from Indonesia.

Cinderella's Rat. Susan Meddaugh. Houghton Mifflin, 1997.

New Versions of "Jack and the Beanstalk" (cited in the text)

Kate and the Beanstalk. Mary Pope Osborne. Illustrated by Giselle Potter. Atheneum Books for Young Readers, 2000.

Jim and the Beanstalk. Raymond Briggs. Sandcastle Books, 1997.

Fiction/Nonfiction Story Writing

Fiction/Nonfiction Stories	TEACH	These Conventions *Unconventionally*
Out-of-the-Ordinary Stories		Genre: Imaginative fiction Literal language

Is It Real or Make-Believe?
  A Story-Writing Game
• A Theatrical Opener
• A Puzzling Opener
• A Fascinating Facts Opener
• Strategies for Writing Real and
  Make-Believe Stories
		Fact and fantasy
		Realistic stories

Extensions: Fictionalized Facts and *Factualized Fictions*		Meanings of fiction and nonfiction

In February 2001, geologic scientists reported an amazing discovery. Rock and mineral deposits from China, Japan, and Hungary revealed that some 251 million years ago, a comet four to eight miles wide slammed into the earth. The force of the impact, one million times the largest earthquake recorded in the last century, triggered planet-wide volcanic activity, climate alterations, and changes in the ocean chemistry that wiped out ninety percent of all life forms during what is now called the "Permian-Triassic Extinction Event."

In addition to being front-page news, the findings continue revising science facts about the dinosaurs, those prehistoric creatures whose lives and sudden disappearance sixty-five million years ago fascinate children and adults. For a century, it was assumed that dinosaurs were slow-witted creatures who died out because they were unable to adapt to the changing environment. Those views were replaced by new theories about a gigantic meteor striking the earth, altering conditions of life throughout the globe, and ending the era of the dinosaurs. The latest findings offer evidence of an earlier, much larger extraterrestrial object hitting the earth with far more global impact. It may be that the first comet strike ushered in the era of the dinosaurs by destroying so much of what came before, while the second comet ended the dinosaurs' reign on earth forever.

When it comes to dinosaurs, fact and fiction are never easy concepts to separate. Facts keep changing—the real becomes make-believe; make-believe becomes real. In the 1993 movie, *Jurassic Park*, the computer-generated dinosaurs were based on the best-known scientific information at the time, but new discoveries soon made those models incomplete and inaccurate. Meanwhile, scientists in several fields have since successfully pioneered cloning of animals, an idea that seemed wildly improbable to moviegoers at the time.

Scientists regularly turn truths into falsehoods and imaginative ideas into facts. Researchers now suggest that plant life existed 150 billion years ago, long before it was previously dated. Astronomers report the presence of more than thirty planets outside our solar system even as engineers ready space crafts to explore them.

Story writers, like scientists, constantly reassess the meanings of fact and fiction, asking the questions "What is real?" "What is make-believe?" "Where does one end and the other begin?" as a basis of their fiction story writing. They write narratives that blend made-up elements—*fiction*—and actual happenings—*nonfiction*—into an intricate tapestry that engages the imagination and the it-really-happened experiences of readers.

"Fiction/Nonfiction Story Writing" presents ideas for using children's fascination with real and make-believe to explore different dimensions of fiction stories. At one level, matters of actual and imaginary in story writing are complex ideas to discuss with young writers. At another level, real and make-believe are wonderfully engaging topics for exploration and examination. By composing stories that combine elements of fiction and nonfiction, children build understanding of how writers attract and sustain the interest of readers.

Out-of-the-Ordinary Stories

Just Another Ordinary Day by Australian cartoonist, Rod Clement, is a unique opener for fiction/nonfiction story writing. In spare description without dialogue, the book chronicles the school day of a girl named Amanda. Arising to an alarm every morning, eating breakfast, riding to school, attending class, eating lunch, visiting the library, going home with her mother in the afternoon, awaiting supper, and reading before bedtime seems so ordinary that the book sounds boring after the first three pages.

The words, however, masquerade illustrations that dramatically transform the meaning of the text. When Amanda is described as "flying downstairs for breakfast," the reader sees a fantastic picture of the girl strapped into wings, swooping down steep stone stairs that connect her bedroom on a butte to the family kitchen on the mesa below. The oldest resident in town, Mrs. Ellsworth, bedazzling in earrings, a bonnet, and a skirt, is a dinosaur who drives Amanda to school in a Model T Ford.

Rod Clement's blend of straightforward language paired with unanticipated illustrations creates the surprise that entertains audiences, young and old. The catalyst for the humor is *literal language*. Language used literally is funny because our everyday communications do not always use words in a precise, concrete manner. If a friend remarks that "My eyes were glued to television last night," she does not mean literally glued, but that the program was so interesting that she could not stop watching.

By juxtaposing common phrases with illustrations of their literal meaning, kids understand how words can be differently interpreted depending on the context they are in. One youngster defined literal language as "You take the expressions and make them come alive." Another child observed, "You make them [illustrations] into what they [words] say." The ways writers use literal interpretations intrigues kids. When Rod Clement illustrates Amanda's "off-road vehicle" as an elephant walking on the grass beside the highway, one of the world's oldest ways to travel where there are no roads, kids gasp and grin.

To introduce *Just Another Ordinary Day* as an opener for fiction/nonfiction story writing, we hide the cover illustrations under paper so as to not reveal the book's premise. Then we read aloud the text of the first several pages without showing the accompanying illustrations. The apparent ordinariness of the words occasions the response "No, not really," if we ask our audience whether they think this is a really interesting story.

"You might enjoy seeing the pictures with the words," is our reply as we reread from the beginning, this time showing the illustrations. The unexpected contrast of words and pictures evokes a totally opposite audience reaction the second time: Laughter, surprise, and delight emerge from this very un-ordinary book. Once the children understand the book's design, they predict what illustrations might accompany the text of the upcoming scenes. As they announce their predictions, they are rehearsing how they might make versions of literal language stories.

In writing their ordinary-day stories, children make full use of the contrasts between words and pictures. Max, a second grader, created a picture book entitled "Just Another Ordinary Weekend," which featured the following scenes (Figure 4.9):

Figure 4.9

Scenes from Max's "Just Another Ordinary Weekend" book. Translation:

(Top) "Today I saw a snowball fight."
(Bottom) "After that I try to sleep, but my mom watches the TV."

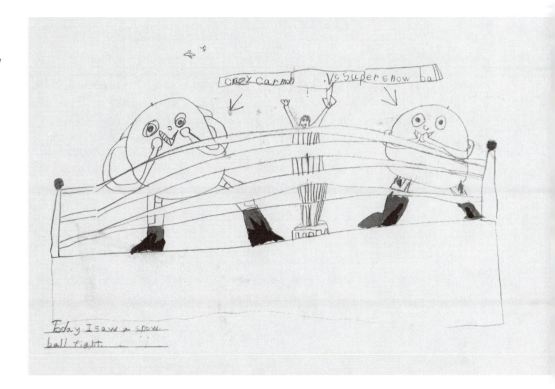

A group of first through fourth graders collaborated on an out-of-the-ordinary story about the daily schedule of their after-school program, crafting images for all parts of their daily routine. "Snack is always fast food" pictures a caricature of one of the program directors dressed as a giant ninja, swiftly cutting pizza with swords. "At clean-up time, everyone rises to the occasion" shows a kid running a super large-scale Eureka vacuum beside a "Two-Thumbs-Up Quick Cleaning Company" truck whose hydraulic lift transports kids high above the floor to trash barrels and recycle bins attached just under the classroom ceiling.

Out-of-the-ordinary literal language play can be developed from common everyday expressions. To add zest to Valentine's Day cards, teacher Jennifer Harris and her third graders brainstormed how many well-known phrases involve the word *heart* ("heart to heart talk," "breaking my heart," "you stole my heart," "eat your heart out," "wear your heart on your sleeve," and "learn it by heart"). Then children illustrated the literal meanings of the terms. One student displayed two big red hearts engaged in a conversation for "heart to heart talk." Another depicted "learn it by heart" as a boy sitting beside a heart while both recited the lines of poetry they were memorizing.

Is It Real or Make-Believe? A Story-Writing Game

Shawn's account of the cactus and his trip to the desert (Figure 4.10) is a first grader's entry into a story writing game we call "Is It Real or Make-Believe?" These stories let children use the elements of fiction and nonfiction to assess how other people react to their words. Discovering the truth or falsehood of someone else's story, as Shawn's classmates tried to do, adds game-like suspense and enjoyment to the learning process. Listening to each other's stories produces a desire to test their powers as story-writers against the audience's desire to accurately discern what is real and what is make-believe.

Real and make-believe stories facilitate learning about language. Kids discover that some words or phrases impart greater plausibility or believability to their writing, even when the events they describe actually never took place. Probing the craft of this story-writing, they see how writers choose particular words to achieve specific effects. As seven-year-old Charlie wondered aloud after hearing a story that was not real, but seemed to be, "You mean, I can fool people by making it sound real?"

"I went to the desert one night and found a dead cactus," said Shawn, reading aloud his one-line story to the class. "How many think this story is true?"

A number of hands went up; at least half the class accepted Shawn at his word.

Pausing momentarily to look at his audience, Shawn continued, "How many think it is not true?"

Again, hands were raised, although tentatively.

"Is it true or false?" asked Sharon.

"False!" declared Shawn happily. "I have a cactus at home."

Figure 4.10   *Sean's "Real or Make-Believe?" story.*

"Is It Real or Make-Believe?" works with any size group. In the game, a writer composes two brief stories—one that is actually happened (true) and one that sounds true, but did not happen (make-believe). The author tries to use words and pictures in such a realistic and convincing manner that audience members are in doubt about which story is a factual account of actual events and which is a cleverly disguised piece of fiction.

Once the writing is done, the author reads each of the stories aloud, giving no overt clues as to truth or fiction, and asks listeners to decide which is the real one. The question prompts thoughtful consideration among listeners who must vote when the author asks, as Shawn did after recounting his adventure finding a cactus:

"Who thinks the first one is the real one? Raise your hands."

"Who thinks the second one is the real one? Raise your hands."

After the votes are counted, fact and fiction are revealed: "The first (or second) is the real story." The fun of trying to identify the true story prompts children to write their own stories and the game begins anew.

A Theatrical Opener

A child-engaging way to introduce "Is It Real or Make-Believe?" requires a plain container—cardboard box or a brown paper bag—holding object(s) the children cannot view. It is important that the item(s) be something the kids will enjoy seeing, adding to their delight when solving the mystery.

"What's in the box?" the children invariably ask.

"Before we look inside," the adult replies, "I am going to tell you two stories about what it might be. One is real and the other is make-believe so listen carefully to decide which one you think is the true story."

At this point, the adult tells two stories about the contents of the box. Maybe the box is filled with new magic markers, enough for everyone in the class, or super rubber balls that bounce high and long, or a puppet or funny mask. The idea is to describe the contents so that both stories sound as if they might be the real one. Once told, the students vote which story they think is true and which is make-believe. After the votes are counted, the contents are revealed for all to see.

The collaboration of two adults telling the stories can involve a theatrical script that heightens listeners' suspense, as demonstrated in the following skit by Ruth and Bob. (Concealed in the bag is a plastic dinosaur mask large enough to cover one's face.) When asked what he thinks might be in the mysterious bag, Bob declares that he always knows when someone is telling the truth, so he cannot be fooled about the contents.

This is the cue for Ruth to begin the dialogue:

Ruth: "Hey, Bob! I have a bag of worms for you."

Bob: "That's not a bag of worms. You're joking me."

Ruth: "OK, If you think this is a joke, then put your hand inside."

Bob: Puts his hand inside and pulls it out quickly. "Ewwe! It feels slippery."

Ruth: "I told you it was a bag of worms."

Bob: "No, it is not. Nobody brings live worms to the school in a bag."

Ruth: "Okay, there are no worms."

Bob: "I knew it. I can always tell when someone is not telling the truth. You can never trick me."

Ruth: "Let's see about that. You [and a small group of kids] go out of the room while we compose two stories about what's inside the bag. We'll see if we can fool you."

Bob and a group of kids leave the room to discuss how they might determine which story is true, anticipating that the other group is trying to fool them. Meanwhile, Ruth shows the kids in her group the hidden surprise and they create two true-sounding stories, making the choice of detecting which is real as difficult as possible.

Invariably, the idea of monsters, ghosts, dinosaurs, or other highly improbable objects hiding in the bag comes up, presenting an opportunity for Ruth to ask if the kids with Bob will believe a story that includes fantastic creatures or implausible happenings. Youngsters decide what may be too wild an idea to make a story sound true.

After discussing how authors make stories sound real, children often, but not always, revise their suggestions to compose convincing possibilities. First graders are less likely than second graders to quickly revise their ideas for making a story sound real, and second graders revise less speedily than third graders. It is through ongoing conversations about how authors revise their writing that youngsters gain the insights needed to easily construct a story that sounds real when it is not.

When Bob's group returns, the kids in Ruth's group tell both their stories. Then they ask "Who thinks Story One is real?" "Who thinks Story Two is real?"

The contents of the bag are revealed, evoking laugher and applause for the story creators. Then children are invited to write their own "Is It Real or Make-Believe?" stories to try to fool the class.

Solving the mystery by trying to decipher which of the stories is true demonstrates how words create a fiction story from elements of nonfiction reality. If a writer presents a highly improbable tale, kids immediately know that it is not true. The fun of determining real and make-believe is lost if no one is fooled. When a writer describes events in ways that might be real, then listeners are really challenged to figure out which is true and which is make-believe.

A Puzzling Opener

A pair of stories written by kids is a different way to open "Is It Real or Make-Believe?"

Rachel's Story

When I went to my Grandma's house over February vacation, we went out to a restaurant called "The Rain Forest Cafe." It was really cool! I had a Sprite and a hamburger with some fries. Then I went and threw a penny into the alligator pond. The Rain Forest Cafe has model animals that are posed and then at a certain time they move. For example, at the cheetah's time, it will growl and move its tail. I also had a root beer float for dessert. It was fun!

Real or Make-Believe?

Elijah's Story

On Sunday I had a basketball game. My team the Blazers played the Sixers. My team is the best team in the league, but we almost lost. I got fouled badly because someone landed on top of me when I was shooting so I got two foul shots. But when the player landed on me my neck got hurt as well as the back of my knee. Then after the game I played one of the referees. I won 10 to 8.

Real or Make-Believe?

(The second story is true; the first never happened.)

Paired stories like these two may be made deliberately more puzzling by one author boldly claiming that her story is the real one, trying to sway the opinions of the audience. The other author then objects, stating that his story is actually the real one. This dialogue heightens the drama for the audience.

A Fascinating Facts Opener

Fascinating facts from everyday life and the school curriculum are two more sources for "Is It Real or Make-Believe?" stories. One teacher told us how she amazed her students with the true story of a dentist who gave away ten thousand tubes of toothpaste after one of his former patients, actress Julia Roberts, won an academy award. The dentist had vowed to give free toothpaste to all of his patients if one of them ever received a major honor. Hearing the story, the children did not believe that a dentist would give away toothpaste. Daily newspapers and *People* magazine report these hard-to-believe, but true events that surprise kids.

Equally amazing are facts from science, geography, and social studies. In the following two-voice poem, Ruth and Sharon test everyone's knowledge of facts that may or may not be real.

Sharon: Do you know how far your veins and arteries stretch if you tie them all together in a line?

Ruth: No! I have been wondering about that for a long time. Please tell me.

Sharon: You won't believe it, but it's true. All your veins and arteries put together measure 60,000 miles, almost two and a half times around the equator of the earth!

Ruth: Wow! That's a lot of miles! I'll bet you can't guess how far your skin will stretch once you take all three layers and put them together!

Sharon: I think it will probably fit all the way over a couch.

Ruth: It would be a VERY large couch. Your skin covers 15 square feet when you take all of it and put it out onto the floor!

Sharon: NO!! Well, do you know how many times a hibernating groundhog's heart beats in a minute? Guess!

Ruth: Okay, I'll guess twenty beats a minute. That's slow.

Sharon: That's not slow when compared to the real count. The heart beats three times a minute, once every twenty seconds! Isn't that amazing?

Fascinating facts that may or may not be true are a part of National Public Radio's weekly news quiz, "Wait! Wait! Don't Tell Me!" whose producers have created games for adults that are fun to play and tricky to solve. One segment of the show has four news stories read by the show's guests. The audience and an on-air contestant try to identify the one story that may sound unlikely but is true. The same basic structure we use with kids is just as intriguing for adults.

Is It Real or Make-Believe? A Story-Writing Game

147

Strategies for Writing Real and Make-Believe Stories

The momentum for writing "Is It Real or Make-Believe?" stories comes from the excitement created by people having to choose between stories. Hearing two tales, voting for one over the other, and learning which is real creates a highly suspenseful format for publishing, for discussing how writers choose language and structure, and for involving audiences in story construction. The following strategies promote real and make-believe story writing by kids.

- When writing "Is It Real or Make-Believe?" stories, especially the first few times, we suggest that kids decide whether to write alone, in pairs, or in trios; collaborate on both stories together or each write one; compose two versions of the same storyline, one real, the other not. This makes it easier for someone without an idea to join a partner and the two can plan together what they will do. These choices take the pressure off the creative process and ensure that everyone participates in creating a story they can share.

- Many youngsters write their first "Is It Real or Make-Believe?" stories autobiographically, recounting events that happened to them or other family members. Starting to explore the ideas of fiction and nonfiction from personal experience gives children a comfortable, familiar point from which to orient their writing. Professional fiction writers do this, incorporating events from real life into the plots of their novels and short stories. To validate that writers use their own and other peoples' experiences in stories, we tell kids, "If I find it difficult to make up a story quickly, I remember something that really happened and change some of it to make it a new story." Statements like this reassure and guide young writers, making writing easier for some.

- We advise kids to write the first story that comes to mind rather than spending too long considering since this can be more confusing than helpful. With experience and after hearing others' ideas, young writers increase their confidence and attempt to combine fiction and nonfiction more imaginatively. Their efforts confirm that they have wonderful and imaginative stories to share.

- Stories do not have to be lengthy to sound true. Someone may choose an event, change only one or two elements of it, and produce a fiction story speedily. Minor modifications of things that actually happened are legitimate parts of the process of exploring fiction. The goal—having children consider the elements of fiction and nonfiction writing to see how easy it can be for authors to change facts to fiction in their writing—begins with short attempts.

- We do not allow publishing in front of an audience to become a contest to see who confuses the most people. Voting between two stories keeps interest high, but the object of writing and choosing one story is for the author(s) to convince listeners and readers that both sound real. The authors are applauded for using creativity and imagination in ways that make the details feel real and a story believable, not simply for confusing or stumping the most listeners.

EXTENSIONS

Fictionalized Facts and Factualized Fictions

Between the ages of two and six, Ryan fervently believed in the existence of an invisible dog named "Shelfie," his constant companion. Playing in the yard or in his room, he would engage in lengthy conversations with the dog only he could see. He would happily tell anyone who would listen about their human/canine adventures. There was the time when Shelfie took off from home, and Ryan not knowing where he had gone, "flew to Africa, found him, and we flew home."

Shelfie possessed great powers and a unique personality. "He can hear a bear fifty miles away," declared Ryan. One day while enjoying ice cream at a roadside stand, Ryan left his unfinished cone on the ground for his dog to eat. As his brother and sister watched intently, the cone remained untouched. "Guess he's not hungry," concluded Ryan.

What adults may regard as Ryan's little fictions are in actuality the beginnings of his imaginative explorations of the realms of fiction and nonfiction. Ryan has created the dog of his dreams and given magical status to their time together. He has invented a world of story that cannot be rigidly categorized as fact or fantasy. Shelfie has many dog-like characteristics, but he is also capable of amazing feats and wondrous accomplishments. He is whatever Ryan wants or needs him to be, a source of stability in the ever-changing world of young childhood.

Once he entered elementary school, Ryan said less and less about his dog. Interactions with classmates and teachers meant Ryan and Shelfie had less time together. Also, Ryan was adopting a more "grown-up" perspective that did not include the existence of invisible companions. Slowly, talk about Shelfie faded away, left only in the memories of family members.

The story of Ryan's dog highlights how matters of reality and make-believe are essential ingredients in children's lives. Kids do not draw rigid lines between the actual events of everyday life and the made-up events of imagination and fantasy. They shift easily between the facts of people, places, and things and fantastic situations where improbable occurrences happen regularly.

Children's intense interest in real and make-believe offers adults the opening to explore how fiction and nonfiction are used in story writing. Authors blend fact and fiction so that factual stories may have some fiction and fictional stories include some facts. Young writers extend their knowledge of stories by achieving some of the same blends in their writing.

To open discussions of how writers use fictionalized facts and factualized fictions, we suggest teachers utilize children's books and discuss the topics sensitively.

Being Sensitive

Showing sensitivity to how young children, particularly preschoolers, make sense of the world includes examining how they experience fiction and nonfiction in their daily lives. Preschool-age children have their own unique and unexpected definitions of reality, a point made abundantly clear one day when four-year-old Christina joined us for a car ride. As we made our way through busy city streets, Bob claimed he had the power to change the traffic lights from red to green. Silently counting the intervals since the previous light, he announced "Abracadabra. Abracadam. Poof!" as the signal changed and the cars surged forward.

"Look, Christina," declared Sharon. "Bob is magic!"

Unimpressed, Christina replied with certainty. "Bob's not real magic. Barney is real magic!"

As Christina's unbending belief in the power of Barney suggests, fiction and nonfiction are not fixed concepts for preschool-aged children. Kids at this age are very literal in their interpretations and responses. Listening to his uncle and a friend discussing the dead battery in a neighbor's truck, three-year-old Alexander declared, "The battery in my green truck is fine." For him a battery is a battery, whether in his toy truck or an adult's automobile. Since the lines between reality and fantasy are still very fluid, many three-, four-, and five-year-olds do not fully understand the humor of some made-up, make-believe situations. Imaginary occurrences may seem perfectly plausible to them.

Even as they enter first grade, improbabilities amusing-to-adults remain as facts in the worldviews of children. There are monsters under the bed, dolls with which one can carry on conversations, invisible playmates, and cartoon characters that intervene directly in the events of daily life. Still, from an educational perspective, first graders are ready to learn more about the meanings of fiction and nonfiction and to use them in their writing.

The lines between fiction and nonfiction are also blurred in the media that pervade the lives of many children. Watching a story on television or at the movies requires some suspension of disbelief from a viewer. But for children, sophisticated special effects make it hard to recognize that fiction is not fact and vice versa. Perhaps characters do travel through time and space, dematerializing in one place and reappearing in another. Perhaps dogs like Wishbone really talk. Perhaps superheroes actually perform fantastic feats. Constantly seeing stories on small or large screens, children find the question "What is real?" not easy to discern.

Given the interweaving of fact and fiction throughout the fiber of children's daily lives, it makes little sense to learn an either/or definition of fiction and nonfiction. Static definitions are commonplace—the school library arbitrarily distinguishes between the fiction and nonfiction sections and dictionaries describe the two terms as mutually exclusive. A more expansive viewpoint looks at the uses of fiction and nonfiction in stories and how one affects the other.

Reading Children's Books

By reading children's books, teachers will see how authors successfully blend fiction and nonfiction in writing. Questions of fiction and nonfiction emerge from children's books, whether they are categorized as fiction or nonfiction. By first grade, most children are prepared to accept that a school bus cannot travel into outer space, even though the space shuttle astronauts do so all the time. The powers of Harry Potter, Jack and Annie in Mary Pope Obsorne's *Magic Tree House* time travel adventures, or Jon Scziezka's *Time Warp Trio* are less easy to categorize. Perhaps time travel or magic mental powers can really happen. From another genre, perhaps there really are people who behave as unwittingly as Sue Denim's *The Dumb Bunnies* or the adults in the Wayside School stories. Here again, children face decisions about what is fact and what is fantasy in the literature they read.

Reading and discussing children's books is a way to show kids how writers regularly incorporate the actual with the make-believe, stretching the dimensions of what happened or could happen. Here are two examples:

Dear Mr. Blueberry by Simon James delightfully contrasts an exchange of letters between a young girl named Emily who sees a blue whale in her backyard pond and her teacher, Mr. Blueberry, who contends that whales cannot possibly reside there. Emily treats her whale the way most kids treat a favorite pet—she feeds it, names it Arthur, and feels great sadness one morning when the whale is gone. Mr. Blueberry on the other hand serves as the voice of science, explaining that whales are migratory creatures who travel great distances in a single day. The book concludes when Emily goes to the beach, sees Arthur, strokes his head, and watches as the whale goes back to the sea.

The Bee Tree by Patricia Polacco begins with a young girl complaining that she is tired of being inside. Her grandfather invites her to go with him to find the bee tree with the sweetest honey. After capturing some bees in a bottle, they let one go and begin following it. Before long, they are joined by Mrs. Govlock and Baby Sylvester, Elinar Tundevold and his squeaky old bike, Olva Lungheigen out walking with Petra and Dorma Hermann, Bertha Titchworth just back from the Yukon, a herd of goats, and three traveling musicians. Eventually, everyone locates the bee tree, starts a fire to quiet the bees, gathers the honey, and enjoys a lovely picnic together.

At the heart of each story is a blend of people and situations that could really happen along with aspects or events that did not actually occur. Each story succeeds because the blending is so clever and enjoyable. In the first story, the fantastic idea of a whale in the backyard is linked to the actuality that children like Emily imagine such wonderful events all the time while adults like Mr. Blueberry dismiss them as false. The realistic elements make the fiction all the more fun to read.

In the second story about the granddaughter and grandfather, the reverse happens—the make-believe supports the real. The reader recognizes that such an event could happen while realizing that the crowd of people and animals that appears along the way to the bee tree is a delightfully improbable addition that adds merriment and uniqueness to the story.

The key for young writers is to observe how the adult writer of each story achieves the mix of what is true with what is not true. Asked to create a story that is not true, many young children immediately turn to wildly impossible happenings involving space aliens, superheroes, time travel, or other fantastic events. These stories miss the more subtle ways that adult authors fuse the actual and the make-believe. As kids read books that carefully weave fact and fiction together, they gain ways to think about how to use these elements in their own writing.

Young Writers' Bookshelf for Fiction/Nonfiction Stories

10 Minutes Till Bedtime. Peggy Rathman. Putnam, 1998. A group of happy hamsters play about the house while a young boy gets ready for bed.

Tom. Daniel Torres. Puffin Books, 1999. A dinosaur visiting New York City goes unnoticed until a little boy named Billy helps him to become a famous artist.

Lily Takes a Walk. Satoshi Kitamura. Econo-Clad Books, 1999. An everyday walk from the point of view of a girl and her dog, one realistic and the other wildly fictional.

In the Attic. Hiawyn Oram. Pictures by Satoshi Kitamura. Henry Holt, 1988. A young boy explores the attic of his house where he makes surprising new discoveries.

Sideways Stories from Wayside School. Louis Sachar. Avon Books, 1998. Madcap adventures from a wild and crazy school.

Stories Julian Tells. Ann Cameron. Random House, 1989. A collection of funny, true-to-life anecdotes from the lives of two brothers. Huey, the younger of the two, looks up to and believes everything his older brother Julian tells him. Julian's

creative imagination leads the pair into episodes reminiscent of real-life adventures and dilemmas. See also *More Stories Julian Tells* and *The Stories Julian Tells* by the same author.

Miss Nelson Is Missing. Harry Allard and James Marshall. Houghton Mifflin, 1985. When their teacher mysteriously disappears, the children are faced with a frightening substitute, Miss Viola Swamp.

Books Cited in the Text

Just Another Ordinary Day. Rod Clement. HarperCollins, 1995. Also by Rod Clement, *Frank's Great Museum Adventure*. HarperCollins, 1999.

Dear Mr. Blueberry. Simon James. Aladdin Paperbacks, 1996.

The Bee Tree. Patricia Polacco. Paper Star, 1998.

The Dumb Bunnies. Sue Denim. Pictures by Dav Pilkey. Scholastic, 1994.

Chapter Summary

Chapter Four, "Stories," introduces imaginative story writing, with the four key elements writers use to craft their tales: characters, setting, storyline (or plot), and problem/resolution (or tension). Since most children are eager to tell stories aloud, oral storytelling games make a delightful introduction to story writing. Writing words to accompany wordless picture books offers another way for children to begin writing stories. So too does composing scripts or storylines for kids' short theatrical productions.

New versions of old tales, stories that are a blend of fiction and nonfiction, and "tall" tales demonstrate how

storywriters use reality and make-believe in their stories. These different story writing ideas give children opportunities to use language to entertain and engage readers. As they write their own versions of old tales, kids change key elements of the story and the characters to make a new story experience for readers. In fiction/nonfiction stories, they try to "stump" the audience into thinking a story that did not happen seems as though it did. They also learn different techniques for transporting readers from the realities of daily life to creative possibilities of imaginative fiction stories.

CHAPTER FIVE

Mathematics

"Can you ever hide from math?" Ruth asked her kindergartners on the first day of school. The children were certain they could; Ruth was adamant that they could not. A yearlong process of mathematical inquiry was underway in response to this challenging question.

The class first investigated patterns—visual and structural. The children were quickly in awe of the many patterns they found in the world around them.

"Look, there's a pattern on my shirt!" declared Blayne.

"You are wearing math," Ruth replied.

"There is one [a pattern] on my pants," added Demetria.

Ruth and the children began listing patterns, drawing patterns, dodging patterns, ducking under patterns. Demetria exclaimed, "Patterns are everywhere so . . ."

"So you can't hide from patterns," a classmate replied.

"Math is all around you," said another.

"Does this mean you can never hide from math?" asked Ruth.

The children looked around the room, at each other's clothing, at the patterns on the rug, the walls, and the floor. They searched the school, the playground, and each other, always finding patterns.

One boy shouted, "I'm going in the closet and shutting the door," thinking that he had found a haven from math.

"Do you see any math?" asked Ruth.

"Yes," groaned the boy, realizing that even in the darkened rectangular closet, the shelves were filled with materials waiting for someone to count them.

A few days later, the class decided to write a list of all the places where someone might hide from math. Mackenzie wrote about digging a hole and hiding in it. But, when she read her theory to the class, one youngster observed, "You are not hiding from math if you are in a hole. You are in a cylinder."

The question "Can You Hide from Math?" energized mathematical learning. While the children were challenging themselves to hide from math, they were constantly discovering it in different and unexpected parts of their lives. It was as if they had acquired spectacles that enabled them to see everything mathematically. Where the math question provided unending curiosity, writing propelled children's inquiries, reflections, and conclusions as they recorded their discoveries in journals, on posters, and in stories.

Chapter Five, "Mathematics," teaches children how mathematics and writing are languages—one based in numbers and symbols, the other in words and sounds. Mathematicians and writers share similar goals as communicators. Each seeks to ensure that readers understand what is being communicated. Each is concerned with process (thinking analytically and imaginatively) and product (using numbers and words appropriately). Each learns by "taking risks, making mistakes without becoming devastated, persisting in independent work, and trusting our ability to solve problems and effect changes in our environment" (Skolnick et al. 11).

Children learn the language of mathematics the same way they learn written and spoken language—by using it for genuine purposes in personally meaningful situations. As well as practicing operations of numbers, educator Alfie Kohn (180) envisions mathematical learning where "students can play with possibilities, think through problems, converse, and revise." The goal is to explore the underlying meaning of terms like estimation, percentage, fraction, and probability as well as learning the math operations that support each concept. In so doing, the study of math is widened from arithmetic to conceptual ideas and real-world applications.

Writing's unique power to make learning happen from the inside out engages kids in the processes of thinking mathematically. Researchers Phyllis and David Whitin (2000) have noted that kids' own language has long been absent from mathematics teaching, yet when children use their own words in their own ways, they give personal meaning to the patterns they discover in their math experiences. The WOWs in this chapter connect mathematics and writing through math riddles, child-conducted surveys and graphs, and math comics. Each activity features math concepts (measuring, counting, place value), math functions (addition, subtraction, division, and multiplication), analytical thinking, and the writing conventions of sentence formation, story construction, and report writing.

- **WOW 16: Math Riddles** pose puzzle problems for kids to solve by thinking analytically and creatively. Every riddle is open-ended and easy to understand so children can solve it on their own. Some solutions are included as starting points for discussion and to inspire more puzzles. Riddles promote problem solving, an essential area of mathematical learning, and show the roles of interrogative sentences, question-asking words, and phrases.
- **WOW 17: Doug's Graph: Children Conducting Surveys and Polls** explores the mathematical concepts of prediction and probability using child-designed polls and surveys. Kids learn about formulating questions, collecting data, displaying results, and reporting findings by using a specially designed bar graph included in the text. Since kids are asking questions about topics that interest them, surveys and polls maintain their curiosity and involvement. Mathematical and written language conventions are crucial: words formulate the question, numbers record the findings, and sentences present the results. "Extensions: The Question & Answer Writing Game" introduces a way to explore synonyms.
- **WOW 18: Garfield Meets Fibonacci: Math Comics by and for Kids** combines mathematical learning with stories written in comic formats. In Math Comics, kids act as writers, illustrators, and mathematicians as they construct a story (real or make-believe), present it as a comic (using one, two, three, four, or more frames), and include a mathematical problem or concept (the key issue or dilemma on which the story is based). Math Comics focus attention on how to craft stories through the use of characters, setting, storyline, and problem/resolution—all in the space of a few frames. And since a comic story is usually conveyed through talk among the characters, Math Comics familiarize children with how writers use dialogue. "Extensions: The Mathematics of Comics" explores fractions, geometry, and scale.

Mathematics

Math Riddles

Math Riddles	TEACH	These Conventions *Unconventionally*
Creating Puzzles with Numbers, Symbols, and Words • Interrogative Sentences and Question-Asking Words • Question Marks • Phrases Are Parts of Sentences		Genre: Riddles Interrogative sentences Question marks Question-asking words: Who, what, when, where, why, and how Phrases
Math Riddles • "When Is the End the Same as the Beginning?" • "When Is the Last Also the First?" • "When Is Any Number the Same As 1?" Fractions • "When Is One Number the Same as Another Number?" • "When Do 1 and 1 Make 1?"		Cycles in nature, science, people's lives, and history Adding to and counting by Palindromes in words, sentences, and numbers Writing numerals as words Addition Sentence formation Division Writing numerals as words Compound words Alphabetical order Using the dictionary Reading and word analysis skills

Kids love riddles! Attracted to and intrigued by amusing wordplays, kids read them, make them up, and tell them to whoever will listen. Humor arises from the way a riddle juxtaposes something unexpected or extraordinary alongside something routine and commonplace to make unusual and funny meanings.

- *A perplexing question:* "What kind of fish do miners catch?"
- *A surprising answer:* "A goldfish."

Whoever heard of a fish that is made of gold? Who would ever think that mining and fishing had something in common? Writers and readers of riddles, that's who.

Creating Puzzles with Numbers, Symbols, and Words

Math riddles pair mathematical concepts, facts, and operations with the humor and surprise of word puzzles, challenging children to think mathematically while using language creatively. As kids explore answers for riddles, they combine imaginative thinking with numbers, symbols, and words to promote problem-solving. For some children, math concepts are more easily understood when introduced through riddles. By solving riddles, children advance their understanding of mathematics and writing as languages of thinking and communicating.

At first glance, the math riddles we pose in this WOW may not appear to be mathematical. Their problems generate more than one solution or answer. Some use no numbers at all. In creating these puzzles, we have purposefully pushed beyond computation and arithmetic to highlight patterns, measurement, and metaphor.

Consider this puzzle: What writing conventions do math riddles teach unconventionally?

Interrogative Sentences and Question-Asking Words

Most riddles start with an *interrogative sentence* (a sentence that asks a question) stating a puzzle for readers to solve. Interrogative sentences begin with *question-asking words*: "who," "what," "when," "where," "why," and sometimes "how." Placing one of these words first in the sentence signals that a question, not a statement, will follow. Each of our math riddles starts with a question-asking sentence.

Question Marks

A *question mark* (?) ends an interrogative sentence to show that the issue is unresolved till an answer is provided. Without a question, there can be no riddle. If the answer is already known or is given away by the opening statement, then the suspense is lost. "Don't tell!" is a frequent response when kids pose math riddles.

Phrases Are Parts of Sentences

Phrases, a group of words without a subject or a predicate, make perfect sense within the riddle genre. For example, the phrase "from a great distance" clearly answers the following riddle:

- *Question:* "How do you talk to a dinosaur?"
- *Answer:* "From a great distance."

While not a sentence, a phrase is often the best conveyor of a quick response, a punch line, or a funny retort to a riddle. The sentence "I would talk to a dinosaur from a great distance" lacks the punch and verve of the shorter phrase. In riddles, sentences and phrases do different but equally necessary jobs. An interrogative states the question and either a sentence or a phrase—whichever better suits the punch line's delivery—conveys the answer. Riddles demonstrate the usefulness of phrases in written communications.

In a sentence, phrases add clarity and detail: "After trailing by five runs in the ninth inning, the Red Sox won the game." The prepositional phrase after trailing by five runs in the ninth inning informs the reader that the team's victory featured, by baseball standards, an impressive come-from-behind rally. Kids are taught that writing a sentence is always better than using a phrase, but since speaking in phrases is so common, recognizing the importance of phrases can help children compose sentences. Rather than revising the child's use of a phrase to make it something it is not (a grammatical sentence), adults can explore what it does (provide clarity and detail that make the writer's intended meaning clear).

Math Riddles

Riddle: "When Is the End the Same as the Beginning?"

"When Is the End the Same as the Beginning?" reveals cycles in nature that unobtrusively influence our lives, cycles of growth and development common to living creatures and plants, and human-made cycles of history and social change. Each of these cycles are parts of the elementary school science and social studies curriculum. Science solutions to the puzzle include night and day, sunrise and sunset, high and low tides, seasonal change, phases of the moon, days of the week, weeks of the year, life cycles, and migrations of animals and insects. Social studies solutions include the rise and fall of governments, shifts in societies' norms, and political movements.

- When the end of spring is the beginning of summer.
- When the end of 2000 is the beginning of 2001 (New Year's Day).
- When the last day of June becomes the first day of July.
- When autumn's fallen sunflower becomes spring's sprouting seed.
- When rain stops and the sun shines.
- When horse-drawn vehicles became old-fashioned and automobiles became common.
- When the end of apartheid in South Africa released Nelson Mandela from prison and granted voting rights to Black citizens.

The ending and beginning riddle inspires children to think anew about everyday happenings and personal events, such as birthdays or family celebrations. Second graders devised responses to the riddle seen in Figure 5.1.

Sometimes, the ending and beginning riddle juxtaposes events that occur simultaneously, but appear unconnected.

- The end of August is the beginning of the new school year.
- The end of the school year is the beginning of summer vacation.

Two recent books are inspiring openers for the cycles that make up ending and beginning riddles. *To Every Thing There Is a Season*, by Leo and Diane Dillon, illustrates verses from Ecclesiastes using artistic styles from Egypt, Japan, Mexico, Thailand, China, Russia, the Middle East, and other cultural traditions from around the world. *This Next New Year* by Janet S. Wong tells about a young boy's preparations for the Chinese Lunar New Year with help from his German, French, and Hopi friends.

- "The end of having baby teeth and the beginning of having big teeth."
- "The end of a chapter and beginning of new chapter."
- "The end of being a teenager and the beginning of being a grownup."
- "When there is daylight here and nighttime somewhere else in the world."
- "The end of the school week and the beginning of the weekend."
- "When it is summer here in Massachusetts and winter in South America."
- [When returning to school after vacation, one boy said that] "I ended my week in Massachusetts after beginning it in New Mexico."
- "When the end of your 7th year is the beginning of your 8th year."

Figure 5.1 *"When is the end the same as the beginning?" riddle answers by second graders.*

Adding to and Counting by Tables Offer Math Answers

"When is the end the same as the beginning?" is a novel introduction to addition tables that always return to where they began. Addends for 9 end with 0 + 9 and begin with 9 + 0. Addends for 10 end with 0 + 10 and begin with 10 + 0. The addition tables below show this idea in full cycle (Figure 5.2).

The demonstration of counting by nines is equally surprising: $9 \times 10 = 90$ is the reverse of $1 \times 9 = 09$ and the pattern continues with 81 being the inverse of 18, 72 reversing the digits 27, and so on. The ending numerals are the beginning numerals in inverse order.

Riddle: "When Is the Last Also the First?"

Wow! Mom! Dad! Sis! Anna! Otto! Bob sees 77, 101, 1001, 10,001, 100,001, 121, 555, and 2332. To answer this riddle, read the words and numbers in the sentence above right to left or last to first. What you see are *palindromes*. These wordplays fascinate second and third graders who, used to reading everything left to right, do not expect to find the same word, phrase, or number reading from the opposite direction (Figure 5.3).

Other surprising palindromes answers to "When is the last also the first?" include: "racecar," "radar," "level," "noon," "solos." Jon Agee has compiled and illustrated three collections of palindromes: *Go Hang a Salami! I'm a Lasagna Hog! and Other Palindromes; So Many Dynamos and Other Palindromes; Sit on a Potato Pan, Otis: More Palindromes.* The palindrome phrases and sentences in these books fascinate kids. It is hard to believe so many of them can be made with words! Marvin Terban and Guilio Maestro combine palindromes with riddles in the book *Too Hot to Hoot.*

Adding to 9	Adding to 10	Adding to 11	Counting by 9
9 + 0	10 + 0	11 + 0	$1 \times 9 = 09$
8 + 1	9 + 1	10 + 1	$2 \times 9 = 18$
7 + 2	8 + 2	9 + 2	$3 \times 9 = 27$
6 + 3	7 + 3	8 + 3	$4 \times 9 = 36$
5 + 4	6 + 4	7 + 4	$5 \times 9 = 45$
4 + 5	5 + 5	6 + 5	$6 \times 9 = 54$
3 + 6	4 + 6	5 + 6	$7 \times 9 = 63$
2 + 7	3 + 7	4 + 7	$8 \times 9 = 72$
1 + 8	2 + 8	3 + 8	$9 \times 9 = 81$
0 + 9	1 + 9	2 + 9	$10 \times 9 = 90$
	0 + 10	1 + 10	
		0 + 11	

Figure 5.2   *Adding to and counting by tables.*

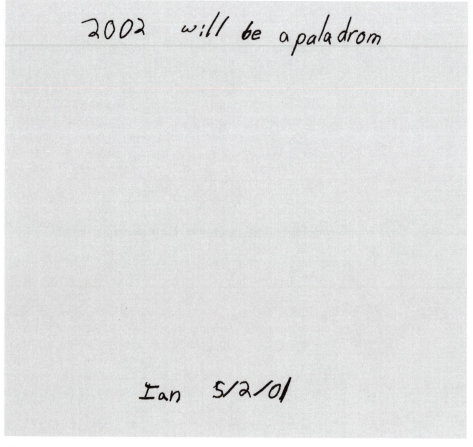

Figure 5.3   *Ian's palindrome.*

Counting by 11s, 101s, 1001s, 10,001s generate palindrome answers. Throughout the year, students can record palindrome numbers and their charts inform the study of place value. Here are some of the palindromes from a second-grade chart:

- 111, 121, 131 . . . counting by 10 starting at 111
- 101, 202, 303 . . . counting by 101
- 111, 222, 333, 444 . . . counting by 111
- 5555, 6666, 7777 . . . counting by 1111

Riddle: "When Is Any Number the Same As 1?"

Fractions, division, and the whole being equal to the sum of the parts all describe ways of thinking about breaking something into smaller pieces. In Marc Harshman's book, *Only One*, a tour of a country fair shows how many things grouped together become one of something completely different as in "100 patches but only 1 quilt." The "Same as 1" riddle reveals different part-to-whole combinations by equating the number one (1) with a group, as in the example by Izzy shown in Figure 5.4.

Figure 5.4 *Izzy's riddle answers.*

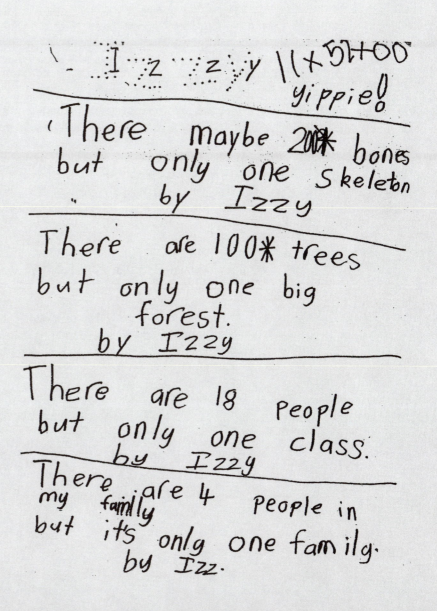

Math Riddle Sentences

Writing equations and descriptions is a different way to solve the "Same as" riddle. Most objects have more than one part and can be described in a math riddle sentence. *Twelve Ways to Get to Eleven* by Eve Merriam illustrates how parts of objects or scenes combine to equal 11.

"Same as" riddles allow kids to transform common everyday events into "same as" riddle sentences:

- 2 eyes, 2 ears, 2 eyebrows, 1 nose, and 1 mouth make 1 face.
- 13 stripes and 50 stars make the American flag.

Children's answers to the "same as" riddle describe things we ordinarily do not think of in terms of their parts:

- *Question:* When is 4 + 2 + 1 + 2 + 1 = 1?
- *Answer:* When 4 legs and 2 ears and 1 nose and 2 eyes and 1 tail make 1 cat (or one dog, one horse, one cow, one goat).
- *Question:* When is 4 + 1 + 1 = 1?
- *Answer:* When 4 legs and 1 back and 1 seat make 1 chair.

Many real-world illustrations appear daily in our lives that we do not recognize as solutions to the "any number is the same as one" riddle. In *More than One* by Miriam Schlein and illustrated by Donald Crews, everyday examples abound. The text includes number words and numerals, demonstrating that riddles can be written in words. Here is an example of how kids might formulate an all-word version:

- *Question:* When is four plus two plus one plus two plus one the same as one?
- *Answer:* When four legs and two ears and one nose and two eyes and one tail make one cat [or one dog, one horse, one cow, one goat].

Adults can point out that numerals let writers present lengthy information in an abbreviated style. For example, the spelled-out numbers one, thirty-eight, or four hundred fifty-five take up considerably more space than 1, 38, or 455. For this reason, numbers over ten are usually not spelled out in writing except when they begin sentences.

Riddle: "When Is One Number the Same as Another Number?"

It is easy to feature numbers other than one as the basis for comparison in the riddle, "When is one number the same as another number?" When two different numbers mean the same thing coincidentally, juxtaposing them creates an unexpected partnership for measurement:

- *Question:* When is 9 the same as 5?
- *Answer:* When the 9th day of school is 5 percent of the school year completed (based on 180 days of school).
- *Question:* When is 22 the same as 1?
- *Answer:* When the 22nd day of September is the same as the first day of fall.
- *Question:* When is 1/2 the same as 30?
- *Answer:* When 30 minutes is half an hour.

Many occasions during a school day and year lend themselves to these comparisons. Since every 9 days of school equals 5 percent of the school year, 18 days is the same as 10 percent and 180 days equals 100 percent! Each seasonal change occurs on a date that creates a riddle: *Question:* "When is 1 the same as 21?" *Answer:* When the first day of winter is the 21st of December.

Riddle: "When Do 1 and 1 Make 1?"

"When do 1 and 1 make 1?" initially appears to have one solution—"When 1/2 and 1/2 make 1 whole." But equivalent fractions will infinitely lengthen the list of numerical answers:

- 2/4 + 2/4
- 3/6 + 3/6
- 4/8 + 4/8
- 5/10 + 5/10
- 50/100 + 50/100

There are hundreds of pairs that make one (1) and answer the riddle, as displayed in the third graders' responses shown in Figure 5.5.

There is yet another solution to this riddle. The following poem offers a hint about what it is:

For the final answer, you may need a clue—
Look—some words, when cut apart, make two,
And when paired back together become one anew:
Inside, outside, upside, uptown, downtown, downsize,
inward, outward, outboard, outlaw, lockjaw, hacksaw,
headache, namesake, forsake, beefsteak, but not cool lake.
Now if you have solved it, you can make a list
Of all the words that you know I have missed!

Compound words pair one word ("shoe") with a second word ("string") to create a third word ("shoestring"). By forming one word from two, writers generate more concise and precise language. "Shoestring" is clear and economical compared with "the string that keeps my shoe on my foot." Other examples demonstrating "When 1 and 1 is the same as 1" include:

- *Breakfast* breaks the fast created by a night's sleep.
- *Motorcycle* refers to a cycle propelled by a motor.
- *Cupboard* is a board for storing cups (and bowls and plates and china).

- 1 husband and 1 wife make 1 couple.
- 1 shirt and 1 pair of pants make 1 outfit.
- 1 pair of snow pants and 1 coat make 1 winter outfit.
- 1 Al Gore and 1 George Bush make 1 argument.

Figure 5.5 *"When Do 1 and 1 Make 1?" riddle answers by third graders.*

- *Spaceship* describes a vessel navigating space, a derivation of a ship that sails the oceans.

The origins of many compound words can be found in the multicultural history of our country. Immigrants coming to a new land encountered situations and objects for which they had no common names. People speaking English, African, Spanish, French, German, or Native American languages found it difficult to communicate with one another. To achieve "directness and instant comprehensibility," notes language historian Bill Bryson (20), early Americans put two older words together to form a new one in English; for example, "eggplant, canvasback, copperhead, rattlesnake, bluegrass, backtrack, bobcat, catfish, bluejay, and bullfrog." Over the years, people continued adding compound terms to the language: "railroad," "baseball," "software," "broadband."

Reading and Word Analysis

Compound word riddles develop reading and word analysis skills of young writers.

- Compound words let beginning readers practice recognizing little words inside bigger words: *Basketball* has *ask*, *all*, *ball*, and *basket* inside it.
- Kids can reverse existing compound words to see if the word makes sense when read in the opposite direction: baseball or ballbase; videogame or gamevideo, outside or sideout. Reversing the words occasions much laughing as well as reading practice.
- An illustration of a word in action reinforces its meaning and its spelling as in Gabrielle's drawing of "sundown" (Figure 5.6).

Compound words initiate a most interesting language investigation question: "When is the meaning of the new word obvious from the meanings of the two words paired to create it?"

- *Race* and *car* (*racecar*) suggest an automobile fast enough to be in a race; *back* and *pack* (*backpack*) indicates a cloth container to pack things in worn across the shoulders and back.

However . . .

- *Skyscraper* conveys an image of a building so tall that from the ground level it seems to scrape against the sky, but neither *sky* nor *scraper* alone suggests their pairing would produce this image. *Fort* and *night* (*fortnight*) give no clues that together they mean a fourteen-day time period, nor do *crow* and *bar* (*crowbar*) suggest a tool that is used in construction.

Compound words are small treasures of discovery—like crystals in rock—awaiting separation and examination of their parts to determine how the meaning of the whole may or may not come from the meaning of the halves. In *Once There Was a Bull-Frog* by Rick Walton, compound words propel the search of a bullfrog who is looking for his hop in a doghouse, on a toadstool, and by chasing a horsefly. This engaging look at combinations provokes conversation about how and why words have become attached and opens the idea that kids might construct new compound words.

Kids enjoy making-up their own compound words to illustrate, define, and read aloud to classmates. These are some of the first compound words invented and defined by second graders.

Toadberries: A toad made out of berries.

Strawfish: Fish made out of straw.

Bullhog: A pig face with half bull body/half pig body.

Figure 5.6
Gabrielle's illustration of "sundown."

Cowcat: A cat that eats grass and catfood and can trample the life out of you.

Toadfly: Eats only grass and has bumps on its wings.

Compiling their words into a dictionary of new compound words practices two language skills: writing definitions of words and alphabetizing them. Definition writing requires a decision about whether or not the compound word will reflect the meaning of either, neither, or both of the words. Alphabetizing requires looking past the first letter(s) which is challenging if all words begin alike, as they do in the following list of new words about snow.

Snowcar: A car with snow on it every season but summer.

Snowchalk: Chalk that was made out of snow so it's hard to find it in the snow and you can write with it in the snow. If you draw with it, it comes alive.

Snowclipboard: A clipboard covered with snow; the part where the paper should go is wide open and shuts fast when it is mad.

Snowgun: A gun that shoots snow; when the snow hits you, you are turned into snow.

Snowlunch: A lunch you have when there is snow on the ground; it tastes like snow and it is cold.

Snowmarker: It draws on snow.

Snowpuppy: A puppy that eats and lives in the snow. He likes the snow and his name is Fuzzy because he is so fuzzy.

Snowschool: Where people who are made out of snow go to school.

Snowtube: Like a sled, but round and goes fast in the snow and it talks language.

New words can be made from any familiar words: "shoechair," "shoetree," "shoecar," "shoephone," and "shoebed." A "shoetree" is a place to store footwear, a "shoephone" was a funny gadget on "Get Smart," an old television show still seen on *Nick at Night*, and the other words might or might not be sensible terms, depending on the writer or the context.

YOUNG WRITERS' BOOKSHELF FOR MATH RIDDLES

Riddles and Puzzles

Sheepish Riddles. Katy Hall and Lisa Eisenberg. Pictures by R. W. Alley. Dial Books for Young Readers, 1996. The same authors have written numerous other riddle books, including *Batty Riddles*, *Snakey Riddles*, *Grizzly Riddles*, *Bunny Riddles*, and *Buggy Riddles*.

Calculator Riddles. David A. Alder. Illustrated by Cynthia Fisher. Holiday House, 1995. Dozens of math equations and riddle questions are answered using a calculator. First, read the numbers on the calculator to solve the equation, then flip it upside down and read the numbers as words to find an answer to each riddle.

City by Numbers. Stephen T. Johnson. Viking, 1998. Join the visual riddle hunt to find the numbers one through twenty-one hidden in different cityscapes.

The Grapes of Math: Mind-Stretching Math Riddles. Greg Tang. Illustrated by Harry Briggs. Scholastic Press, 2001. Visually eye-catching, this book's combination of bright mathematical illustrations and rhyming riddles challenges readers to discover problem-solving strategies that stretch beyond the obvious. See also *Math for All Seasons* (2002).

One Riddle, One Answer. Lauren Thompson. Illustrated by Linda S. Wingerter. Scholastic Press, 2001. An ancient tale of finding a husband suitable for a Persian princess rests on the power to solve a mathematical riddle with only one answer.

Riddle: "When Is the End the Same as the Beginning?"

This Next New Year. Janet S. Wong. Pictures by Yanksook Choi. Francis Foster Books, 2000. (Cited in the text.)

To Every Thing There Is a Season: Verses from Ecclesiastes. Leo and Diane Dillon. Blue Sky Press, 1998. (Cited in the text.)

Twelve Ways to Get to Eleven. Eve Merriam. Illustrated by Bernie Karlin. Simon & Schuster Books for Young Readers, 1993. (Cited in the text.)

Riddle: "When Is the Last also the First?" (Palindromes)

Go Hang a Salami! I'm a Lasagna Hog! and other Palindromes. Jon Agee. Farrar, Straus & Giroux, 1991. See also *Sit on a Potato Pan, Otis: More Palindromes* (1999). (Cited in the text.)

Too Hot to Hoot. Marvin Terban. Illustrated by Guilio Maestro. Houghton Mifflin, 1985. (Cited in the text.)

Riddle: "When Is Any Number the Same as 1?"

The Doorbell Rang. Pat Hutchins. Greenwillow Books, 1986. With each chime of the doorbell and the arrival of a new guest, the children redivide the cookies that grandma has made for them.

Only One. Marc Harshman. Illustrated by Barbara Garrison. Cobblehill Books, 1991. (Cited in the text.)

More Than One. Miriam Schlein. Illustrated by Donald Crews. Greenwillow Books, 1996. (Cited in the text.)

Tops & Bottoms. Janet Stevens. Harcourt, Brace, 1995. When asked if he wants the top of a plant or the bottom, a rabbit outsmarts a bear by choosing crops that grow below the ground one year and above the ground the next.

Riddle: "When Do 1 and 1 Make 1?"

Once There Was a Bull-Frog. Rick Walton. Illustrated by Greg Hally. Gibbs Smith Publisher, 1995. (Cited in the text.)

Doug's Graph: Children Conducting Surveys and Polls

Doug's Graph	TEACH	These Conventions *Unconventionally*
The Whole Poll		Genre: Surveys and polls Asking questions
Formulating Questions		Parts of an interrogative sentence • Capital letter • Question mark • Question-asking word order
Collecting Data and Displaying Results		Bar graphs Equations Percentages
Reporting the Findings		Writing information in words and numbers Making predictions Data analysis
Extensions: The Question and Answer Writing Game		Synonyms

THE SURVEY RESULTS ARE IN:

- Nine out of ten like ice cream.
- One hundred percent enjoy computer games.
- Six in ten prefer pizza to french fries.
- Forty percent say blue is a favorite color.

These statistics are not from a national survey of children's likes and dislikes but from a poll of ten classmates conducted by first and second graders. These young pollsters obtained their findings using a multifaceted survey, graphing, and writing tool we call "Doug's Graph," named for its original designer, educator Doug Roupp. While the number of respondents in the student poll is small (ten), the WOW potential of surveys and polls is huge when the mathematical operations of graphing, percentages, and predictions pair with the writing conventions of question-asking, interrogative sentence crafting, and report publishing.

One Whole Poll

Doug designed his graph so kids could carry a clipboard, ask a question, take a poll, and display the results. We added math equations and analytical description. Doug's Graph equally features and teaches math concepts and writing conventions. Using language to convey information opens and powers every part of the process:

- Creating a survey question and taking the poll.
- Tallying responses and displaying them on a bar graph.
- Summarizing the findings in a short report or paragraph that communicates quantitative information in written language.
- Using math concepts of measurement, graphing, and percentages.
- Playing the role of adult professionals—pollster, opinion surveyor, market researcher, graphic designer, and social scientist.

The graph asks children to complete a series of sequential steps until the poll is completed. Along the way, a child's thoughtfulness and focus combine with interest and purpose to produce intense effort. Because different kinds of questions can be posed, the graph's teaching potential comes from repeatedly taking polls and publishing the results.

To show how the graph works, the letters (**A**) through (**H**) label and explain each feature (Figure 5.7). The first four (A, B, C, D) are standard survey tools; the last four (E, F, G, H) are different data-presenting options to explore with kids.

- (**A**) The space where an "either/or" (forced-choice) survey question is written using an interrogative sentence beginning with a capital letter and ending with a question mark.
- (**B**) Spaces for identifying two possible responses to the question.

    (Yes/No) "Do you like to play in the snow?"

    (Pizza/Spaghetti) "What is your favorite lunch, pizza or spaghetti?"

    (Ice cream/Jello) "Would you rather eat ice cream or jello?"

    (In/Out) "Would you rather go out or stay in for recess?"

- (**C**) Spaces where ten people record their names and their responses to the survey. Ten (10) is an ideal number for completing a survey quickly, for comparing the results in percentages, and for recognizing ten as the basis of our numeration system.
- (**D**) Three columns for creating a bar graph to display the survey results. The left-hand column is for children to number upward from 1 to 10. The middle and right-hand columns are filled in according to the number of responses for each choice.
- (**E**) An eleventh line under the list of names for an equation (or whole number sentence) reporting the poll results: "One whole poll means 10 is the same as 7 plus 3."
- (**F**) An eleventh line at the top of the bar graph for a fractional equation based on the poll results: $7/10 + 3/10 = 10/10$.
- (**G**) A space for reporting the poll results in percentages: 70%/30%
- (**H**) The reverse side of the page is a space for children to explain the survey results using words and numbers that analyze and summarize the data.

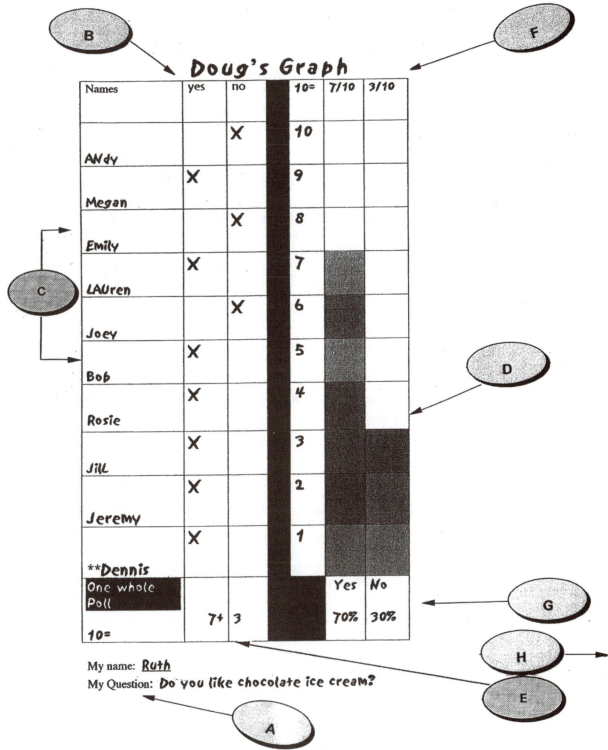

Doug's Graph

Names	yes	no	10=	7/10	3/10
Andy		X	10		
Megan	X		9		
Emily		X	8		
Lauren	X		7		
Joey		X	6		
Bob	X		5		
Rosie	X		4		
Jill	X		3		
Jeremy	X		2		
**Dennis	X		1		
One whole Poll				Yes	No
10=	7+	3		70%	30%

My name: <u>Ruth</u>

My Question: Do you like chocolate ice cream?

Figure 5.7 *Doug's Graph.*

Doug's graph appears to be a simple, easy to use tool and therein lies its power. It can flexibly accommodate the simplest objectives for younger students (by taking away E, F, G, and H) or adding the dimensions of reporting fractions and percents for older students (by including E, F, G, and H).

Formulating Questions

Surveys and Polls let children practice formulating questions and writing them using the conventions of an interrogative sentence. An interrogative sentence asks a question. With kids, we call these word formulations question-asking sentences.

Kids continuously ask oral questions, correctly ordering the syntax of the words and using the vocal intonation that signals a forthcoming query. Throughout the school day adults hear many variations of the following: "Can we stay in?" "Can we go out?" "Is the computer on?" "Where's Brianna?" "Do we have gym or art today?" Speakers and listeners have no doubt a question is being asked.

Writing grammatically correct questions is a skill acquired through practice. Because children ask more questions than they write, when they do write questions, they often do not use all the conventions of an interrogative sentence: a capital letter at the beginning, a question mark at the end, and a question-asking subject/verb word structure. Doug's Graph focuses attention on each of these features of written language sentences.

- *Capital letter*. Every interrogative sentence starts with a capital letter, announcing to a reader that a new thought is being expressed.
- *Question mark*. A question mark is a beacon of the writer's intent in an interrogative/question-asking sentence. It signals that this is an inquiry, not a comment, cueing the reader to use the vocal intonation of a question, as one would do in oral speech.
- *Question-asking word order*. Orally, "You see the sailboat" might be a declarative or an interrogative sentence, depending on the speaker's vocal intonation. In written language, the arrangement of the words makes clear the intent of the sentence: "Do you see the sailboat?" puts words in a question-asking order. Doug's Graph requires young writers to use question-asking structures to elicit responses from listeners and readers.

Three subtler but equally important characteristics of interrogative, question-asking sentences emerge as kids design their own polls and surveys:

- Doug's Graph poses questions in an "either/or" structure that offers two possible responses. Questions beginning "Can you," "Are you," or "Do you" are the easiest to answer with "Yes/No" or "Either/Or" choices.
- Doug's Graph can expand to increase the number of responses by adding a third column next to sections (B) and (D). Choices can include "Yes/No/Maybe" (Do you like ice cream for dessert?) or "Either/Or" (Which is your favorite? Pizza, Pancakes, Macaroni).
- Slight variations of words make big differences in results when gathering information about people's opinions or attitudes. "Do you like movies?" tells who enjoys movies and who does not but "Do you prefer movies or books?" indicates who prefers one medium over the other. As kids realize that different inquiries produce different results, they see the ways words work while

discovering other questions they can ask to expand the information they are collecting.

Collating Data and Displaying Results

After formulating a question and interviewing ten people, kids collate their data and relay their mathematical findings on a bar graph by:

- Numbering the left column, 1 to 10, from bottom to top.
- Recording the two choices in the bottom spaces of the two right columns.
- Coloring and decorating the columns above each choice to display the results. (Neon pens, combinations of colors, drawing interesting patterns or pictures in the squares, attract attention to what would otherwise be a plain two-color, two-column bar graph.)

A five and five split in the survey results makes the two bars the same height, but findings of 6/4, 7/3, 8 /2, 9/1, or 10/0 move the heights of the two columns farther apart from each other. Math equations derived from the poll results are displayed on the bar graph.

- Ten responses constitute 100 percent of the poll—8 affirmatives is 80 percent "yes," 2 negatives is 20 percent "no."
- Two children may combine their two ten-response graphs to acquire twenty responses to the same question. They calculate percentages counting by fives. Each answer is 5 percent of the whole—sixteen affirmative is 80 percent "yes," four negatives is 20 percent "no."
- Ten kids or ten pairs of kids collect ten responses to the same question and then calculate their one hundred responses. Each answer is 1 percent of the whole—80 affirmative is 80 percent "yes," 20 negatives is 20 percent "no."
- A collective graph done by a team of pollsters offers another way to collect and calculate percentages. If four kids ask the same question of five respondents, they have twenty responses together. Each youngster has acquired 1/4 or 25 percent of the whole poll.

A bar graph is only one way to publish survey results. To introduce kids to other types of graphs, adults can consult "*USA Today* Snapshots," informational graphs found daily in each section of that newspaper. Another resource is the book *Tiger Math: Learning to Graph from a Baby Tiger* by Ann Whitehead Nagda and Cindy Bickel, which uses full-color photographs, descriptive text and four kinds of graphs—picture, circle, bar, and line—to chronicle the story of how a Siberian tiger cub named T. J. grew to be a five-hundred-pound adult.

Once kids begin to think in terms of fractions and percentages of a whole, they also try out different ways to present information visually (Figure 5.8). Bruna designed her own bar graph to record the results of an experiment involving kids racing racquetballs down a playground slide. Christine used a graph to record the results of a poll about who would like to live on a farm.

Graphing programs for computers easily convert data into many different data formats. "The Graph Club," an easy-to-use CD from Tom Snyder Productions, features picture, bar, line, and circle graphs as well as data interpretation activities. An interactive, online "Create a Graph" program (and many other math activities) is available free of charge from the National Center for Education Statistics at http://nces.ed.gov/nceskids.

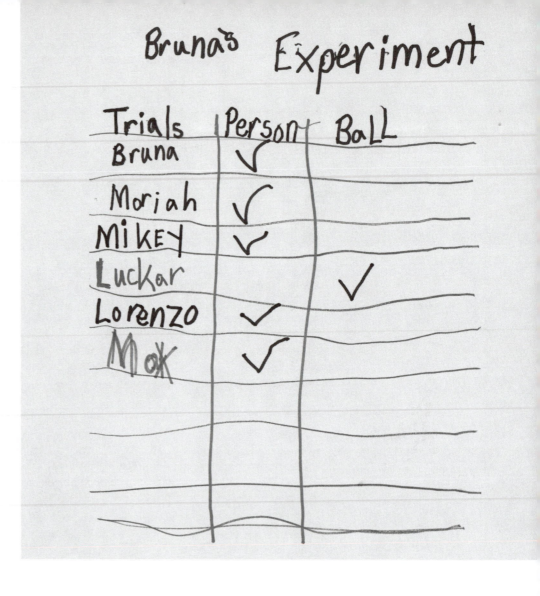

Figure 5.8

Bruna's and Christine's graphs.

Trials	Person	Ball
Bruna	✓	
Moriah	✓	
Mikey	✓	
Luckar		✓
Lorenzo	✓	
Max	✓	

Reporting the Findings

Reporting survey results presents an authentic reason for children to explore the different ways a writer connects with an audience. Television, the Internet, and global communications mean that the twenty-first century is becoming the information presentation age, an era where not only what one has to say, but how one says it, matters greatly. Writers and mathematicians need effective strategies for communicating information easily and clearly.

Doug's Graph displays various ways to communicate information collected in the survey—visually on a bar graph, numerically in equations, or descriptively through written language. The information may appear in writing as a short nonfiction report, a paragraph, or a sentence.

To see how survey writers might use sentences to communicate with readers, consider the child's survey question, "Who likes ice cream?" The young pollster has the option of reporting data in numerals and words—"80 percent like ice cream"—or solely in words to see how numbers are spelled in written language—"Eight out of ten like ice cream." Of course, she could write both! Consider the humorous results if everyone surveyed likes ice cream. The results will show "No nos." This is a funny pun on "No nose" and the younger kids like to comment to others, "I have no nos!"

A report on survey findings can be expanded into a more detailed piece of writing. A prediction about possible findings could be written in advance of the survey, and then a

Would you like to live on a farm?

BAR GRAPH

young writer could discuss whether the survey results confirmed or disputed the initial hypothesis or prediction, and why. Kids can engage in analytical thinking about what caused the survey results: Who were surveyed? What kinds of questions were asked? and What might happen with a different example?

Reporting on the ice cream survey, the child might write, "I predicted that at least 50% would say yes. 100% answering yes really surprised me. I think if I asked only adults, instead of kids, they would not all say yes. Then I would have some nos on the graph."

EXTENSIONS

The Question and Answer Writing Game

This amusing game for answering questions requires two things: questions that can be answered by "Yes" or "No" and synonyms for "Yes" or "No." Small groups of kids are ideal for the game. One group writes questions on sticky notes and attaches them to the sides of a tetrahedron folded from oaktag. The second group writes "Yes" and "No" synonyms on sticky notes and attaches them to another tetrahedron folded from oaktag.

To begin, the question team rolls its tetrahedron. The question appearing on top is read aloud. Then the answer team rolls their tetrahedron, and whatever is on top is read aloud. While synonyms do not change the overall meaning of "yes" and "no," they produce surprising retorts—some funny, some nonsensical, some ordinary.

Synonym Phrases for "Yes" and "No"

YES (or affirmative responses)	NO (or negative responses)
decidedly so	not likely
of course	not in your dreams
it is for sure	don't hold your breath
it will be in your future	in no way
do not doubt it	not soon
consider it done	do not believe it

With many possible responses, the probability of one response appearing more often than others adds to the suspense and novelty of the game. What is the probability of "decidedly so" appearing once in the game? What is the probability that one question will come up five times in a game? Ten rolls of each tetrahedron constitutes a game, making easier calculations of fractions and percentages.

Charts listing questions and synonym phrases can be kept with tally marks for the phrases that appear most often as the game is played. Since new questions can be posed and new synonyms can be devised, the likelihood that this game will get stale is small.

As new synonyms are created, the meaning of "yes" and "no" can be broadened to include other kinds of affirmative and negative phrases. There is no end to the creative variations that are possible:

Question: "Will school be cancelled tomorrow?"
Answer: "Rain is in the forecast" or "Only if the Red Sox win."

YOUNG WRITERS' BOOKSHELF FOR DOUG'S GRAPH

Anno's Counting Book. Mitsumasa Anno. HarperTrophy, 1986. Wide-angle watercolor illustrations show a country town scene, changing as winter becomes spring and summer becomes fall while a graph alongside the page keeps track of ascending numbers of people and objects, from zero to twelve.

Does a Kangaroo Have a Mother, Too? Eric Carle. HarperCollins, 2000. The names of animal babies and adults (kangaroos, penguins, sheep, dolphins, and more) are introduced by a question-asking sentence that ends with a question mark.

Hottest, Coldest, Highest, Deepest. Steve Jenkins. Houghton Mifflin, 1998. Pictorial representations of scale showing some of the earth's most dramatic and imposing physical features that are also described in one succinct paragraph.

Counting on Frank. Rod Clement. Gareth Stevens, 1991. Mathematical facts and calculations enliven this story about a boy and his dog.

Big Numbers: And Pictures That Show Just How Big They Are! Edward Packard. Illustrated by Sal Murdocca. Millbrook Press, 2000. An ever-expanding pile of peas introduces children to numbers of all sizes, stretching their mathematical knowledge exponentially.

Tiger Math: Learning to Graph from a Baby Tiger. Ann Whitehead Nagda and Cindy Bickel. Henry Holt, 2000. (Cited in the text.)

Garfield Meets Fibonacci:
Math Comics by and for Kids

Math Comics	TEACH	These Conventions *Unconventionally*
Telling Mathematical Stories		Genres: Comics Writing word problems Sequencing ideas Mathematical concepts • Numbers and operations • Measurement • Communication • Connections • Geometry • Representation • Problem solving Combining the ingredients of stories • Characters • Setting
Strategies for Writing Math Comics		• Plot • Problem and resolution Dialogue is talking on paper Speech bubbles and quotation marks Character development
POW!er of Comics in Teaching Conventions *Extensions: The Mathematics of Comics*		Mathematical concepts • Fractions • Geometry and spatial sense • Problem solving

Young children naturally seek the humor and joy in everyday situations. Play is their preferred mode for learning, even at the most inopportune times—at worship, during meals, in the car, or whenever sustained silence is expected. Not surprisingly, children are drawn to the unusual language, imaginative stories, and vivid pictures in comic strips, comic books, and cartoons.

Kids revel in the surprising twists and turns of comics, the slapstick adventures that unexpectedly upset conventional norms. While kids are drawn to the fun of these visual and verbal stories, often they relate most directly to the characters. They imagine themselves living out the action, performing amazing escapades as superheroes and superheroines, sports stars, or intergalactic travelers. Other times, children connect the situations in comics to problems and complexities in their own lives, reconsidering the consequences of personal decisions in light of the choices made by the characters.

Most adults, by contrast, think about comics from two opposing points of view. On one hand, they enjoy the stories. This is part of the reason why there are so many sitcoms on prime-time television; adults are amused by the predicaments facing the characters. At the same time, many adults view comics as unacceptable diversions from real learning. They regard inviting kids to write comics as a frivolous activity that holds little to no literacy or literary value. Some, intensely concerned by children's fascination with war-like, violent images and themes of power and conquest by mostly male characters, find nothing entertaining or worthwhile about comics.

Fortunately, children's book authors and illustrators are presenting more and more thought-provoking stories in comic format. In *Tommy Traveler in the World of Black History* by Tom Feelings, a young boy reads books and then journeys in his dreams to meet Phoebe Fraunces, Crispus Attucks, Frederick Douglass, Emmet Till, Aesop, and Joe Louis. *Art Fraud Detective* by Andrea Bassil and Ann Nilsen asks readers to carefully examine thirty-five famous paintings to find inconsistencies that may have been left by a gang of master forgers.

Children's affinity for learning through humor and drawing make comics an attractive engaging writing experience. Asking youngsters to author their own comics amounts to asking them to do one of their favorite things—express their creativity and imagination using words and pictures.

Telling Mathematical Stories

The following formula unites comics, mathematics, and writing to create a unique WOW.

Mathematical Thinking + Story Crafting + Drawing = *Math Comics*

Math Comics, in the space of a few frames, power learning in three ways:

- Exploring the mathematical concepts of number and operations, measurement, communication, problem solving, geometry, representation, and connections.
- Using the story writing elements of character, plot, setting, and problem/resolution as well as the writing conventions of dialogue, speech bubbles, and letter fonts.
- Recognizing geometry, fractions, and chronological order as integral features of comic story presentations.

Math appears as a central part of the comic in language, illustrations, and children's thinking through the following strategies:

- *Mathematical situations from real life can be portrayed in story form.* Consider the following story: "On the way home today, I stopped at the park and picked 8 leaves from the ground. In my neighbor's yard, I found 4 more. My mother asked me how many leaves I had and I replied 12." Mathematically speaking, 1 group of 8 and 1 group of 4 makes 1 group of 12 (8 + 4 = 12).
- *Fictional characters can resolve real-life problems.* In Figure 5.9, three second graders, Allie, Izzy, and Siobhan, constructed a fictional tale based on an actual

Frame 1 One day after school, Allie rang up Izzy and Siobhan to see if they wanted to come over.	Frame 2 At her house, Allie invited them to have some apple pie that her mother had just made. "You two have half and I'll have half," said Allie.
Frame 3 Siobhan said, "You have more pie than me and Izzy. That is not fair."	Frame 4 Then all of a sudden there was a flash of light.
Frame 5 Out of the flash of light there appeared Math Chinchilla, Math Puppy, and Math Kitten.	Frame 6 The math animals asked the girls, "Do you have a problem?"
Frame 7 The girls were so amazed that the animals appeared right out of thin air. "We do have a problem," said Allie.	Frame 8 "We can help you with your problem," said the math animals.
Frame 9 "Oh please help us," said the girls.	Frame 10 10) "We will cut the pieces of pie so that all you girls have two pieces of pie," said the math animals. (Izzy gets 2/6 or 1/3) (Siobhan gets 2/6 or 1/3) (Allie gets 2/6 or 1/3) *[drawing of a pie cut into pieces labeled Izzy, Izzy, Siobhan, Siobhan, Allie, Allie]*
Frame 11 "Thank you so much," said the girls.	Frame 12 "You're welcome," said the math animals.
Frame 13 BOFF! There was a flash of light and they were gone.	Frame 14 BOFF! There was another flash of light and they appeared.
Frame 15 We forgot to say bye so "Bye, Bye, Bye!"	Frame 16 BOFF! They were gone for the rest of the year. Bye!!!

Figure 5.9 A Math Comic by Allie, Izzy, and Siobhan.

incident that is solved by the intervention of make-believe characters. The girls composed a written text to accompany their frame-by-frame drawings of the problem and its resolution.

- *Word problems can be inserted in comic frames to practice whole number operations and computation.* Many word problems are written in language that is hard for kids to understand. Kids must choose which operation(s) will solve the problem. Note how Maddie finds the missing addend through subtraction, creating the action in "Froggy the Problem Solver" (Figure 5.10).

- *Mathematical concepts and mathematical vocabulary can be featured in comic stories.* As kids learn math language, they return to what they know to help them understand new ideas and concepts. In "The Adventures of Math Dude," a group of fourth-grade girls mix and match the new—common factors—with the known—missing addends—to set the scene for a make-believe character to solve the mystery of how 2 might connect to 5 in the equation: $2 + \times = 5$ (Figure 5.11).

"Measurement," "estimation," "probability," "statistics," "geometry," "fractions," "patterns," and "relationships" are all possible topics for math comics with vocabulary specific to each; for example,

- Measurement: "inches," "feet," "meters," "centimeters."
- Probability: "prediction" and "percentage."
- Patterns: "place value" and "division."

To inspire children's ideas, adults might write a math comic or compose a math story to enact with characters, dialogue, and a narrator (if desired). For "estimation," we perform a sketch featuring "The Great Estimator," a take-off on the circus midway performer who attempts to guess someone's weight or age. In our play, the Great Estimator encounters a boy wearing three thick winter coats, and declares that for the wager of one dollar, she can guess the boy's weight within five pounds. After the Great Estimator states her guess, the boy removes his heavy coats before stepping on a scale. With the coats off, the difference between the estimated and actual weight is much greater than five pounds foil-

Froggy is walking down the street to go to school.	He was working on a worksheet, but suddenly	His phone rang! The police said the necklace was stolen.
Froggy ran to the jewelry store.	Oh No! First there were 24 and then there are only 8 beads left. What is 24 − 8? Froggy thinks hard. How many did they steal?	24 − 8 = 16! 16 beads were stolen.

Figure 5.10   *"Froggy the Problem Solver" by Maddie.*

2:	*"I want to be friends with 5."*
5:	*"I want to be friends with 2."*
3:	*"2 does not go into 5."*
2:	*"If only Math Dude were here!"*
Math Dude:	*"I'm Math Dude."*
2:	*"I want to be friends with 5. Can you help me?"*
Math Dude:	*"Well, since your best friend is 3, take 3 and 2 and add together to get 5. Then you can all be friends."*

Figure 5.11 *"The Adventures of Math Dude."*

ing the Great Estimator's plan, much to the delight of the audience. While the skit is obviously tongue-in-cheek, the math lesson is real: Without a way to measure, any estimate is a guess.

Strategies for Writing Math Comics

Story structure is intrinsically part of math comics. Solving equations, using operations, thinking about measurement, practicing counting, or seeing math in everyday situations naturally become part of the storyline when kids make math part of their comics. This is a two-for-one payoff where the practice of story construction and the solving of math problems simultaneously support each other—as in "Froggy the Problem-Solver" with the use of "equations," "subtraction," "difference," and "algebra" or "The Adventures of Math Dude" with the use of "fractions," and "wholes." Here are strategies for promoting math comic story writing with kids.

Start with the Characters

We urge kids to start their math comics by choosing the characters: "Who are they?" "What do they look like?" "What are they doing in the story?" Readers (and writers too) care about characters for they bring humanity and sincerity to a story. Kelly, Maggie, Megan, and Kira created the following characters for their comic "The Math Times." These characters make a reader eager to discover what happens.

> *Mathimillion*, Mayor of Mathville
>
> *Division Man*, a superhero
>
> *Multiply*, Division Man's sidekick
>
> *Evil Villain I. H. M.* (the initials stand for "I Hate Math")

Once the characters are established, a storyline can emerge. And even when the story is short, the presence of interesting characters gives the comic a way to succeed for many readers.

We are going to the mall in our blue convertible.	We are looking at the lamp.	The lady at the counter says it is $50.00.
"Oh, no! We only have $40.00."	We are going on the escalator looking for friends to give us money.	We split up. "I go left." "I'll go right." "I'll go straight ahead."
Caroline meets Katie and asks for ten dollars but she can only give us two.	Jasmin says "Hi" to Mona and asks for ten dollars and she says "I only have four."	River says "Hi" to Alea and says "We need $10.00" and then she says "I only have four."
	Cool. We got $10.00 more. We can buy the lamp now.	2 + 4 + 4 = 10

Figure 5.12   *A Math Comic by Caroline, Jasmin, and River.*

Make the Problem Clear to the Reader

Every story has a key problem, an amusing predicament or a basic tension around which the plot revolves—even a one- or two-frame comic. Seeing how the characters get in and out of a complicated situation is what keeps the audience reading on to find out what happens next.

In math comics, solving the math problem also resolves the dilemma facing the characters. Here is a unique way for young story-writers to practice creating and resolving tension in story plots. In the math comic in Figure 5.12, three friends—Caroline, Jasmin, and River—try to figure out how to get enough money to buy a lamp at the store. The comic story reads left to right.

Invent Different Situations and Settings

Every story, whether a comic, picture book, or chapter book takes places in a setting, the "world" of the story in which the characters live. One way to create interesting mathematical settings is to imagine places that incorporate math concepts as parts of everyday life. Bob and a group of kids created a version of a setting called "Mathland" using math vocabulary in amusing wordplays.

"Let's Go to MathDonald's (where the Golden *Arches* are filled with *yellow numbers*).

Ten pin bowling is open *24* hours a day.

The "Harry Potter Square Library" is *square* in shape and has only books about Harry Potter.

At the dog *pound*, every pet gets weighed on a *scale*.

People in town shop at the *Seven/Eleven*, but not at the *Twenty-Four/Seven*.

POW!er of Comics in Teaching Conventions

Writing about comics for the Smithsonian's 1989 traveling exhibition on the history of American cartoon art, M. Thomas Inge urged adults to "use the power of comics" to acquaint children with humor, drama, narration, dialogue, arranging ideas in sequence, artistic styles, political satire, racial and ethnic stereotyping, language, and value systems. As kid-sized entry points to complex writing concepts, comics offer a large-angle lens through which children and adults can explore many conventions unconventionally.

Young cartoonists engage in the decision-making process at the center of good writing: "How does an author get ideas across to readers and listeners?" Comics depend on how the writer unites words and pictures. Even though the pictures convey lots of information, the words are vital to understanding the message and meaning of the story. Since so much has to happen in such a short space, words and pictures must work together as a team.

The daily newspaper's comic page offers wonderful models for kids to consider. Many adult cartoonists are gifted storytellers. They blend words and pictures so skillfully that readers can easily miss the amazing connections being made in just a few frames. Discussing what adult writers do to transmit ideas gives children valuable insights that will carry over into their own writing—both in comics and other genres. For example, kids can produce a balance of words and pictures by illustrating some of a story and including words for the rest or by writing most of the story and incorporating pictures to accompany it. The writer is in charge of the creative process, and decides which predominates—words or pictures—in a piece of writing.

Talking on Paper

Comics tell stories through dialogue. In a comic, much of the story is contained in the dialogue among characters, as in Julio's story where different animals talk to each other about a math equation (Figure 5.13). Sometimes the talk is a monologue, as when Snoopy sits on the roof of his doghouse and reflects on life.

Dialogue is another term for "talking on paper." Writers have two ways to show talk in their writing:

- *Speech bubbles*—used with a picture to identify who is saying what.
- *Quotation marks*—used when there are no pictures to distinguish between characters talking and descriptive writing.

Speech bubbles and quotation marks are usually not switched, one for the other. Talk in comics is set off in speech bubbles, but rarely in quotation marks. (One notable exception are the cartoons in *The New Yorker* magazine that always use quotation marks.) In virtually all other genres, quotation marks identify when the characters in a story are speaking or when people are being quoted as part of a newspaper story or nonfiction report.

Dialogue acts as a personality megaphone for the characters in a story. The words a character speaks communicate that individual's hopes, fears, emotions, and feelings. Illus-

Figure 5.13 *Julio's one-frame comic. Translation:*

What is 2 + 2?
Hmmm, I think it is 72.
No! It is 4!
I knew that all the time.
Me too.
So did we.

trations show what the character looks like on the outside: tall, short, wide, skinny, light or darker skin shades, male or female, and so on. Dialogue reveals what the character is thinking and feeling on the inside.

If a young writer decides to make a cat the main character in a comic, pictures of the outward appearances of size and shape and color start to define the cat distinctly. But when the cat begins to talk, its unique personality is displayed. Perhaps it is a "bully cat," acting rough and tough, or a "good friend cat," offering a helping hand to one and all. Maybe it is a "new-in-the-neighborhood" cat who is unfamiliar with the way things work around there. Different words show different personalities. The author decides who the characters are and what they will be like.

Drawing characters and adding dialogue becomes one of the exciting features of writing math comics. As comic readers, children relate to favorite characters, acting and reacting with them throughout a story. They imagine themselves present in the scene as well, struggling along with their heroes and heroines to figure out what to do and how best to do it. As comic writers, children bring that same passion to their stories. The characters kids create and the words kids have those characters speak are heartfelt and real because as writers, kids care about what happens in their stories. Featuring math as the comic's storyline creates additional dimensions of interest for young writers.

The Mathematics of Comics

Mathematics is inherent in the design and delivery of every comic strip and comic book.

Geometric Shapes

Comic layouts are framed in geometric shapes and sizes. While rectangles and squares are the predominant shape, occasionally circles and triangles appear in comic books and comic strips. The popular *Family Circus* uses circles as often as squares.

Not-often-seen shapes catch the eye of the reader who wonders why the illustrator chose to use them. Even bolder ideas appear occasionally—pictures separated by frames that are leaning slightly, or are saw-toothed instead of being straight up and down. *Zippy the Pinhead* uses this unexpected technique—titling lines between frames, edging frames as if pinking shears had cut them, or making all frames circles. *Mother Goose & Grimm* mixes different shapes; sometimes a circle overlaps an unframed rectangle—or the opposite—creating an illusion of movement from left to right. Kids can modify geometric conventions to create variety and innovation in their comics.

Scale

Words and pictures in comics introduce the concept of scale. In comics, some words are larger than others and use different fonts, providing emphasis or signaling excitement and alarm. Pictorially, objects that are farther away are smaller, illustrating the measurement concepts of more than/less than and nearer to/farther from.

Fractions

Comic strips present stories in fractions. Fraction is action in a comic strip. When a cartoonist uses only one box or frame, the reader sees a whole story in a single glance. More than one box, whatever the sizes and shapes, creates a more-than-one-scene movie so readers must slow down to read what is happening inside each frame. The story is revealed as readers connect frames, one to another, left to right or top to bottom.

Three or four frames of equal size produce a different feel of movement and time than many frames of smaller size. The smaller-sized multiple-frames format provides space for more action or for sustained motion. A frame larger than the rest shows more of the story or emphasizes one part. Kids become fascinated by these mathematical devices when they examine comics—size of frames, fractioning of the story, and the combination of both are unique features of comics and picture books.

Different-sized frames, in addition to showcasing the importance of scenes in a story, fraction a comic's parts into wholes. Single or one frame (1/1), double or two frame (2/2), triple or three frame (3/3), and quadruple or four frame (4/4) are standard divisions of comic strips. Monday's through Saturday's newspapers usually illustrate all of these fractions in a week. Sunday's comics demonstrate a bonanza of other ways to divide a whole— 8/8, 10/10, 12/12, 16/16, and more.

In developing their own comics, young writers experiment with how to fraction a story. Generally, kids do not know how many frames they need when they start writing a comic, nor the sizes of the frames. Sometimes they fit the story to an existing outline of four, five, or six rectangular frames. Sometimes they draw their own frames and continue adding frames until the story is finished. Either way is fine, for as they illustrate the story they adjust the number of comic frames accordingly, adding or subtracting as needed. If a child is dissatisfied with the result, cutting and pasting the strip onto a different background and inserting the changes revises the frames.

One way for third graders to practice fractioning the action in comics uses the wooden building blocks designed by Lucy Sprague Mitchell, co-founder and director of the Bank Street College of Education in New York City established in 1916. Her blocks are proportioned so each smaller size is half of the next larger one. Not only are these the most popular blocks for building, they are fractions of each other, perfect models of equivalent fractions for children to use in designing their comics.

With paper cut to the same proportions as the building blocks, kids can use the blocks as comic cubes. A twelve-inch-long rectangle block equals a one-frame comic; two six-inch rectangles represent a two-frame format; and four three-inch-square blocks become a four-frame comic arrangement (see below).

One frame

Two frame

Four frame

On paper cut to fit the sides of the wooden blocks, kids draw their comics. When finished, they lay out the frames or stand them up on the blocks. Using movable blocks lets them decide if they need to add more frames to make the comic easier to understand. Here is an ideal introduction to the usefulness of scale. If a block is double the size of another, it gives room for more of the story to occur in that frame than in a smaller frame.

YOUNG WRITERS' BOOKSHELF FOR MATH COMICS AND MATH STORIES

2 × 2 = Boo!: A Set of Spooky Multiplication Stories. Loreen Leedy. Holiday House, 1995. Halloween characters do multiplication activities in spooky stories. Also see *Mission: Addition* (adding, 1999), *Measuring Penny* (units of measurement from inches to dog biscuits, 1997), and *Big, Small, Short, Tall* (pairs of opposites, 1987).

Fraction Action. Loreen Leedy. Scott Foresman, 1994. Five short

stories in comic format show Miss Prime teaching her students about fractions.

Anno's Mysterious Multiplying Jar. Masaichiro and Mitsumasa Anno. Putnam, 1983. The multiplication concept of factorials is revealed in a steadily expanding story that takes place inside a magical jar.

The Shape of Things. Dayle Ann Dodds. Illustrated by Julie

Lacome. Candlewick Press, 1996. When you see a square, be sure to look again; squares, circles, rectangles, and other shapes become suddenly transformed into familiar objects, each described in a rhyme.

Too Many Kangaroo Things to Do! Stuart J. Murphy. Illustrated by Kevin O'Malley. HarperCollins, 1996. Kangaroo has no one to play with because all of his friends are secretly preparing his birthday party, the plans of which are displayed in eye-catching multiplication equations.

The King's Chessboard. David Birch. Illustrated by Devis Grebu. Penguin, 1988. The mathematical power of doubling is shown in this tale of a king who after promising to pay a man a single grain of rice—doubled every day for a month—realizes his entire supply will be depleted if he keeps his word.

Ed Emberley's Picture Pie 2: A Drawing Book and Stencil. Little, Brown, 1996. Kids see how to draw by combining parts or fractions into a whole. See also *Ed Emberley's Drawing Book of Animals* (1970) and *Ed Emberley's Halloween Drawing Book* (1980).

Tommy Traveler in the World of Black History. Tom Feelings. Black Butterfly Children's Books, 1991. (Cited in the text.)

Art Fraud Detective: Spot the Difference, Solve the Crime. Andrea Bassil and Anna Nilsen. Illustrated by Andy Parker. Larousse Kingfisher Chambers, 2001. (Cited in the text.)

CHAPTER SUMMARY

Chapter Five, "Mathematics," explores how mathematical learning supports and sustains children's writing. Both mathematics and writing are languages of communication—one using numbers and symbols, the other using letters and sounds. Mathematicians and writers are engaged in similar activities, using the structures and symbols of their languages to convey information, solve problems, and express themselves creatively.

Math riddles invite problem solving and imaginative thinking while demonstrating how to pose questions and provide answers using written language. Doug's Graph is a multifaceted tool for child-designed polls and surveys that asks children to present their findings using mathematical and written language. Math comics link children's enjoyment of math with their attraction to the visual display of comics. Math stories require kids to make mathematical and writing decisions about how to communicate their ideas within a comic format. Young writers invent characters and settings, fraction the action within comic frames, construct a problem solved by the story, and convey the plot to readers through dialogue between the characters.

CHAPTER SIX

Science

Marble machines, wooden block structures that use gravity to propel tiny spheres down straight and curving runways, is an annual building and design curriculum in Sharon's first-, second-, or third-grade classroom. From the top of three foot-high child-designed structures, marbles zip through tunnels and fly over bridges with the hope that they will land in a floor-level catch basin several feet away from the launch site. In theory, the marbles will race with stealth-like speed down the ramps. The initial runs, however, are not totally successful—blocked by obstacles, marbles abruptly halt, fly off the ramp, or disappear inside a camouflaged crevice.

Lively conversations, problem-solving activities, and analytical thinking among the children accompany the design process. One young builder suggests testing different-sized marbles. Other designers tinker with the central ramp's elevation, adding more height near the top and rounding a curve near the bottom—not the easiest thing to do using rectangular wooden blocks. These physical changes, along with rolling the marbles more forcefully from the top of the structure, send marbles cascading down the incline, resulting in one or two reaching the target. "Perhaps the big ones are chasing the little ones down the ramp," observes one youngster while the others nod their heads in agreement.

Marble machines power the curiosity of child scientists because kids must consider so many different characteristics and combinations as part of the design process—height, width, and number of blocks; sizes of marbles; curved or straight runways; sidewalls to enhance speed or redirect movement. The success of the ramp designs comes from the builders' creativity and persistence. Their open-ended explorations have no fixed starting or ending points, no right answer, no single best solution. Rather than dismantling an entire structure and rebuilding it, the children discover ways to design modifications as part of their ongoing problem solving. After adjusting one part of his construction, Peter announced to everyone, "You can take one thing and change it. I revised it."

Imagine every classroom as a child-sized science research center where exploratory activities like marble machines are happening every day. The center does not require expensive equipment or costly supplies. What it needs are ongoing opportunities for children to act first as scientists conducting research and then as writers who communicate what they are learning using nonfiction reporting forms and styles. In these learning centers, kids enthusiastically investigate real science questions, practicing the methods of experimentation with their own ideas or with topics from the school curriculum.

Fundamental to the science/writing connection are the characteristics of exploration and discovery, what educators Jerome Harste, Carolyn Burke, and Kathy Short (257) call "curriculum as inquiry," where children behave as "*problem-posers*, not just problem-solvers." Rather than organizing science learning around formal procedures, preset questions, and factual content to memorize, they urge starting with children's questions as a way to build an "attitude as an inquirer" into every youngster's habits of mind. In inquiry learning, kids observe everything more closely and "ask questions about aspects of the world that puzzle them. Then they systematically investigate those questions or tensions and create new understandings, new questions, and issues they want to explore further."

Investigating the natural and social world opens a doorway to exploring how writers communicate information in compelling, engaging writing styles. Young writers discover methods to convey what they are learning about science in written language that is "aggressive, bold, assertive, and full of spirit *throughout* the process of composing a work of nonfiction" (Harwayne 22). In this way, writing becomes a powerful catalyst for engaging children with the principles and practices of science.

The WOWs in Chapter Six: "Science" explain how children use writing throughout the processes of the scientific investigation and discovery. Writing lets kids share their scientific thinking as they explore topics as diverse as "What causes seasonal change?" or "What is a workable design for marble machines?" Writing propels the investigation of questions kids want to answer for themselves using what we call "I Observe, I Think . . . Because" cards. Writing makes kids more accomplished communicators of nonfiction information through interest-grabbing reports that discuss research in clear terms, propose thoughtful explanations for the results, and present succinct summaries of the findings.

- **WOW 19: Thinking and Acting as Scientists** uses the seasons' cycle to introduce how science and writing promote children's learning. Kids become scientists of seasonal change by using their natural curiosity to ask questions and seek explanations and by practicing the steps of the scientific method: observing, questioning, hypothesizing, experimenting, collecting/analyzing data, drawing conclusions, communicating findings. Kids see the methods of science in action through three investigations: Tracing Shadows, Spinning Tops, and Compiling Data. "Extensions: "Doorway in Time" has kids write about the seasonal changes they see through the doorways and windows of their classroom. Each young writer practices describing events accurately and vividly so that readers not present to see for themselves are still able to understand the changes taking place in the natural world.
- **WOW 20: Investigations and Discoveries** links writing to formulating hypotheses, conducting experiments, and analyzing data, the middle phases of the scientific method. A system of "I Observe, I Think . . . Because" cards make writing a central part of the process as children record their thoughts on paper and then revise them when new information is discovered. "Extensions: Writing Research Notes" discusses how to write about research activities in two different formats, notes about activities and summaries of what has been learned.
- **WOW 21: Attention-Grabbing Science Reports** presents strategies for teaching children about the "research report," a writing genre that every elementary school student is asked to do by grade four. Research reports must present information accurately while also maintaining the interest of readers. Reports relaying facts copied from the book inform but rarely entertain readers. Voice, a quality of personality and uniqueness in someone's writing, is a key to attention-grabbing research reports. Different strategies for voice are outlined, giving kids techniques to try in their reports. "Extensions: Great Paragraph Journeys" offers ideas for how to paragraph, an essential skill in conveying information clearly and concisely.

Thinking and Acting as Scientists

Acting as Scientists	TEACH	These Conventions *Unconventionally*
How Things Work and Other Puzzles		The scientific method • Observing • Questioning • Hypothesizing • Experimenting • Collecting/analyzing data • Drawing conclusions • Communicating findings
What Causes the Seasons? • Investigation 1: Tracing Shadows • Investigation 2: Spinning Tops • Investigation 3: Compiling Data		Genre: Science observation reports Science concepts • Causes of seasonal change • Planetary motion
Extensions: A Doorway in Time		Writing for different audiences Details and description in science writing

It's normal to want to know how things work and why the world is the way it is. At its most basic level, this is what science is all about. And scientists are just professionals at doing what children do so naturally.

Michael Shermer (4–5)

Most kids have no idea what scientists actually do. Movies and television portray specialists in lab coats with wild hair and glasses who perform incredible experiments, move through time and space, invent robots that function like humans, or concoct substances that defy all present laws of science. Meanwhile newspapers and magazines feature adults—mostly white males—describing their studies in hard-to-understand language. Rarely do kids see scientists systematically investigating the natural world and then communicating their findings through writing. Small wonder only a fraction of children consider science as a future career. They need ways to connect their daily living and learning to connect with the excitement and adventure of science.

How Things Work and Other Puzzles

At the core of science are puzzles and mysteries—the questions of "how," "why," "where," "why not," "what if," and "when." Since science is powered by questions, not by answers, and kids ask the most questions of anyone we know, a natural learning connection is created when children engage in both inquiry and investigation.

As curious inquirers, children are intrigued by recent developments from many different scientific fields: astronomers locating never-before-seen planets outside our galaxy; paleontologists finding a dinosaur skeleton with a possible four-chamber heart and an intact skull that challenge what is known about the evolution of reptiles, birds, and mammals; inventors changing how people communicate using wireless technologies; researchers exploring and mapping the human genome. Each new discovery generates more questions that lead to more discoveries that pose more questions.

As active investigators, children are eager to explore the world around them. The importance of science lies in the unknown, in what might be possible to understand or accomplish. The unknown and the what-might-be-possible attract children's attention, hold their interest, and engage them in asking questions and conducting inquiries about the natural and social world. These habits of mind are essential for the future. In the world of the twenty-first century, every member of society will need to be active inquirers in the processes of change. Confident elementary school scientists today are practicing the skills of inquiry, investigation, reflection, and revision that will enable them to become the thoughtful decision makers of tomorrow.

Despite these attractions between children and science, many adults think they must teach kids how to engage in science study. They introduce topics of study and then give step-by-step assignments instead of watching to see how much science students do naturally when they set up their own experiments with items like wooden blocks, water and paints (to make shades of color), or spinning tops. Sometimes adults assume that since the scientific process requires recording information, they must wait till children are proficient writers before introducing science learning.

But being able to complete assignments and write English proficiently are not the sole gateways to inquiry-based scientific thinking. For children to become engaged by science, adults need to capitalize on what children already know how to do well, find easy and interesting, and can do anywhere, anytime—observe, question, wonder, explore, discuss, and analyze.

There are direct parallels here between children's naturally occurring thinking patterns and habits of mind of professional scientists whose work engages them in the steps of the scientific method:

making observations,

asking questions,

formulating and assessing hypotheses,

designing experiments,

collecting and analyzing data,

drawing conclusions,

and communicating results (Skolnick 161).

Carrying out scientific inquiry by combining kids' own questions with teacher-assigned activities strengthen the habits of mind that increase children's involvement in learning. Excitement about observing and recording events fuels self-directed explorations where young minds practice sustained focus on a topic and detailed analyses of real-world happenings—skills vitally important for success at every educational level.

What Causes the Seasons?

"What causes the seasons?" a much-studied topic throughout elementary and secondary school, offers a puzzling yet engaging way to start children thinking, acting, and writing like scientists.

The process of seasonal change is easily confused or misunderstood. Many nonscientists, including an astonishing percentage of college graduates, do not realize that the 23.6-degree tilt of the earth in space produces seasonal change. Without its tilt, the earth's year-long revolution around the sun would be in a straight, upright position. This would produce twelve hours of light and twelve hours of night, all year long, everywhere on the globe, as occurs daily at or near the equator and twice a year in the northern and southern hemispheres at the September and March equinoxes.

Instead, because the earth tilts in its orbit, locations on the globe receive more or less sunlight at different times of the year causing a cycle we call the seasons. As a result,

- Amherst, Massachusetts receives fifteen hours, seventeen minutes of light at the summer solstice in June, but only nine hours, four minutes of light six months later at the winter solstice in December. This six-hour, thirteen-minute difference in length of day is twelve minutes short of a typical school day—a fact that amazes adults as much as it surprises youngsters.

- The northernmost parts of Alaska receive twenty-four hours of light in June, July, and August before and after the summer solstice and twenty-four hours of night in November, December, and January before and after the winter solstice. In summer, sports teams start baseball and softball games at 12:00 midnight and play without electric lights. Antarctica experiences the same cycle at opposite times—winter darkness for twenty-four hours in June, July, and August and summer daylight in November, December, and January.

- For three months, the North Pole tilts toward the sun while the South Pole tilts away; for three months the opposite occurs—the North Pole tilts away from the sun as the South Pole tilts toward it. During the other six months, daylight grows and shrinks because the tilt is more or less pronounced.

Demonstrations of the seasonal cycle are easier to understand when kids engage in three different observational experiences—tracing shadows, spinning tops, and charting a seasonal almanac. These simple science activities arouse curiosity and impart information about how and why shadows move as they do, how and why spinning tops behave like planets in space, or how and why the lengths of daylight and nighttime change throughout the year. Children's investigations of these questions feature observing, experimenting, and writing (activities that will produce more questions and more research), all part of the scientific process.

Our three seasonal change investigations require the following items:

- assortment of toy tops
- sidewalk chalk
- an outdoor area with sunlight
- pencils, markers, and paper for charts
- a home-made or store-bought sundial
- a strong light from a slide projector or overhead projector with small model globes

Investigation 1: Tracing Shadows Demonstrate Day/Night Cycles

Tracing kids' own shadows collects data, focuses attention on natural events, and interests youngsters in scientific research about something they think they already know how to explain—the cycle of daylight and nighttime. The purpose of shadow tracing is to instigate a conversation about why shadows move, an often-held confusion by young children. Noting the movement of the sun in the sky during the day, they logically assume that it is moving while the ground they stand on—the earth—remains still. Here is a way to demonstrate that the earth is moving around the sun in planetary motion like a gigantic spinning top in space.

Any object large enough to cast a shadow can be used for shadow tracing, but we start with the children themselves going outside on a sunny day in early September to trace each other's shadows on the ground. With different-colored sidewalk chalk, kids work in pairs. One traces around the other's shoes before tracing the person's shadow. They switch roles to repeat the process, writing their names in the outline of their bodies.

Kids trace their shadows at one specific time of day—between nine and eleven in the morning—and return to re-trace again between twelve and three in the afternoon. Observing their outlines, kids see every shadow behaving the same way, moving along the ground west to east as the earth spins its 360-degree, 24-hour rotation from west to east on its axis.

The combination of tracing their own shadows and watching them move astonishes kids. They can hardly believe that changes occur in just minutes or that dramatic differences appear in two hours. Having introduced the idea of shadows on the move, other things can be traced and studied. Tall objects, like trees, flagpoles, or street signs, provide compelling examples of lengthening and shrinking shadows moving across the ground. A large box is another good choice for shadow study because its perimeter is easy to trace on the ground so if it is accidentally moved, it can be exactly replaced in its outline and then transported from place to place to observe its shadow's shape and size in different spots.

Repeating shadow tracings at the same time of day for several days in a row or over a two-week span is important. Ancient astronomers and chronologers who first understood the principles of planetary motion did not base their conclusions on a single set of observations. Neither should children. They need to see that shadows move in the same way day after day. It is the regularity of procedures used and patterns discovered that allow children to see similarities and differences in shadow length and direction cast by different objects.

Sharon's class traces shadows three times before they do a series of experiments in the classroom with the light of an overhead projector shining against a wall or a plain sheet of paper. Children choose a small object to hold in the light to see what happens to its shadow as they turn the object. Paper is then tacked up for recording the object's different shadow shapes. The children trace various shadow shapes in different colors on the paper as they turn their objects. In effect, they become models of the spinning earth and their objects become them on the earth.

One simple, but surprisingly dramatic, shadow-making object is a piece of paper or a 3 × 5 index card with a shape or hole cut out of its middle. As it turns, the change in the paper's shadow is astonishing. Held sideways toward the light, the paper's edge produces a slender straight line of darkness that looks like a line drawn by a ruler and pencil. When the light illuminates the complete face of the paper, its shadow is a rectangle with a hole of light through it. The shadow shapes produced by the different angles of the card against the light as it turns from side to side are hugely surprising to kids. After experiencing indoor shadow tracing, Sharon takes the class outside hourly to trace the shadows of different-sized blocks or objects to see how they change with the angle of the sunlight.

It is desirable to trace outdoor shadows for several days in a row at noon during different seasons. Beginning in September around the autumnal equinox in New England, Sharon's children observe the length of shadows at noon as summer becomes fall. Tracing one child on a long length of paper that can be placed in exactly the same spot makes it easy to repeat the observations in December, March, and June. This shows the differences of sun height in winter, spring, and summer sky through the length of noontime shadows.

Children's observations provide a direct and wonderful historical connection to the calendars of ancient peoples, including one unknown group of Native Americans whose cliff drawings in southern Utah are visible only twice a year at the equinoxes when sunlight strikes the rock face at exactly the angle designed by the stonecutters to reveal the pictures.

Investigation 2: Spinning Tops Demonstrate Planetary Motion

To begin the second investigation, children spin different styles and sizes of wooden and plastic tops, including

- bowl-bottom tops that flip over and spin on their handles
- magnetic tops that propel slithering metal snakes back and forth or spin flat circles around their magnetic tips.
- transparent tops with multicolored beads spinning inside
- tops that light-up and play a tune as they spin
- large flat wooden tops that spin on a penny at the center
- dreidels with Hebrew letters on each of the four sides
- gyroscopes that tilt as they spin, seemingly defying gravity

Playing with new versions of one of humankind's oldest toys serves to focus children's attention to what is happening with each top. Such close observation is an essential starting point for kids investigating how things work scientifically. If one of the tops' accomplishments is focusing attention, another is inspiring different investigative questions:

- "Which one will spin the longest?"
- "What happens when tops collide or carom off nearby walls?"
- "Will a top continue spinning if it drops from a table onto the floor?"
- "Is there another way to make the bowl-bottom top flip over?"

Figure 6.1

Quitze and Chelsea's science observations.

Each question becomes the basis for observations and experiments that are recorded in a science journal or a newspaper reporter's notebook (Figure 6.1).

Quitze's Science Observation

I discovered that when I make orange spirals on paper and put pipe cleaner on it, it makes sparks around it. I discovered that when I put shiny paper on a top it looks like lightning.

Chelsea's Science Observation

the First top looks Like a Cd. when its Spining. on the seckent one it Looks Like a butterfly Stiking its touing out When it is not spining.

Chelsea May 21, 2000

[*Translation:* The first top looks like a CD when it is spinning. On the second one it looks like a butterfly sticking its tongue out when it is not spinning.]

Spinning tops illustrate many curricular topics, notably, how planets behave in our solar system. Earth and the other planets are different-sized spinning tops, although unlike tops, planets do not slow down, stop moving, or behave wildly in their orbits. Each planet has a fixed rotation around the sun, held in place by the force of gravity. A top with a magnetic tip demonstrates this concept of orbiting around a larger body in space. This top is sold with a circular metal disk. As the top spins, the circular metal disk is attracted by the magnet causing it to revolve around the top, thereby simulating the movement of a smaller body around a larger body in an orbit.

Kids themselves can simulate spinning planets in a large space with a center pole (flagpole, signpost, or tall stake) to represent the sun. One child becomes each planet, positioned from nearer to farther away from the center point using the distances in the following chart. The other children in the class position themselves as stars, meteors, or comets. Orbits are marked on the ground with colored sand so kids can see how the planets' placement in relation to the center pole simulates actual distances of planets from the sun using the following model.

Planet	Distance from Sun	Distance from Center Pole
Mercury	36 million miles	3 inches
Venus	67 million miles	6 inches
Earth	93 million miles	9 inches
Mars	141 million miles	14 inches
Jupiter	483.4 million miles	48 inches or 4 feet
Saturn	886.7 million miles	88 inches or 7 feet
Uranus	1,783 million miles	178 inches or 15 feet
Neptune	2,794 million miles	279 inches or 23 feet
Pluto	3,666 million miles	366 inches or 30 feet

As the children walk in circular orbits, they see how much longer it takes the more distant outer planets to complete a single rotation around the center of their class-made solar system. In this activity, the child who is Mercury, the planet with shortest annual cycle, has the shortest orbit. The child who is modeling Pluto is one hundred times the distance from the sun as the child who is Mercury. Children can swap places to experience the different lengths of orbits.

Investigation 3: Compiling Data Over Time by Charting a Seasonal Almanac

Seasonal change is measured by steady increases or decreases in the number of hours of daylight, except near the equator. The predictable two to three minutes a day gained or lost in Massachusetts visually illustrates the passage of the seasons. Second and third graders using data from the weather page of a local newspaper or from information on the Internet can chart an "Hours of Daylight Calendar" throughout the year. The following selection is from a two-week period in September around the 2000 fall equinox when the daylight drops below twelve hours a day for the first time in six months.

Hours of Daylight, Autumnal Equinox in Boston Massachusetts,
September 18 to October 1, 2000

Monday	Tuesday	Wednesday	Thursday	Friday	Saturday	Sunday
18	19	20	21	22	23	24
12:20	12:17	12:14	12:12	12:09	12:06	12:03
25	26	27	28	29	30	1
12:01	11:58	11:55	11:52	11:49	11:46	11:43

Depending on where one lives in North America, there are interesting local weather phenomenon to record and analyze, including daily high and low tides, snowfall, rainfall, wind speed and direction. Usually these are different throughout the year, providing additional information about seasonal change. Fall and spring's arrival features wide variations in temperatures in many parts of the country. Kids might chart mid-day temperatures for a month, displaying the fluctuations on a wall-sized line graph. Regardless of the source of the data collection—newspapers, online, or thermometers placed outside the classroom in sunlight and in shade—learning comes from collecting information over time and recording it to display on wall charts and large graphs.

Using the wall charts, children can review their recorded observations of weather patterns and formulate written hypotheses about what is happening and why. When kids practice this type of writing regularly, by the end of a school year, they are able to explain different aspects of seasonal change because they have been actively engaged in asking questions, doing experiments, and developing theories based on real-world observations and written records.

EXTENSIONS

"A Doorway in Time"

In her wordless picture book *Window*, Jeannie Baker creates a powerful visual account of environmental change seen though the window of a small house over twenty-four years. Each page offers a view of the same location, but the scene changes as urban sprawl devastates a lush natural habitat. Dilapidated buildings, carelessly thrown trash, and abandoned cars rusting by the side of a road occupy what was once a green meadow with tall trees and abundant wildlife. Baker's point is clear: to prevent the ravages of unfettered development, people must first stop and look carefully at the world around them, a world that humans, busily preoccupied with personal day-to-day pursuits, easily overlook.

While the readers of Jeannie Baker's book peer out a window, visitors to New Castle, New Hampshire, gaze through a different kind of portal in time. The island's lookout and picnic area features a black metal sculpture of an artist with a paintbrush and watercolors standing next to an empty square frame of an easel. Looking through the frame from different angles, one sees an ever-changing scene of water and land at the mouth of the Pisquash River, rendered artistically in each viewer's imagination.

Like Jeannie Baker and the New Castle sculptor, children delight in seeing what happens when they look closely at a small place for a sustained period of time. Our portal is the back door of Sharon's classroom, a comfy place for children to observe grass, plants, trees, bushes, and sky from a new perspective, a viewing and analyzing experience we call "A Doorway in Time." Children become so immersed in their everyday activities that they often fail to see what is happening right in front of their eyes. The view out the back door is changing every day, but in small ways that must be carefully traced through regular observations.

We begin the "Doorway in Time" by having the children note all the environmental features that can be seen from this single vantage point. It is a lovely New England college campus. Green grass, tall trees, and large hedges frame a sprawling brick building that houses both the elementary school and the University of Massachusetts School of Education. A driveway with parking spaces for visitors circles around a small grass island where the children have planted flowers. Alongside the driveway sits a two-story, colonial-style house belonging to the University. In the distance, other academic buildings are visible above the bushes, most notably the top half of the twenty-two-story W. E. B. DuBois Library.

The seasonal passages of fall, winter, spring, and summer provide dramatically different views of buildings, grounds and skyline. October's red and gold leaves become November's bare branches and January's starkly white sculptures of ice and snow. The muted browns and grays of March become vivid shades of green in May and June. Even the daily weather creates vastly different nature scenes. One rainy Spring morning, when the clouds hung low in the sky camouflaging the top floors of the library, seven-year-old Tilly playfully suggested that perhaps a dragon had "come during the weekend and eaten part of the building."

"Doorway in Time" observations may start during pivotal periods of seasonal change. We use September to November or March to May, the times in New England when warmth of summer becomes the chill of fall or when the last snows of winter melt into the new grass, leaves, and flowers of early spring. The transitions from fall to winter or winter to spring are filled with change. In other parts of the country, any natural seasonal change or weather cycle can be the basis for "A Doorway in Time" project.

Standing in the side doorway in March, children first observe the overall scene from different angles, noting what they can see by looking left, right, straight ahead, up, and down. Moving outside, they concentrate on smaller parts of the environment—melting piles of snow, the first signs of green grass and flowers, buds on the trees, insects and worms on the ground, patterns of clouds in the sky.

Pairs of children then choose specific locations—the center island in a small parking cul-de-sac, bushes in front of the nearby building, trees along the small hillside, flowers and grass to the left of the doorway—to observe for a week, first from inside and then, weather permitting, outside and close-up. The idea is for the children to microscope their observations and record whatever earth changes might be happening in their specific area.

At the end of the week, each pair of observers summarize their observations in a journal using words and pictures. The journals are then passed on to a new pair of observers for the next week. These children begin their week of observations by reading what the previous week's recorders have written before adding their own entries to the journal.

These young scientists are producing a written record of seasonal change. Their commentaries and illustrations form descriptive word pictures of science as it happens to share with classmates, as in the second graders' observations of winter and spring scenes seen in Figure 6.2.

"Doorway in Time" science study can go on for many weeks or for an entire school year. Journeying outside lets young scientists examine what is happening during all sorts of events, from shadows and sundials to plants and the growth cycle. Investigating processes of change in a familiar environment promotes the learning of important science concepts. By year's end, the first, second, and third grade scientists become adept at using and explaining terms such as atmosphere, earth motion, water cycle, and the sources of all kinds of precipitation.

Audiences for Writing

Learning to write for an audience is key to "Doorway in Time." It would be easy for children to describe everything they observed without writing in journals. Pairs of youngsters could make daily trips outside and share their findings orally in class meetings; then adults could summarize the key results on worksheets and exam questions. Science study could proceed, as it often does, without including writing as a centerpiece of the learning.

By writing journal entries that are read by other children, science observers discover that they are writing not only for themselves or for a class assignment, but for those who are going to observe their area over the next several weeks. An audience of classmates makes it important for each observer to record clearly and completely what has been happening. Readers depend on what reporters write. Without understandable and accurate information, readers will not fully understand the nature changes their reporter/peers are observing outside the classroom.

Winter Time Observations by Allie

Outside I see snow everywhere, the sky is bright blue, everything is clear. There's an evergreen, it's dark green. The ground is brown. I also see a tree with a lot of branches.

Winter Time Observations by Izzy

Outside I saw the wind blowing the snow off the trees and I saw it was lightly snowing. Outside there was lots of snow on the ground. Outside two big balls of snow stuck to the other snow. Outside no leaves are on the trees.

Spring Time Observations by Elijah

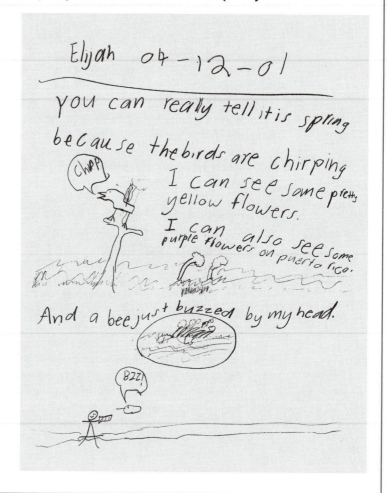

Figure 6.2   *Children's Winter Time and Spring Time observations.*

"Doorway in Time" purposefully creates multiple audiences for writing while the pace of seasonal change gives real importance to each set of written observations. Since small groups write journal entries, not every child gets to observe every area first-hand for several days at a time. They must rely on what their classmates write to fully appreciate what is happening in the flower beds, trees, bushes, or other parts of the yard. Once a new group starts viewing the scene, the rest of the class now depends on them to describe their parts of the whole. It is through the collective writing of the entire class over a number of weeks that a full picture of seasonal change emerges.

Recording the events of seasonal change helps children learn to include details in their writing. The goal for each journal entry is conveying an accurate picture to readers about what is happening outside. The key for the writer is to keep looking intently to record happenings that might be easily overlooked by a more casual observer. In the entry below, written as spring arrives, Garrett focuses on the details he sees in an outdoor scene (Figure 6.3).

Details are even more interesting to readers when they are presented in descriptive language. "They are like wedding flowers," remarked one youngster, witnessing a New England spring for the first time, after noticing the first plants of the season in bloom. This observation not only informs the audience that the first spring flowers have arrived, but by

There is still grass. Even though it snowed, it still didn't cover the island [middle of a traffic circle in the school driveway]. Half of Puerto Rico [name the class gave to the traffic circle] is snowy and grassy.

I think the snow bank on the right is the biggest. There are other snow banks, too. Some are small and some are medium sized.

There is smoke coming out of a tube and it is blowing left into the field. On a garage there is snow on top of it. On the ground are puddles. And I see some leaves on the bottom branches of a tree. The other leaves evaporated, I think, or got blown away.

I saw a squirrel outside so I knocked on the window and he got so scared he ran up the tree! When I looked over there again, he was digging a hole. Then he ran away.

You can't see the sidewalks because they are buried in snow. There are not icicles except for on the house over there and there are snowballs in the road. There is snow up almost half of the tree trunk. I see another tube with smoke coming out of it.

Figure 6.3   *Garrett's "Doorway in Time" report.*

adding a metaphorical phrase, makes the report more engaging for those who did not see the flowers bloom. It conveys an image in a sensory manner—anyone who has seen flowers at wedding celebrations can picture what she has written—while bringing readers directly into the experience of the moment.

YOUNG WRITERS' BOOKSHELF FOR THINKING AND ACTING LIKE SCIENTISTS

Scientists and Their Work

Mary Anning and the Sea Dragon. Jeannine Atkins. Pictures by Michael Dooling. Farrar, Straus & Giroux, 1999. A twelve-year-old girl, possessing curiosity and persistence, discovers the fossil remains of an ichthyosaur along the English seashore in 1811, determining her life's work as a paleontologist.

The Librarian Who Measured the Earth. Kathryn Lasky. Illustrated by Kevin Hawkes. Little, Brown, 1994. The true and amazing story of Eratosthenes who measured the circumference of the earth (within two hundred miles) more than two thousand years ago.

Seasonal Change

The Autumn Equinox: Celebrating the Harvest. Ellen Jackson. Illustrated by Jan Davey Ellis. Millbrook Press, 2000. Harvest festivals around the world including North American Thanksgiving, Jewish Sukkah, Iroquois Green Corn Dance, southern India's Pongal celebration, and African feasts.

Gather up, Gather in: A Book of Seasons. M. C. Helldorfer. Illustrated by Judy Pedersen. Viking, 1994. A story told in prose poetry with acrylic paintings displays the beauty of the seasonal cycle.

The Winter Solstice. Ellen Jackson. Illustrated by Jan Davey Ellis.

Millbrook Press, 1994. Folklore and science facts tell all about the shortest day of the year.

In for Winter, Out for Spring. Arnold Adoff. Illustrations by Jerry Pinkney. Harcourt Brace Jovanovich, 1991. Young Rebecca records a year of memories about changing seasons and family activities in poetic verses that stretch long and march short across each page in a captivating cadence of words and images.

The Seasons Sewn: A Year in Patchwork. Ann Whitford Paul. Illustrated by Michael McCurdy. Harcourt, 1996. The seasons of year on the nineteenth-century American frontier is depicted in quilt squares and scratchboard illustrations.

The Seasons and Someone. Virginia Kroll. Illustrated by Tatsuro Kiuchi. Harcourt Brace, 1994. Questions and answers about the changing seasons of the year in Alaska are revealed through the life of a young Eskimo girl.

Exploring the Sky by Day: The Equinox Guide to Weather and the Atmosphere. Terence Dickinson. Firefly Books, 1998. See also *Exploring the Night Sky: The Equinox Astronomy Guide for Beginners*. Terence Dickinson. Firefly Books, 1998.

Window. Jeannie Baker. Greenwillow, 1991. (Cited in the text.)

WOW
20

Investigations and Discoveries

Science Investigations	TEACH	These Conventions *Unconventionally*
I Observe, I Think . . . Because • "I Observe" Statements • "I Think . . . Because" Statements		Noticing details Making predictions Formulating hypotheses
Extensions: Research Notes and Summaries		Genre: Note writing Communicating factual information Drawing conclusions

"I Observe, I Think . . . Because" is an approach to science-based thinking and writing that blends children's natural curiosity with sensory awareness. The idea is for kids to begin science study by making close and systematic observations of something interesting (I Observe). Observations are followed by speculative thinking (I Think) as children propose possible explanations for what they have seen (Because). These initial, tentative reasons must then be examined to determine their accuracy and usefulness as scientific findings. A week of investigation using this method can be organized according to the following outline.

Activity Outline for "I Observe, I Think . . . Because"

Day 1: "I Observe" . . .	Day 2: "I Observe" . . .	Day 3: "I Think" . . .	Day 4: "I Think" . . .	Day 5: "Because" . . .
Initial Oral Observations	Sensory Data Written on Cards	Educated Guesses Written on Cards	More Bright Ideas Written on Cards	Tentative Explanations Written on Sticky Notes

"I Observe" Statements

Ruth piloted "I Observe, I Think . . . Because" with five- and six-year-olds by first displaying the dismantled center tube of a brass towel rack and asking her students to observe it carefully. Unassembled, the tube lacks apparent meaning or function and thus is a mysterious item in the eyes of the children.

"What can you say about this?" Ruth asked, holding the tube aloft for everyone to see. The children wrote (Figure 6.4):

"It is hollow."

"It feels like a bell."

"It smells like metal."

"I see a circle; I see bubble letters."

"I hear ringing."

"It's gold."

Figure 6.4   *Children's "I Observe" statements.*

As the list of their comments grew, Ruth gently questioned the origins of the children's ideas: "How do you know that the tube is gold?"

"I can see it" was the collective reply, demonstrating how scientists use "I Observe" observations and statements as tools for beginning their investigations. In scientific inquiry, sensory data, like that being recorded by these children, is an appropriate starting point. When scientists observe the natural or physical world first-hand, "an interest or feeling of tension begins to grow, we discover what we want to pursue, and that interest gradually forms into a focused question or issue" (Short, Harste, and Burke 266).

Ruth reminded the children to complete their observations before drawing definitive conclusions. When kids leaped from what they saw to what they thought they knew, declaring, "It's a pipe," Ruth re-emphasized the need for systematic observations, asking, "How do you know that?"

"It looks like one my grandfather has," said one student.

"Pipes feel cold and shiny," said another.

Each day for several days, Ruth unveiled other parts of the towel rack, including the screws used to attach it to a wall, asking the children to state what they observed about each piece. She explained that the human brain uses all of the five senses to create a clearer picture or a more complete story about what is happening around us:

"You collect information with your body all the time. Your eyes tell you that the table is brown, your skin tells you the table is smooth. Your ears tell you what things are going on around you and when you taste or smell something you decide whether or not you like it and want more."

"All of your senses silently talk to you all of the time. Your brain is constantly getting phone calls and recording messages from your senses. I see, I hear, I smell, I touch, I taste. Now we are going to practice writing down information that our body tells our brain."

Ruth gave each of the children 3″ × 5″ white index cards, held together on a small ring. The children wrote their sensory responses, one on each card. Lily's cards for the week of observations and discoveries, written in a kindergartner's spelling, were as follows:

- Its loing (*It's long*)
- It fis lic a bez (*It feels like a bell*)

- It smals (*It smells*)
- I see haw it lucx (*I see how it looks* accompanied by an illustration of the individual parts and how she thought they should fit together)

After a week of observations, every child had a ring of six to nine personal "I Observe" data statements.

"I Think . . . Because" Statements

Children were now ready to move on with the inquiry process. Using their "I Observe" cards, Ruth asked them to create "I Think" statements—"educated guesses" based on the data collected and written down. In scientific language, "I Think" statements are possible explanations or "hypotheses" about what the object might be as gleaned from the information available to the children. Ruth's students offered the written conclusions about the center section of the brass towel rack shown in Figure 6.5.

After complimenting each student on the thoughtfulness of her or his ideas, Ruth reminded the class that the validity or accuracy of possible explanations can only be supported or rejected by further investigation and data collection.

She then gave the children neon-colored index cards for their "I Think" statements. The bright cards signified "bright ideas" evolving from children's observations and interpretations. Formal science terms—"hypothesis," "experiment," "theory," "validity," "prediction," "cause and effect," "comparison and contrast"—were introduced in conversations and explanations. Kids heard Ruth use these words paired with kid-friendly synonyms (validity means truth or reality) and they began expressing these new words in relation to their own inquiries.

To go beyond first impressions and immediate explanations, "I Think" statements require supporting evidence. Ruth called these "Because" statements. A child might write: "I think the gold tube is a pipe *because* there is a hole all the way through." A "Because" statement highlights supporting details or factual information. In this case, other people are able to see for themselves that the tube is hollow all the way through.

Ruth chose sticky notes for recording "Because" statements. This choice proved as valuable to the process of thinking and acting like a scientist as had the white "I Observe" and the neon-colored "I Think" index cards at earlier stages in the process. When a "Because" statement was written it was attached to the "I Think" card it supported. Combining "I Think" and "Because" statements provided additional factual support to the "I Think" statements, verifying or denying the child's initial hypothesis. Adding or taking away sticky notes on the "I Think" cards easily revised or changed the information.

Kids like to use sticky notes. They are attractive and because of their self-adhesive application, they offer the flexibility that scrap paper or index cards do not. They have other positive features as well:

"I think it's a curtain holder."

"I think it is a telescope."

"I think it is part of the sink."

"I think it is a curtain hanger."

"I think it is part of something; maybe it is part of a table."

Figure 6.5   *Children's "I Think" statements.*

- Different facts can be written on different colors of sticky notes to attach to an "I Think" card, showing various points a child might include when reporting information.

- The pull-off and stick-on notes allow arranging and rearranging them on an "I Think" card in the order that the child wants to share them with an audience.

- Sticky notes can be lifted off "I Think" cards and displayed on a class chart for everyone to read.

- Sticky notes uniquely support speaking and listening. Quiet or shy children have written and arranged their ideas already, making an oral presentation easier. Loquacious children report the information written on their cards without becoming overly informative.

Getting kids involved with science using "I Observe, I Think . . . Because" cards is easy. The materials needed are inexpensive, the process is endlessly repeatable, and teachers, parents, and children spontaneously propose child-engaging topics to investigate. Here are more strategies for promoting "I Observe, I Think . . . Because" science inquiry.

- Encourage kids' natural inquisitiveness by listening carefully to their comments and conversations. When topics for investigation arise, remark, "That's interesting. What do you see happening?" Instead of waiting for children to raise topics, ask, "What are you wondering about this? Let's look at it more closely."

- Take trips to a museum, watch television shows such as *Bill Nye, The Science Guy* or *Kratt's Creatures*, and read children's books about everything from dinosaurs to seasonal change to get kids to experience and investigate the many worlds of science.

- Use an inexpensive, hand-held voice recorder during science exploration and investigation so children can orally record data while paying close attention to their thoughts instead of either child or adult immediately writing everything the child wants to say.

EXTENSIONS

Research Notes and Summaries

Observations and investigations of science topics focus children's attention on two forms of nonfiction writing: *research notes* and *research summaries*. Research notes are brief written descriptions of facts and questions that kids find when they interact with scientific events. Research summaries are longer written statements of what kids say they have learned after conducting experiments and analyzing data. Each is recorded in journals and notebooks and are often included as part of classroom reports. While notes and summaries are sometimes written solely for a writer's own learning, these materials, when shared, are a source of new information for everyone in a group.

Research Notes

Many children do not think about writing research notes while they are observing scientific phenomena. Investigations can be so attention-consuming that stopping to write notes seems to distract from the real action happening in an experiment or in the world outside the classroom. Plus, writing research notes is an unfamiliar role for many kids. They are unsure what to write about or what kind of language to use to record their experiences.

Research note writing emerges from *active observation* and *thoughtful conversation*. While it may seem obvious, without something to observe kids have little to write about in their notebooks. When kids pay close attention to real-world events, they can make notes about what is actually happening. Active observation does not just happen. Children need to be taught to look closely, to notice subtle changes, to treat each observation as a new situation where what happened the previous time is not necessarily going to happen the same way again. Daniel's notes record his experiment to determine whether a tennis ball or a racquetball would be the first to reach the bottom of the playground slide (Figure 6.6).

An active observer does not merely glance, but looks intently and intensely to discover patterns and changes. Then the observer writes notes, trying to capture the important details of what is happening. Notes help the writer to relive the event long after it has taken place. After spinning many different kinds of toy tops, Moriah recorded both her questions and discoveries in note form (Figure 6.7).

Thoughtful conversations promote active note taking. In our classes, all the children observing an event share their ideas with one another in small and large groups. As kids talk to each other, they help each other to look more closely. Quite naturally, they become interested in finding out what someone else saw that they might have missed. An oral exchange of research observations gives children reasons to go back and look again to confirm or change their initial impressions. Their talk is the rehearsal for writing ideas and information.

In a context of active observation and thoughtful conversation, kids learn that research notes are factual statements based on actual data. The role of the note writer is to record events. For example, observing the appearance and disappearance of shadows on a partly cloudy day, a young scientist might write: "I see my shadow and sometimes I do not." State-

---

On the red slide the blue ball went the farthest. But at first when they were on the slide, they were a tie. Then the blue ball got off the tennis ball somehow and it rolled up on the side of the slide and it went past the tennis ball so that's how the blue ball won.

Figure 6.6 *Daniel's notes.*

Why do some tops go faster than others?

Some tops look like airplane propellers.

Some tops look like there are pennies stuck in them.

How do tops change colors?

Some tops are shiny.

I like shiny tops.

I like designs.

Figure 6.7 *Moriah's "questions and discoveries."*

ments like "I like shadows" or "Shadows are my friend" do not reveal what the observer has seen. Research notes function as detailed statements that produce a picture of an event in a reader's mind.

Encouraging children to make observations over and over again is an essential ingredient to writing research notes. As kids do repeated observations and discuss them, they are using unfamiliar vocabulary in a real context where the words and their meanings make sense. Terms like "equinox" or "solstice" are difficult to remember because of the unfamiliarity and the strangeness of the spelling. After a year of investigations and observations of seasonal events, kids will have heard, read, and written the terms often enough to use them appropriately in many different forms of writing.

Research Summaries

At some point in the process of scientific inquiry, research notes are transformed into research summaries. The purpose of writing summaries is to inform others about the findings of the research. Two elements are essential for effectively incorporating research notes into research summaries: Facts must be accurate and the presentation of data must be clear. Erroneous information or overly complex language distorts the message and confuses the audience.

When communicating factual information, essayist Patricia T. O'Connor (50) urges writers to keep the "words few and simple." When discussing the impact of rain on the price of corn, a writer does not need to say, "predictions of increased precipitation have in the present instance proved accurate." The words may sound impressive, but readers get lost in the phrasing and no one is sure whether the precipitation is rain or snow or whether the price went up or down.

For young writers, summary statements based on their science observations are opportunities to practice crafting sentences that convey key information clearly, as in the summaries written in response to the question, "Why do shadows happen?" (Figure 6.8).

The goal in writing summaries is to convey the maximum amount of information in few words, like the weather sentence templates presented in WOW 6. Rather than fill a page with text, a writer seeks specificity and clarity, as in Brianna's summary of what she learned about rocks and dinosaurs after a class trip to a museum (Figure 6.9).

Figure 6.8

Children's research summaries about shadows.

> Reflections made shadows. Shadows are a kind of reflection. Black and white light make you see the shadow, the black is the shadow.
>
> We saw our shadows outside. The sun and our body makes our shadows.
>
> The sun is what makes shadows. We need the sun or we would not have shadows.
>
> The earth moves around which makes the shadows move.
>
> Shadows are made from sun and your body. If we did not have the sun we would not have any shadows.
>
> Shadows are like clothes that don't fit.

Drawings accompanying a research summary further explain the writer's ideas. Taken together, words and pictures create a museum-style display that focus readers' attention on a key point or insight. Such summaries are a useful beginning for the preparation of research reports, a longer form of science writing required in elementary classrooms and discussed in detail in WOW 21.

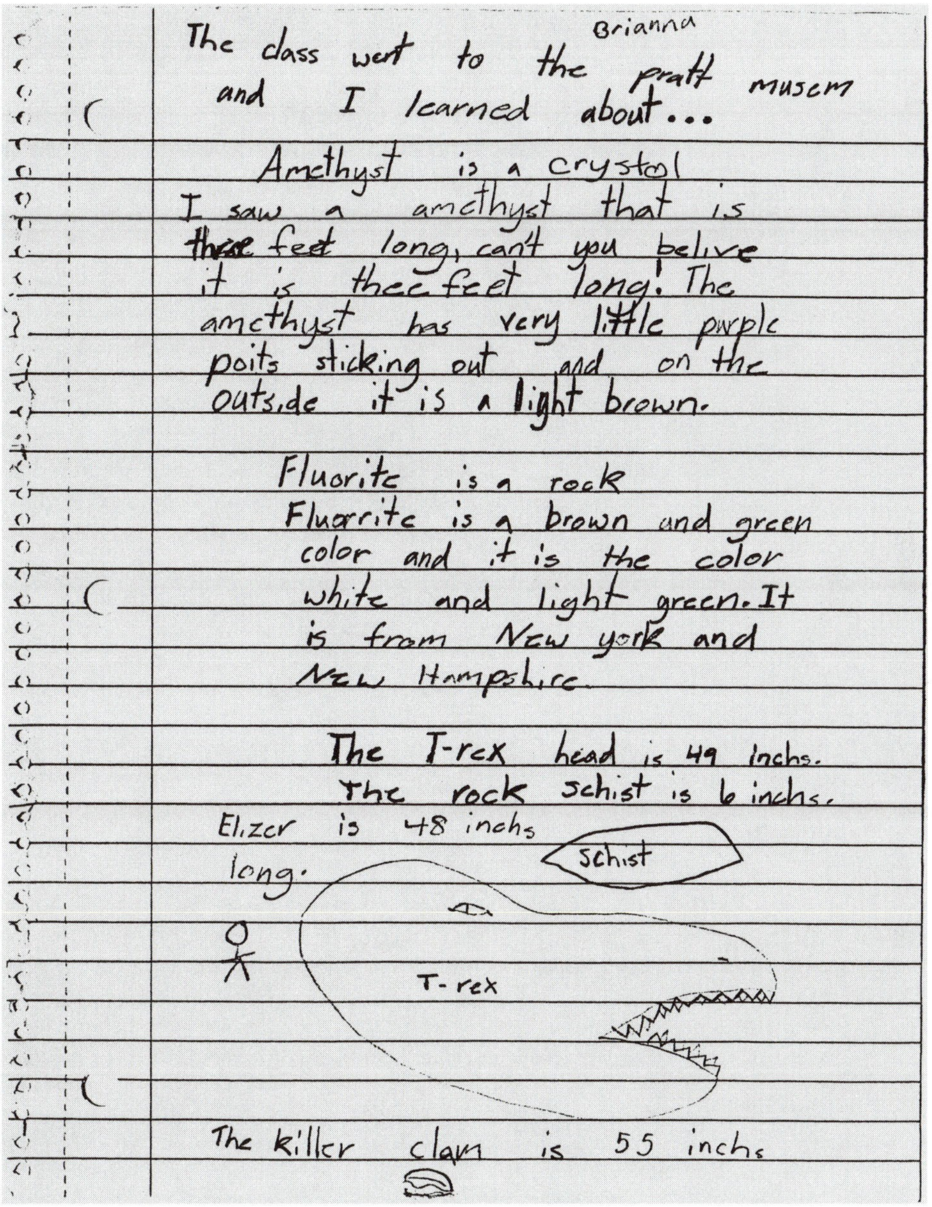

Figure 6.9 *Brianna's research summary. Translation:*

The class went to the Pratt Museum and I learned about . . .

Amethyst is a crystal. I saw an amethyst that is three feet long, can't you believe, it is three feet long. The amethyst has very little purple points sticking out and on the outside it is light brown.

Fluorite is a rock. Fluorite is a brown and green color and it is the color white and light green. It is from New York and New Hampshire.

The T-Rex head is 49 inches. The rock schist is 6 inches. Elizer [a classmate] is 48 inches. The killer clam is 55 inches.

Technology Supports Research

Many youngsters enjoy using voice-activated tape recorders and digital cameras as part of their science research. Ruth introduces these devices by explaining their usefulness to scientists when they do not have time to, or cannot easily, write as they work. The tape recorder lets researchers save their ideas to return to later. The digital camera provides a visual record of events. Kids can listen to their tapes, view their pictures, and then transfer their thoughts to idea cards or science notebooks.

Kids view tape recorders and digital cameras as professional tools, and using them imparts an expectation that what kids are doing or saying has importance to them and to an audience with whom they share their discoveries. Such tools encourage children to recognize that their ideas are serious and worth paying attention to. Observing and recording—habits of mind that are distinguishing features of scientists, artists, poets and writers—are talents that can be developed in children through first-hand experience supported by technology.

Using voice recording technology builds kids' confidence as oral language communicators. They have been practicing speaking for years. Talk gives kids a way to hear what they are thinking as they are thinking it. Later, when they sit down to write their research notes, the ability to hear their own words repeated exactly as stated the first time creates a unique opportunity for reflection, contemplation, fine tuning, and revision.

Tape recorders and digital camera easily capture data and detail, ingredients that add interest to kids' writing. With easily accessible information to draw upon, sentences lengthen and word structures become more complex. And as kids' explanations become more expansive, adults can invite children to consult their audio and video records to build analogies, metaphors, and similes in written descriptions. New digital cameras come with a video feature. Using an I-Mac computer, kids can combine moving pictures and still images and edit them for presentations that include sound effects and voice-overs.

YOUNG WRITERS' BOOKSHELF FOR "I OBSERVE, I THINK . . . BECAUSE"

A Handful of Dirt. Raymond Bial. Walker, 2000. Beautiful color photographs show how close observation reveals the many forms of life found in soil.

ABCedar: An Alphabet of Trees. George Ella Lyon. Illustrated by Tom Parker. Orchard Books, 1996. Fascinating information about trees is presented in a unique alphabet.

Where Fish Go in Winter and Answers to Other Great Mysteries. Amy Goldman Koss. Price Stern Sloan, 1988. A model of how to answer science questions.

Questions: Poems of Wonder. Selected by Lee Bennett Hopkins. Illustrated by Carolyn Croll. HarperTrophy, 1992. Many science puzzles are explained in verse.

Is a Blue Whale the Biggest Thing There Is? Robert E. Wells. Albert Whitman, 1993. Big numbers and large sizes tickle the imagination as objects on our planet are grouped and compared with parts of the galaxy that are even larger.

What's Faster Than a Speeding Cheetah? Robert E. Wells. Albert Whitman, 1997. Facts about the speeds of some of the fastest moving animals on earth are presented using different parts of speech.

What's Smaller Than a Pygmy Shrew? Robert E. Wells. Edited by Christy Grant. Albert Whitman, 1995. A companion to *Is a Blue Whale the Biggest Thing There Is?*, this book focuses on the many forms of smallness.

I Wonder Why series from Kingfisher Books, including *I Wonder Why the Sea Is Salty: And Other Questions about the Oceans* (1997); *I Wonder Why the Sun Rises: And Other Questions about Time and Space* (1996); *I Wonder Why the Wind Blows: And Other Questions about Our Planet* (1994); and *I Wonder Why I Blink: And Other Questions about My Body* (1993).

Angel Hide and Seek. Ann Turner. Illustrated by Lois Ehlert. HarperCollins, 1998. The importance of looking closely is illustrated because seemingly familiar objects in the woods, sky, ice, and other places may also take the form of angels, depending on how one looks at things.

Attention-Grabbing Science Reports

Science Reports	TEACH	These Conventions *Unconventionally*
Writing Research Reports		Genre: Research reports
		• Opening
		• Body
		• Summary
Report Writing Strategies		Voice in nonfiction writing
• Presenting Facts Accurately and Engagingly		Analyzing and interpreting findings
		Descriptive writing
• Displaying Information Visually		Writing in the first person
• Using First-Person Narratives		Similes, metaphors, and analogies
• Drawing Research Conclusions		
• Making Scientific Models		
• Including Figurative Language		
Extensions: Great Paragraph Journeys		Paragraphing

"New Spin on Mars" announced the *Boston Globe* in June 2000 when high-resolution images from the Mars Global Surveyor revealed apparent signs of water erosion on pole-facing slopes far from the planet's equator. "I was dragged kicking and screaming to the conclusion that [the] grooves and channels must have been carved very recently by flows of running water," noted one of the scientists who authored a report based on the findings (Chandler A1, A16).

The story of the latest Mars discoveries grabs a reader's attention. As in so many other cases in science, existing theories about the solar system now must be revised because scientists did the research and then published their findings for a wider audience. In fact, writing is an essential feature of scientific inquiry, a way for scientists to enlarge and clarify the knowledge of each field of science study. To show young children ways to share the science information they are learning, virtually every elementary school teaches how to write a research report. Making children's research reports interesting and attention-grabbing is the approach we explore in this WOW.

Research reports are intended to provide factually accurate and readily understandable responses to clearly posed questions. Their format—opening, body, summary—asks writers to introduce a topic or question for investigation, present explanatory information in a series of paragraphs, and summarize the findings along with personal observations about what has been learned from the research. Some reports recreate the steps of the scientific method, beginning with an hypothesis statement, including examples of evidence collected, and ending with conclusions based on the findings.

Too often, children write their research reports in a formal, just-the-facts style, using either short, simple sentences or material copied directly from library sources. The reader has few clues about what it was that originally interested the writer in the subject. "How frustrating it is," observes teacher, principal, and researcher Shelley Harwayne (27), "to read a dull report on box turtles copied from an encyclopedia, and then find out the student shares a bedroom with a box turtle."

Enlivening children's reports beyond uninteresting recitations of facts involves what Harwayne (20, 22–26) describes as writing with "*chutzpah*, the Yiddish word for gall, guts, nerve, or brazenness." In her view, *chutzpah* translates into a willingness to confidently explore different ways to present ideas, viewpoints, and conclusions. Harwayne draws this potential for bold, assertive writing from three key strategies used by adult nonfiction writers: taking one's "*learning* seriously," interpreting and expressing information in a personal voice, and finding many ways to engage readers with the material.

Writing Research Reports

From a practical standpoint, adults can assist young children to become dynamic science report writers by reminding them that first and foremost what excites a young writer will also likely engage their audience. Kids need guidance in order to write about what they find intriguing, amazing, or wonder inspiring so that their intense feelings will energize their research writing.

At the center of report writing is a convention known as *voice*, a highly desirable quality that teachers want children to develop in their writing. *Voice* means a lively, compelling writing style where words "carry with them the sense that someone has actually written them" (Fletcher 68). Through voice, the personality and perspective of the writer becomes apparent by how she or he uses language and arranges words and sentences on a page. Voice gives children uniquely personal ways to share information or tell a story.

Children can use the following strategies to write interesting nonfiction reports. Each strategy is a vehicle for imparting voice, vibrancy, and uniqueness to a written presentation.

Report Writing Strategies

Presenting Facts Accurately and Engagingly

Accurate facts in research reports is vital: Information that is incorrect or out-of-date is of little value to readers. Yet factual writing does not need to be dull or uninteresting writing. Readers expect accuracy but also appreciate information presented in ways that spark their curiosity and maintain their interest.

Newspaper reporters, science magazine writers, and nonfiction book authors use many different formats to engage readers while still communicating facts. In his reports about meteors and rocks, Ben uses capital and lower case letters for dramatic impact in a short paragraph, easy-to-understand vocabulary in a report that sounds like an oral conversation, and a personally voiced opinion to finish a news story about the Lenoid Meteor Shower (Figure 6.10).

Capital and Lowercase Letters

Meteors can be as small as gravel or as BIG AS TEXAS.
I find that amazing.
How about you?

Factual Report

There are lots of ways rocks get formed. Here's two ways rocks are formed. 1) Sometimes when volcanos erupt the lava stays in one place, and after about a year later the lava cools down and it forms rock. 2) When sand clumps together and other stuff. After about 100 years a rock about this big will be formed. (Ben)

Personal News Story

Me and my Dad heard there was going to be a meteor shower tonight [the Lenoid Meteor Shower]. We heard it on the radio. They found this out because the satellite picked up signals and sent them to the space center, NASA. I'm staying up and watching it. I think it will be really neat. It starts at 9 and ends at ten.

Figure 6.10 *Ben's reports on meteors and rocks.*

Displaying Information Visually

Pop-up, see-through, fold-out science books depict animals in motion; produce cross-sectional views of the human body; present castles, pyramids, and cathedrals in three-dimensions; and display all sorts of information in unique ways. These books are popular because readers understand science ideas more easily when description and explanation can be seen as well as read.

The same principle is true for children's research reports. Words combined with pictures and diagrams are an effective way to capture an audience's attention. Many science topics benefit from visual presentations. Ben used a diagram to show how rocks are formed from the lava flows. Ian provided visual step-by-step directions about how to assemble a paper airplane (Figure 6.11).

Using First-Person Accounts

John McPhee (*Annals of the Former World*), Peter Matthiessen (*The Snow Leopard*), Barry Lopez (*Arctic Dreams*), and Carl Safina (*Song for a Blue Ocean*) are a few of the well-known science and nature authors who present material through first-person narrative accounts. A first-person voice takes readers inside the writer's thoughts to share the writer's personal reactions to events.

Figure 6.11 *Ian's and Ben's diagrams.*

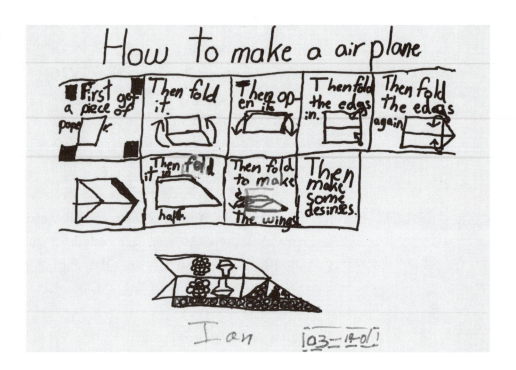

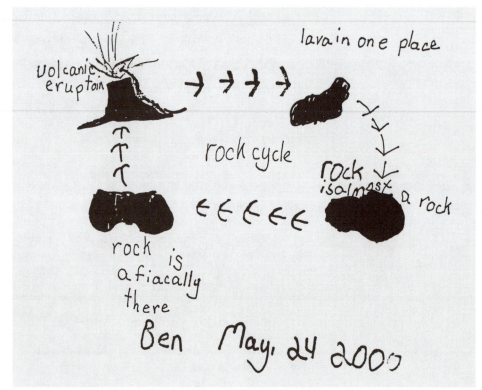

A first-person writing style is natural for children, since they are the fact-finders. It is easy for them to explain what "I" or "we" have found. This writing style gives readers a sense of what it was like as young scientists make discoveries. In the reports above, Siobhan and Izzy describe the results of their experiments with long cardboard tubes angled against a five-foot-high structure the kids could climb. They were dropping objects down the tubes from the top or propelling items up the tubes from the bottom to see the force of gravity at work (Figure 6.12).

Figure 6.12

Siobhan's and Izzy's long cardboard tube experiments.

Translation of Siobhan's report: (**A**) Today with the tubes I did an experiment. This is how I did it. I tried throwing a blue ball up the tube, but it wouldn't go up the tube. I think it is because the tube was on a slant.

Translation of Izzy's report: (**B**) I put down a yellow car that was squishy and a car that was made out of metal. The metal car won [the race] because the yellow car was squishy.

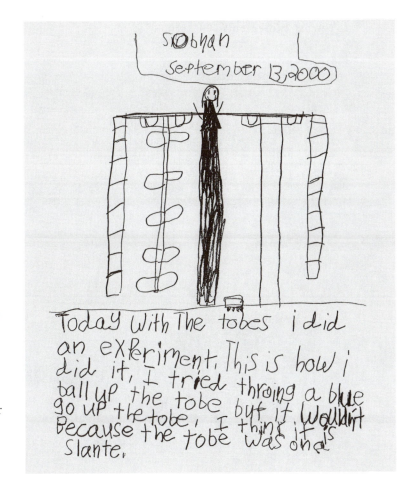

(A)

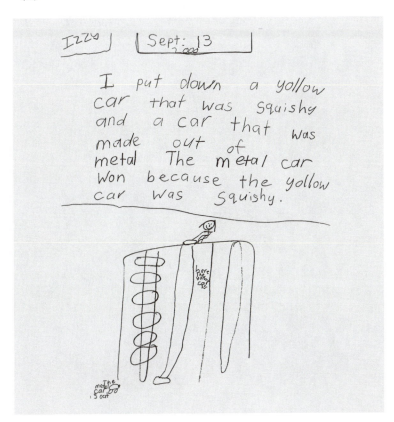

(B)

Drawing Research Conclusions

Kids can enlarge their first-person accounts by drawing conclusions about what happened and why it happened that way. Conclusions stretch thinking, giving writers a chance to pause, reflect about the "whys" of events, and consider what might change the experience the next time.

A racquetball and a notebook give kids an action-based way to practice writing conclusions. Small, bouncy, and pliant, racquetballs are an ideal source for experimental data. Kids can take them outside the school or even home overnight to conduct all kinds of short investigations: How high will they bounce on different surfaces? How far will they roll? Will they hop into different-sized containers when tossed? After observing the behavior of racquetballs, second graders drew the conclusions shown in Figure 6.13.

Figure 6.13

Children's racquetball investigations.
Translation: Gravity Works: If you put more pressure on the ball, it will go higher. If you drop a ball down the stairs, it will go faster.

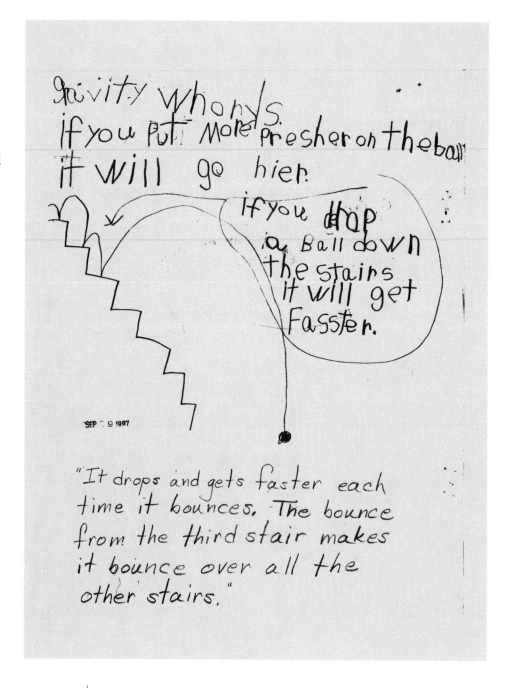

Making Scientific Models

Kids love to build with boxes, blocks, clay, sand, Legos, or whatever will stack or stand. Constructing is a form of imaginative play that teaches about design and engineering—size, shape, weight, height, cause, effect, and revision. Building is practice for making models of science events that try to recreate what happens in the real world.

Model-making occasions all kinds of writing possibilities as kids experience the mystery and uncertainty of science research: Will the model work? How should the design be modified to achieve better results? What forces or processes are causing things to happen the way they do?

Young scientists—three girls and three boys—in Sharon's class built domino structures in the shapes of snakes on two different table tops and connected them via a cardboard ramp. They wanted to see if the falling dominos from one table could push a small toy car down the ramp and make the dominos fall on the other table. As part of their work, they wrote about their experimental models and drew diagrams of the construction (Figure 6.14).

Scientists build models so that they and other viewers can more easily understand complex scientific information. They combine written language with diagrams and/or figures in a model that informs and demonstrates. When young writers construct science models, they too focus on readers as they decide what information to emphasize within their designs.

In Ruth's class, the children studied reptiles, learning among other things, that these creatures lay eggs and have scales and spines. "How would you tell others what a reptile is?" Ruth asked as an opener for science model building. "What are the important ideas you want to get across? If someone were walking by, how would you interest them in what you know?"

Fiona sculpted a clay model alligator, then added separate drawings of the scales, eggs, and shell mounted on black paper. For the scales, she used shiny textured paper that looked and felt rough to the touch. Alongside the model, she wrote "an alligator eats a mouse for lunch." Torey constructed a clay snake with its eggs, specifically labeling the nest and the spine. Other children made drawings of reptiles highlighting important information in bright colors and making arrows pointing to it. In so doing, they learned how a model

---

Report One

Hey you! This is the domino structure. It is built by: Mike, Me, Brianna, Chantel, and Quitze. Brianna knocked it down twice! Chantel made up the idea. We did not only make the big snake, we made a small baby snake! I invented a tower to knock a car to knock the head [of the snake on the other table].

Report Two

Me, Julio, Mike, Quitze & Brianna found a way to not knock the dominos down. Julio put ten blocks and if the dominos fell it would not knock [them] down.

Figure 6.14 *Children's domino structure reports.*

that communicates information is different from an experimental model that does something (like a marble machine or a domino structure). At the same time, each model shares a common purpose, communicating what someone knows so that others understand it.

Including Figurative Language

Figurative language in research reports lets readers "see" ideas and concepts in action while also appreciating the emotional response of the writer to the event. Writers use similes (explicit comparisons), metaphors (implicit comparisons), or analogies (explaining the unfamiliar in terms of the familiar) to draw readers into the material, and children can too. Here are figurative language responses to trees, rain, and the sun by a group of second graders:

- The branches look like a rocking chair, back and forth, back and forth.
- The trees are swaying to the rhythm of the wind drums.
- Sun is like hot lava pouring on you!!! And if you come too close you will melt!!!
- The rain is falling like rice on the ground and then I eat it.
- The clouds are like a sponge.

To include figurative language in her volcano report, Brianna created a pretend dialogue between an author and readers and finished with a descriptive metaphor in the final sentence (Figure 6.15).

Figurative language also enhances the description of models such as the one Jamie made of a hypothetical solar system. To assemble her design, she took seven small white paper plates and colored the ridged edges on the front of the plates red and blue all the way around the seven centers. Then she covered their backs with silver paper. Next, she taped the six plates (planets) surrounding the seventh plate (sun). In the sun plate's white middle, she colored red, orange, green, and yellow rings. Finally, she poked a small hole through the center of the sun, looped a length of shiny ribbon through it, and held the entire system in her hand. She wrote: "This is a solar system that I made. When you hold it by the string, it looks like a hat and a light, and when you put it down flat it looks like flowers."

EXTENSIONS

Great Paragraph Journeys

Attention-grabbing science reports are opportunities for investigating how and why to construct paragraphs. As a writing convention, paragraphs aid readers' comprehension by organizing sentences into groups where each group explains one main idea. In report writing, the goal is to convey known facts and current theories to readers so they clearly understand a topic. Paragraphing and report writing work together as an information-sharing team.

Reading a report of well-arranged paragraphs is like reading a map clearly designed to get someone to a destination with ease. This is why paragraphs commonly begin with a topic sentence stating the main idea, followed by additional sentences explaining the main idea with illustrative and informative details. A new topic, a shift in thinking, or further explanation necessitates another paragraph.

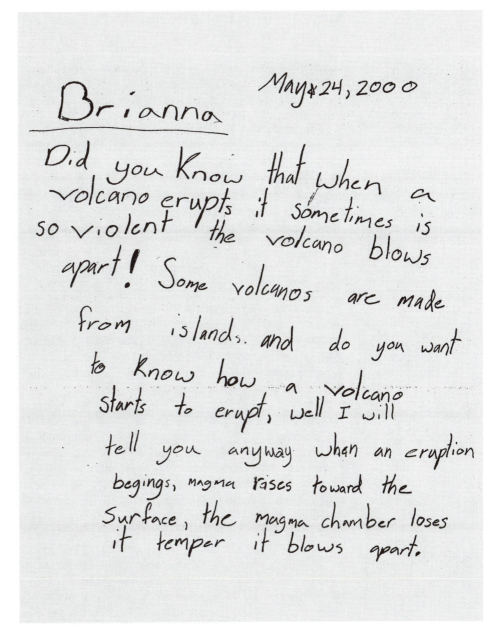

Brianna   May ♯ 24, 2000

Did you know that when a volcano erupts it sometimes is so violent the volcano blows apart! Some volcanos are made from islands. and do you want to know how a volcano starts to erupt, well I will tell you anyway when an eruption begings, magma rises toward the Surface, the magma chamber loses it temper it blows apart.

Figure 6.15

Brianna's volcano report.

As inexperienced paragraphers, children's sentences often flow together into one long narrative without any sorting of ideas. Or, children copy vocabulary, phrases, and sentences verbatim from books and websites, regardless of whether they understand the meaning of the terms. Sometimes they do both, producing a confusion of writing that leaves readers unenlightened by the report.

Since crafting paragraphs is inextricably part of the process of report writing, learning how paragraphs transport readers through a text requires that young writers know:

- Why writers use paragraphs.
- How to make sentences into interesting and informative paragraphs.
- Why paragraph order is important.

Why Writers Use Paragraphs

Writers use paragraphs to present information clearly to readers. In science, events like the phases of the moon, growth of plants and animals, and the orbits of planets around the sun happen in cycles, making them natural topics for practice in arranging reports into informative paragraphs. Ideally, paragraphs flow easily, one to the next, creating a smooth current of thoughts and ideas.

Clearly organizing reader-friendly writing into paragraphs is an essential skill when elementary school students are asked to respond to open-ended essay questions on achievement tests, as in the following taken from a statewide Massachusetts science exam for fourth graders:

> Jamal wanted to learn the fastest way to melt ice on a road. His teacher, Ms. Gonzalez, asked the class for some ideas on how ice on a road is melted.
>
> a. List at least TWO ways that ice on a road can be melted.
> b. Design and describe an experiment you could use to see which of the two ways is fastest.

Achieving a good score on the ice-melting experiment question requires a writer to combine scientific knowledge about heat, light, and chemical interactions with a clear presentation of information in a series of paragraphs. A report might use two paragraphs to describe how to melt ice on the road and then use additional paragraphs to explain how the writer proposes to turn ice into water quickly. A child who knows the information may easily receive a low score if the science answer is presented in a random order—for instance, if the middle of the planned experiment is discussed before the beginning, or if the conclusions of the essay are given before the different ways ice can be melted.

One way to explore paragraph construction is through a game that resembles making a map of a tourist attraction. To begin, everyone researches a topic together. This may be a short research project over a few days or a longer one that is part of the science curriculum. Either way, at the end of the research, kids will know enough about the topic to write separate facts and information on pieces of paper or index cards. If the topic is rocks, kids might record ages, colors, sizes, where rocks are found, and how they are formed—one sentence or phrase per paper. These papers hold the information that readers (or visitors to the tourist attraction) will enjoy learning about "Rock Land."

Randomly placing the cards on a large blank paper laid out on the floor creates what looks like a snowstorm of information, blown every which way. It is visually apparent that no one can navigate through all of these pieces of paper without some order. Kids need to create the roads, parks, and attractions of Rock Land to get visitors to their destinations easily. The cards are scooped up and returned to each writer so the group can sort them into topics as they would arrange playing cards into suits.

The class begins to structure the information by drawing streets and attractions on the paper. Someone names a road: "Color Avenue." Everyone with information about rock color puts her or his papers along this road. Someone else suggests "Big and Little Park" where information about rock sizes all congregate. Naming areas and streets, moving and sorting facts, discussing which ones should be where continues until every card has a group—or until a single paper sits on a road alone, signaling more information could be added to it. With all of the information collected and sorted, visitors can make their way through all the locations of Rock Land!

If kids desire to go one more step, 3-D constructions could be built from cardboard boxes or milk cartons and decorated, with paragraphs written on them that states the information laid out on the cards. Then the cards are replaced by a 3-D model of Rock Land.

As a map of a town helps someone go from one place to another, a sequence of paragraphs lets readers enjoy their journey to learn the information about rocks, or any other topic. A map or outline could now be made to guide the visitor so the content of the trip makes sense. One might begin with a paragraph describing how the earth was formed as one huge rock, before moving to a series of paragraphs about the main types of rocks (sedimentary, metamorphic, and igneous), and concluding with a paragraph about how rocks are formed. It is the writers in the class who are in charge of making the map. They decide in what order the visitor should read the paragraphs to create the most informative and interesting visit.

A second way to practice structuring paragraphs is an old idea but an entertaining one that kids enjoy repeating. A two- or three-paragraph text from a science book or magazine is copied, cut into sentences, shaken up in a basket, and introduced as an activity called "Paragraph Puzzles."

To begin their work, kids pair up as Topic Detectives. One youngster from each pair of detectives picks a sentence out of the basket. Then the second detective of the pair reads the sentence aloud to the class. Other detective teams listen, trying to identify sentences that contain information similar to theirs. When a similarity appears, the two Detective Teams join to become a Topic Team. This procedure continues until all of the sentences are read aloud and a few Topic Teams exist. Some sentences must be reread in an effort to determine which of the Topic Teams they should join. The teams assemble their sentence puzzles, constructing a paragraph that makes reading and understanding the information clear and easy. Then they tape the sentences together.

When all of the teams have finished and the class is back together, each Topic Team reads their paragraph aloud. The kids then suggest how the paragraphs might be sequenced to help readers understand the information. The paragraphs are hung on a chart in the order that the class decides makes the best sense. Now copies of the original paragraphs are handed out to each Topic Team to compare how the author of the piece arranged the sentences and the paragraphs for readers. A discussion ensues about which version seems clearer and how writers construct paragraphs in their writing.

How to Make Sentences into Interesting and Informative Paragraphs

Importantly, notes teacher Barry Lane (122), "students don't need to learn how to write paragraphs, but rather, how to identify ones they have already written." Like a potter, sculptor, or other craftsperson shaping raw material into a finished piece of work, young writers can revise the content and the order of their sentences to improve clarity for readers.

Arranging sentences into interesting and informative paragraphs is the next piece of the paragraphing puzzle. This is how youngsters display enthusiasm for a topic in their writing while still maintaining scientific relevance and factual accuracy. Ideally, every paragraph includes voice and verve rather than a "just the facts" style series of simple sentences. Livelier paragraphs make readers feel that their trip through the information is worth taking.

It is important to let children write first, form paragraphs later. For example, as kids take notes in "I Wonder" journals or on "I Observe . . . I Think . . . Because" cards, they are not yet ready to form their paragraphs. They need to be able to record their questions and observations in a free-form style. Written notes, even fragmentary ones, can be used later to transport the writer back to the moment when important events took place in the classroom aquarium, at the playground sundial, as the magnets attracted and repelled different objects, and so on. Questions like "What do you see happening?" invite children to theorize about "What might explain this phenomenon?"

Here are some strategies for children and adults to use in shaping sentences into interesting and informative paragraphs, starting with initial drafts.

- *Ask the question "What is the point I am trying to make?"* Writing is a way to make clearer what a writer wants to communicate to readers. Physicist and Nobel laureate Richard Feynman, whose career spanned the Manhattan Project to the Challenger Space Shuttle disaster, insisted on writing down his lectures before he gave them so he could be clear about what he was going to say. Ask children to reread their writing and the writing of their classmates. If they find themselves confused, rearrange the order of the sentences. Many times the information is already there; it just needs to be presented more clearly using a reader-friendly sequence of points. Sometimes, more sentences must be added before readers will understand the main idea.

- *Find the main idea.* Writing guides and grammar books are unanimous in their insistence that each paragraph have its own main idea. Too many pieces of information grouped together leaves everyone confused about meaning and message. We are using bullet points in this section and in many other places in this book for just this reason. We want readers to digest one idea at a time. Kids might map out the main points and make each one a separate paragraph. This may result in several brief statements that can be expanded into separate paragraphs or combined into a sequence of related points within one paragraph.

- *Let different paragraphs have different lengths depending on their purpose.* Commonly, a paragraph signifies that a new idea is being introduced, a new person is speaking, a new point is being emphasized, or it is time for readers to pause and consider what has been said (Lunsford and Connors 46). Invite young writers to read over their drafts and see where new ideas or new speakers show the need for a new paragraph.

- *Avoid letting paragraphs go on and on without breaks for readers.* Our colleague, educational economist Byrd Jones, used the word processing program on his computer to count the number of words in his draft paragraphs. When a paragraph was more than 125 words, he either edited out words or created two paragraphs to do the work previously done by one for ease of reading and understanding. Young writers can look over their writing and see if their paragraphs have too many words, then modify them to make the information easier to read.

- *Plan out the roles for the different sentences that make up a paragraph.* Generally, the lead sentence is the topic sentence that introduces what the paragraph is about. Sometimes in writing a first draft, a good topic sentence ends up somewhere else in the paragraph or is missing altogether. Ask young writers to think about which sentence best communicates the major point and make that the topic sentence. Once the topic sentence is clear, the next several sentences can be used to support and elaborate the main idea. The last sentence in the paragraph also has an important role, providing a transition to the next point or building a dramatic tension that heightens a reader's interest about what is to follow next.

Paragraph Order

Some Bugs Glow in the Dark (I Didn't Know That), *Mighty Machines: Truck,* or *Wild, Wet and Windy: The Weather from Tornadoes to Lightning* by Claire Llewellyn are visual models for paragraphing science information. Each of the pages explains different science facts using attractively arranged illustrations and a series of numbered paragraphs. Pictures and facts connect together to present a complete explanation, showing children how paragraphs organize a text into bite-sized groups of information rather than making a reader consume everything at once in one long descriptive narrative.

Like clearly organized travel plans that make for a satisfying journey, well-arranged paragraphs produce an entertaining reading experience. One way to demonstrate how writers order paragraphs is to use the well-known analogy of a bus trip where:

the bus driver	is the writer
the passengers	are the reader/audience
the bus	is the writing
the stops along the route	are the paragraphs
the bus route	is the paragraph order
the destination	is the explanation of the topic

A bus trip has a destination, scheduled stops, and an arranged distance for the complete trip. Writing has a destination (communicating or explaining a topic) and scheduled stops (paragraphs and their order) as well as distance (the length and breadth of a report). All of these are determined by the writer, acting as the bus driver, who designs the writing for the learning and enjoyment of the readers or travelers. As with real bus trips, passengers/readers may ride the whole distance (read the entire report) or board the bus for a portion of the route (scan the text and read only a few paragraphs).

One way to illustrate the bus trip analogy uses a model yellow school bus, a paper road with bends and turns, bright paper arrows, and small paper billboards (or small write-on/wipe-off boards that serve as billboards) on which to write topic sentences or central points from the first draft of a report. These props appear to be game pieces. Their purpose is to enable individuals, pairs, groups, or the whole class to plan a writing journey from beginning to end: determining the stops, deciding the topics, ordering the progression or sequence of paragraphs, and establishing the central points that the report will explain.

The props let kids write topics on the billboards to post on the roads. While comparing which order they think is preferable, they develop awareness of how paragraphs present information to gain and sustain reader interest. Zachary's science report, a one-paragraph summary of what he learned about rocks after a visit with a librarian, parallels a nonstop bus trip down only one street (Figure 6.16).

A one-paragraph journey is one of Zachary's options as a reporter, but he could also create a longer report by adding more information using more than one paragraph. He might have bus stops at volcanoes, minerals, and each of the three types of rocks. Creating paragraphs for these ideas makes a longer, more informative trip for readers.

Brianna's seed report has more length, but now needs paragraphs to communicate its chronology clearly to readers—since she wrote it over several days (Figure 6.17).

Ask young writers what questions they have after reading Zachary's and Brianna's reports. By its very nature, a single paragraph can answer only a few questions, concentrating on what can be learned in a one stop trip. When the bus stops three, four, or even five times during its journey, more information or facts can be added through the use of paragraphs. Every writer must consider what she or he wants to communicate to readers and then decide how many paragraphs will help do the job well.

> Did you know that the lava goes up and then it comes out and it cools? And did you know that a crystal can be mostly all rocks? Did you know that there are three kinds of rocks that's on most mountains? They are called igneous, sedimentary, and metamorphic. These rocks I'm holding are wet and smooth.

Figure 6.16   *Zachary's report about rocks.*

Original Text

My seeds are getting soft and scrunchy and when I first checked my seeds my lima bean was starting to get soft and then a few hours later my bush bean was starting to get soft. Then the lima bean looked even softer and the lima bean looked like it got bigger. The seeds look like little scrunched up clouds. When you touch the seeds they feel like the skin of the seed. Ms. Edwards's seeds are starting to sprout but the bush bean has a bigger sprout and the lima bean just started to sprout. My seeds don't have skin anymore because it lost its skin. I know that my seeds are going to grow unless something bad happens. Now my seeds look like regular beans. Today the seeds look like they got a little bigger.

Paragraphed Text

My seeds are getting soft and scrunchy and when I first checked my seeds my lima bean was starting to get soft and then a few hours later my bush bean was starting to get soft.

Then the lima bean looked even softer and the lima bean looked like it got bigger. The seeds look like little scrunched up clouds. When you touch the seeds they feel like the skin of the seed. Ms. Edwards's seeds are starting to sprout but the bush bean has a bigger sprout and the lima bean just started to sprout.

My seeds don't have skin anymore because it lost its skin. I know that my seeds are going to grow unless something bad happens. Now my seeds look like regular beans.

Today the seeds look like they got a little bigger.

Figure 6.17 *Brianna's report about seeds.*

Young Writers' Bookshelf for Science Reports

Cow. Jules Older. Illustrated by Lyn Severance. Charlesbridge Publishing, 1997. Basic facts about cows spring to life with rhythm, rhyme, and illustrations by the same artist who created the *Ben and Jerry's* ice cream font.

If You Hopped Like a Frog. David M. Schwartz. Illustrated by James Warhola. Scholastic Press, 1999. Lavish illustrations and amazing science facts explained in one paragraph compare what would happen to humans if they could do what animals can do.

The Icky Bug Alphabet Book. Jerry Pallotta. Illustrated by Ralph Masiello. Charlesbridge Publishing, 1986. Every letter explains a science fact with colorful illustrations and entertaining language that is one paragraph long. See also *The Yucky Reptile Alphabet Book* (1989), *The Frog Alphabet Book* (1990), *The Freshwater Alphabet Book* (1996), *The Butterfly Alphabet Book* (1995), and *The Dinosaur Alphabet Book* (1990), among many by the same author and illustrator team.

Out of the Ocean. Debra Frasier. Harcourt Brace, 1998. A beautifully illustrated first-person story of a little girl and her mother who collect things that wash up along the beach near their home. Photos and science facts about many of these objects are included.

From Seed to Sunflower. Gerald Legg. Illustrated by Carolyn Scrace. Franklin Watts, 1998. Every page is a new paragraph of facts about the life cycle of sunflowers.

Picking Apples and Pumpkins. Amy Hutchings. Photographs by Richard Hutchings. Cartwheel Books, 1994. Every page is a new paragraph about the delights of freshly picked fruits and vegetables.

CHAPTER SUMMARY

"I'm an explorer, okay? I like to find out," Richard Feynman once observed, framing science as a process of limitless investigation and exploration. Chapter Six, "Science," explores the connections between scientific investigations and creative writing. Children are scientists, constantly trying to figure out the world around them. Intrigued by so many different mysteries, they are eager to explore and discover new information about virtually every scientific topic that is part of the elementary school curriculum.

The science and writing connection features three concepts: the scientific method, inquiry-based learning, and nonfiction writing. The scientific method offers children a way to organize their science study by posing questions, conducting research, formulating initial hypotheses, testing those tentative explanations experimentally, drawing conclusions, and communicating findings to different audiences.

Inquiry-based learning emphasizes the importance of children being active investigators rather than passive recipients of science ideas. Inquiry methods place kids directly in the role of a scientist who is constantly "re-searching" questions to discover how and why things work the way they do.

Writing is a key ingredient for children learning about the scientific method through inquiry-based learning. As they do their work, young scientists write for themselves, recording questions, taking notes, and drawing conclusions. Writing allows kids to organize their investigations while reflecting on their results. Children also write about science for wider audiences, conveying activities and findings in a research report. Such research reports benefit from attention-grabbing, interest-maintaining writing styles that use elements of nonfiction, fiction, and poetry in the presentation.

CHAPTER SEVEN

Social Studies

Who Came Down That Road? a powerfully evocative picture book by George Ella Lyon opens with a mother and her young son walking in the woods where they happen upon a rarely used pathway, barely visible as it recedes into the forest.

"Who came down that road, mama?" asks the child.

His mother's answer describes a very ancient road that has been traveled by settlers in covered wagons, civil war soldiers, native peoples farming the land, ice age mastodons, and before that, a primordial sea teeming with early life forms. Spare prose and cinematic illustrations illuminate a timeline of human experience.

Present-day roads, rivers, and passageways invite explorations of past, present, and future. Standing on the sidewalk of North Pleasant Street, which bisects the University of Massachusetts and runs in a mostly straight line from north to south through the town, Sharon asked her students: "Who came down this road to our school?"

"I came down that road two years ago," replied Sasha who was in her second year at the school.

"I came down that road last year," added Julio.

"I just came down that road," said Michael, the newest student in the class who had just arrived in the community.

Children's books extend the study of roads and rivers to the modern-day lives of people all over the world; for example:

- *My Painted House, My Friendly Chicken and Me* by Maya Angelou uses striking photographs and a first-person narrative to describe the daily life of Thandi, an eight-year-old Ndebele girl living in South Africa.
- *The Block* combines reproductions from Romane Bearden's mural with poems by Langston Hughes to portray life in one Harlem neighborhood.
- *Children of Clay* by Rina Swentzell shows how three Tewa children are learning their family's craft of clay pottery in the Santa Clara Pueblo in New Mexico.
- *Gabriella's Song* by Candace Fleming describes the musical tones heard by a young girl as she makes her way along the streets and beside the canals of Venice, Italy.

Standing alongside a street, river, or trail, every child is an active participant in an immense human story and a unique individual whose choices, actions, and decisions affect not only her or his own life, but the lives of other people in the community, nation, and world. Chapter Seven, "Social Studies," invites children to think of themselves as part of a parade of history-making individuals, neither the first nor the last people to live in their community.

Futurist Alvin Toffler has suggested that eight hundred lifetimes (of approximately sixty-five to seventy years per generation) recede into history behind contemporary people, stretching backward in time more than fifty thousand years to the beginnings of humanity. While no one is sure when the first peoples arrived on the North and South American continents (thirteen thousand years ago is one recent estimate), kids can start from any local pathway and engage in inquiries and investigations about:

- *The Past*, by asking: "Who came before them to this place?" "How did they live?" "What did they eat and wear?" "What struggles and successes marked their lives?" By asking about the past, kids expand their thinking beyond the here and now while learning how to differentiate chronologically between present, past, and very ancient times. Natural history study can be included as well by exploring what kinds of birds, animals, fishes, insects, and other creatures lived here too.
- *The Present*, by asking: "Who am I?" "How am I the same as and different from other people?" "Who are my close and ancient ancestors and how do they affect my life today?" By locating themselves as members of families, schools, and communities, kids affirm their place in the long and evolving cycle of human experience.
- *The Future*, by asking: "Who will arrive in the years, decades, and centuries to come?" "What will their lives be like?" "What values and ideals will they express?" By envisioning the future, children reinforce their own positions as history makers whose choices and decisions today are integral parts of creating the world of tomorrow.

Learning about oneself and learning the histories of many peoples, cultures, and civilizations, notes the National Center for History in the Schools (1), "directly contribute to the education of the *public citizen*, but they uniquely contribute to the nurturing of the *private individual* as well. Historical memory is the key to self-identity, to seeing one's place in the stream of time, and one's connectedness with all of humankind." The WOWs in this chapter frame a context for children to consider their own actions in relation to others:

- **WOW 22: A Child's EncycloMEdia** focuses children's attention on the events of their own lives as members of schools, families, and communities. An encycloMEdia combines portfolio, scrapbook, and journal into a living museum of the person. In it, kids record personal milestones, recall memorable activities, and save creative writing and drawing. "Measuring Me" investigations explore the physiological and biological commonalities among human beings: pulse rate and blood pressure, body temperature, how eyes regulate light, how skin blocks germs, and how the human skeleton stands and stretches. "Extensions: His-Stories and Her-Stories Make History" uses multicultural autobiographies and biographies as well as historical fiction to generate writing personal memories.
- **WOW 23: Community Rules!** uses codes of conduct and behavior, topics of great interest to kids, as a foundation for exploring how and why rules are formed—both in the microsocieties of classrooms, schools, and families as well as in larger social groups of communities and countries. As kids participate in the writing of rules, they also learn about how sentences communicate different messages to readers. Expectations for behavior expressed in an interrogative or question-asking sentence carry different meanings than the same rules presented in an imperative or command-giving sentence. "Extensions: The Rules of Democracy" draws a parallel between rulemaking in schools and voting and active citizenship in a democratic society.

A Child's EncycloMEdia

EncycloMEdias	TEACH	These Conventions *Unconventionally*
Creating an EncycloMEdia		Genre: Personal narratives First-person writing Historical concepts • Past, present, and future • Chronological thinking
"Measuring Me" • Investigation One: Measuring Pulse Rate and Blood Pressure • Investigation Two: Body Temperature • Investigation Three: Eyes Regulate Light • Investigation Four: Skin Blocks Germs • Investigation Five: Skeletons Stand and Stretch		
Extensions: His-Stories and Her-Stories Make History		Genre: Autobiography and memories Multicultural his-stories and her-stories One paragraph memories

Allie wrote "My Christmas Day—Chapter 1: The Chair" after returning from her school's holiday break. It recorded an important historical event in her life—the Christmas gifts she received and so enjoyed. Sharon asked her to write about her presents so she would not forget how happy she felt about them.

Allie's memory introduces an EncycloMEdia, a child's ongoing personal record of past and present, compiled and arranged as a reference book. An EncycloMEdia is a place for children to write and illustrate events, places, and people that:

- Define "Who am I?"
- Describe "What is important to me?"
- Record "What do I want to remember?"

An EncycloMEdia builds an autobiographical portrait of a young writer by collecting important facts, ideas, and memories from a child's own point of view.

Creating an EncycloMEdia

The term *encycloMEdia* comes from a two-part play on the word "encyclopedia." First, it is entirely about one person, hence an encycloMEdia features "me." Whatever a writer finds meaningful becomes part of a record of the past and present to be read in the future. Second, it uses many "media" as recording tools. In this collection of a child's personal history appear writing and drawing, illustrations, photographs, art, sculptures, voice and video tapes, and computer CDs. Just as an encyclopedia fills a shelf, an encycloMEdia might fill a suitcase!

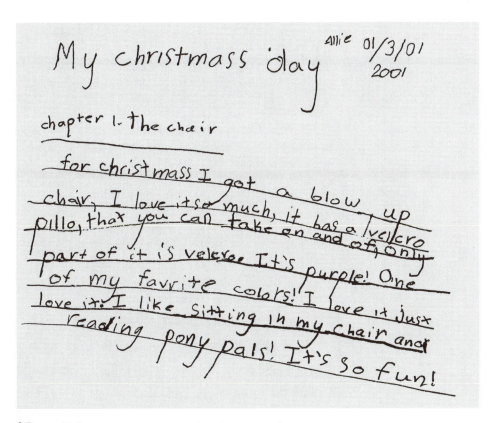

Figure 7.1   *Allie's "Chapter 1: The Chair." Translation:*

My Christmas Day   01/3/01

Chapter 1: The Chair

For Christmas I got a blow up chair. I love it so much. It has a Velcro pillow that you can take on and off. Only part of it is Velcro. It's purple. One of my favorite colors. I love it, just love it. I like sitting in my chair and reading Pony Pals. It's so fun!

Many elementary school students construct personal timelines or assemble "All About Me Books" that record information about themselves and their classmates. These writing activities initiate the study of history and social studies by viewing each student as a history maker whose choices and decisions matter in the larger course of events. Adult authors compose memoirs or autobiographies that tell personal stories in unique ways. These invite readers to become acquainted with the author through first-person descriptions of aspirations, disappointments, and reflections set within a context of the time in which the writer is living.

An encycloMEdia builds a "museum of the person" by combining features of three different types of record keeping systems that children and adults use to save personally meaningful information:

- *Scrapbooks* where children keep track of notable accomplishments and achievements. "Dear Ms. Edwards," wrote second-grader Gabrielle, "I broke two world records. I held my breath for 1 minute and 13 seconds." This note could easily become an entry in an EncycloMEdia as can Jacob's account of a swim meet (Figure 7.2).

  Kids can save clippings from newspapers, pictures and photographs from family trips, letters from relatives and friends, or autographs to affix onto pages of a blank book.

- *Journals or Diaries* that preserve children's written commentaries about memorable events or day-to-day activities as well as kids' reflections about and responses to what happened, like Rachel's description of the day she got her picture taken at school (Figure 7.3).

- *Portfolios* that store collectible examples of children's creative self-expressions— stories, drawings, poems, pictures, arts and crafts projects, or other types of writing and art.

The idea of starting and maintaining an encycloMEdia is very appealing to children. The word itself is intriguing, and kids learn its pronunciation, spelling, and meaning when its purpose becomes clear to them. By definition, an encyclopedia is a resource book containing all known information, arranged by important topics. Many youngsters have used an online computer database, consulted a multivolume library collection, or read informational books on topics from dinosaurs to dolls. They recognize that something "encyclopedic" is comprehensive, and they welcome the idea of an encyclopedia about themselves as an exciting challenge, different from anything they have made before.

> Today at swimming I was doing twenty-five free style and my time was a 16, that is 16 seconds. I needed to knock off two seconds to get the record for twenty-five free style, and if I knock off three seconds I will break the record time. Last year at age groups my time was for twenty-five yard free style was seventeen seconds and eighteen milliseconds. But I got one second off. That's very fast. Whoa! I'm the fastest eight and under in the world, or galaxy, or universe, or galaxy and the universe put together.

Figure 7.2 *Jacob's account of his swim meet.*

Figure 7.3

Rachel's description of herself.

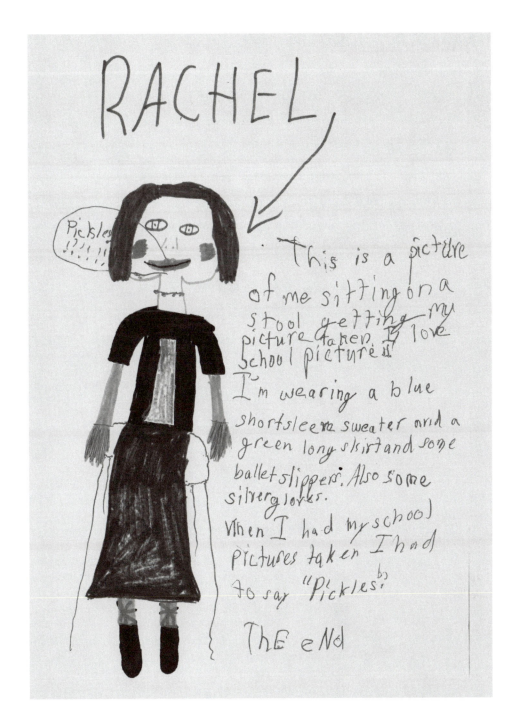

There are many ways to store the different "media" that kids decide to include in their encycloMEdia. A large-size, heavy cardboard pizza box is one good system. Different-sized sheets of paper fit easily inside, letting kids save everything from small notes to large picture poems or drawings. Photographs and other materials that should not be folded or bent fit inside as well. The exterior of the pizza box is a large palette where kids may design a personal display that makes the container uniquely their own. Just as cereal boxes display pictures and information about famous athletes, this container reflects the owner.

Another way to organize an encycloMEdia is with big sheets (9″ × 12″ or 12″ × 18″) of art paper made into a scrapbook format. Using different-colored paper for various sections and putting more than one piece of writing on one sheet, several sheets can be spiral bound together to form an issue or section of a larger collection.

"Measuring Me"

"Measuring Me" is a way for children to begin an encycloMEdia by recording information about anatomy and physiology. The resulting measurements are simultaneously unique to each individual child, yet universal to the human race. Children learn that they have much in common biologically with every other person in the community, country, and world—regardless of skin color, nationality, home language, or physical appearance.

Human genome research reveals that 99.9 percent of all humans share the same genetic makeup. The remaining one-tenth of one percent is responsible for variations in external appearance among population groups. Genetically, people are more alike than commonly assumed, contradicting the idea that "race" is a biologically meaningful delineation. DNA studies reveal that "on average, 88 percent to 90 percent of the differences between people occur within their local populations, while only about 10 percent to 12 percent of the differences distinguish one population, or race, from one another" (Angier 1, 6).

Skin tone, hair and eye color, and other external features are the basis for harmful stereotypes and superficial judgments ("blond is prettier than brown" or "tall is better than short"). Kids hear such statements all the time in the daily culture or among peers. When derogatory remarks are left unchallenged by adults, kids assume that surface characteristics actually make substantive differences in who people are or what they can do. Prejudice and discrimination have roots in such misinformation about people and their creative potentials.

To focus children's attention on features human beings share in common and to highlight specific information that makes a difference to each child's health and well-being, we investigate five biological topics:

- Pulse rate and blood pressure
- Body temperature
- Eyes measure and regulate light
- Skin protects us from germs
- Skeletons and bones

Each investigation is part of the standard health curriculum taught in most school districts. Some of them require specialized equipment and an experienced person such as the school nurse for accurate measurement. The information-gathering process allows kids to "see" not-visible-from-the-outside features of themselves that are part of the human body's self-regulating and self-protecting systems.

Writing is an integral part of the data collection for "Measuring Me," both as a way to record measurements and to describe kids' reflections about what they learn through these investigations. As writers, children formulate "I Wonder" questions, record research notes, and author interest-grabbing science reports about different topics.

Following are the procedures and materials needed for "Measuring Me" investigations.

Investigation One: Measuring Pulse Rate and Blood Pressure (at rest and after exercising)

Materials needed: Blood pressure cuff (called a sphygmomanometer), a stethoscope, and a data recording sheet.

Blood flow is one of the human body's self-regulating systems that must be kept free from obstruction in order to function well. An elaborate system of arteries and veins carries blood to and from the heart giving the body's organs the oxygen they require while clearing away the waste. To learn how the vascular system functions, students first make a pictorial representation of the arteries and veins of the blood system leading to and emerging from the heart on a generic human figure. They consult resource books to view scientific illustrations of the arteries and veins.

As kids draw and discuss the vascular system, adults measure children's pulse rates and blood pressure readings, while sitting and after vigorous exercise—jumping rope, running outside, or walking fast inside. Students or adults then record these figures on a child's personal data sheet. Kids see the contrast between the "at rest" and "after exercise" numbers for blood pressure and pulse rate, prompting observations and questions such as those Izzy put on her data recording sheet (Figure 7.4).

Investigation Two: Body Temperature (at rest and after exercising)

Materials needed: Two disposable body thermometers (for under the tongue or under the arm) and a data recording sheet. Measuring body temperature may be done simultaneously with Investigation One if there are enough adults to assist. If not, the two investigations can be done on different days.

Thermometers record the body's temperature before and after exercising. The data recording sheet includes a thermometer with Fahrenheit and Celsius scales on the left and the right, so when kids mark their temperatures they can read the numbers on both scales. Kids find that they are not all registering 98.6 for a normal temperature. Some are lower and that is normal for them.

Body temperature introduces the differences between cold-blooded and warm-blooded creatures. Reptiles, birds, fish, and other cold-blooded organisms regulate body temperature by moving from warmer to cooler spots. In winter, for example, birds and Monarch butterflies migrate to warmer climates while squirrels, chipmunks, frogs, turtles, and skunks hibernate or sleep to conserve energy. Warm-blooded mammals have internal systems that register and regulate temperature. Human pores open to cool the body by letting sweat form on the skin and warm the body by closing pores and inducing shivering.

Investigation Three: Eyes Regulate Light

Materials needed: Different sources of light including a penlight or a small flashlight and a mirror.

The human eye is light sensitive so it can act as a self-regulating system. As the amount of light increases, the iris enlarges making the pupil smaller; as the amount of light

---

I Wonder Questions
How long are your bones if you pull them out and put them together?
How long is your brain if you stretch it out?

Research Notes
Did you know that if you pull out all of your veins and arteries and put them together, they are as long as 60,000 miles?
Your kidneys clean your blood. They are like a big dishwasher.

Figure 7.4 *Izzy's "I Wonder" questions and research notes.*

decreases, the iris contracts so the pupil expands. Expansion and contraction allow the eye to protect itself from being harmed by excessive light and to see in dark or near-dark conditions.

Shining a flashlight or a penlight (from a short distance) into the eye while looking at their reflections in a mirror enables children to see how their pupils expand and contract when light increases and decreases. This experiment can also be done by going outside on a bright day, then coming back inside to a darkened room and viewing the changes in the size of the pupil. Observations are then written on a data recording sheet.

Investigation Four: Skin Blocks Germs

Materials needed: Goo-Glow and a black light or roll-on glitter cosmetic.

The "Germs-on-the-Hands Simulation" is designed to show how the human skin acts like a coat of armor, protecting the body from germs and other damaging agents. To begin, kids apply Goo-Glow, a harmless thick orange liquid to their hands. Once applied, the liquid becomes invisible except under a black light. The orange Goo-Glow mimics the germs that are present, but unseen, on human skin. Roll-on glitter cosmetics can be applied to achieve the same effect, and it can be seen on the hands without extra light.

Next, the children wash their hands thoroughly with soap and water and look again at their hands under the black light if they are using Goo-Glow or in bright regular light if using roll-on glitter. Ostensibly, hand washing will remove the Goo-Glow or the glitter just as hand washing removes germs. In both cases, a casual washing has little effect. Kids are always surprised at how much of the orange liquid or roll-on glitter remains after what they think has been a thorough cleaning, letting adults remind them that even the protective power of human skin cannot control all germs, but careful hand washing eliminates many of them. Kids then write their reflections for their encycloMEdia, as Siobhan did in the report below (Figure 7.5).

Investigation Five: Skeletons Stand and Stretch

Materials needed: Tape measure, white art paper, scissors, and tape.

The human skeleton is an impressive collection of 206 bones, including 32 just from the ball and socket joint of the upper arm to the ends of the fingers. Measuring and recording even some of the major bones lets kids see how the human skeleton is put together to

Figure 7.5
Siobhan's Measuring Germs report.

> At school, my class and me did a body experiment today. We checked our pulse and we heard it with this weird kind of machine. When I got home I told my parents about it. My dad laughed when I told him about the paint and germs. Now I'll tell YOU! I put a little bit of orange paint on both of my hands. So did the rest of my group. Then we washed our hands. After that, we went to the darkest place in the school and we used a flashlight that shows you things that you can't see with your real eyes and we could see the paint. After that we washed our hands two more times and we tried it once more and we got more and more paint off every time.

let the body bend and move freely. It can be pointed out that while not everyone's physique looks the same on the outside, most bodies have the same bones inside. The names of the bones for the "Measuring Me" skeleton activity are

- skull
- collarbone (clavicle)
- breastbone (sternum)
- backbone (spine)
- ribcage
- upper arm bones (humerus)
- lower arm bones (radius and ulna)
- hipbone (pelvis)
- thigh bones (femur)
- kneecaps and lower leg bones (patella and tibia)
- calf bones (fibula)

Using illustrations and plastic models of skeletons as guides, kids work in duos and trios to measure each other's bones. Feeling under their collar, they are surprised to find the collarbone stretching from shoulder to shoulder, meeting in the middle at the breastbone.

To cut a model of it, one child measures her partner from breastbone to shoulder—half the length. Then the partner folds a strip of paper in half lengthwise, drawing from the fold toward the edges she has a bone the same length as half of her own. She cuts on her outline but does not cut the fold. When she opens the paper, there is the whole bone. She holds the paper model against herself, shoulder to shoulder to assure that the length is correct and labels it "Chantel's collarbone." Refolding it, she places it in her "My Bones" envelope.

This process continues for the other bones by:

- Locating the bones under the skin.
- Looking at illustrations and models to see whether the major bones are singles (upper arm and leg) or doubles (lower arm and leg).
- Measuring a partner's bones.
- Drawing the bones on a folded paper so after cutting there are two: a left and a right.
- Labeling each bone in standard spelling ("Chantel's upper leg bone").
- Storing the paper bones in personal envelopes.

The lower leg and the lower arm bones—fused at the tops and bottoms—are made by double folding the paper so four bones are cut out at once. Then two are stapled together, top and bottom for the lower legs and lower arms.

To cut a hipbone, kids fold a rectangle of 12-inch by 6-inch white art paper in half to make a 6-inch by 6-inch rectangle. From the fold, they outline a wide half butterfly—the top and bottom wings. After cutting on their outline, they open up the paper and a whole butterfly appears. They then re-fold it to see only half the butterfly again and fold the top wing down so the top and bottom are flat against each other. Next bending the paper so the right side touches the left, they cut a half circle on the bend. With the half circle removed and paper opened, the hip bones appear approximately their correct shape and size, resembling a butterfly with holes in its top and bottom wings.

The skull's length and width are measured and kids draw their own renditions, resulting in uniquely interesting skulls. Some youngsters cut out eye sockets, nose hole, and a mouth, others draw the holes on the paper. Speech bubbles are attached by some.

One hand and one foot are traced onto folded paper. After cutting around the tracing, the student has two of each—hands and feet. Looking at photographs and illustrations in books, children draw the bones and joints that they can feel in their fingers and on the backs of their hands. Then they sketch the foot bones onto their paper feet.

The spine is cut first into long strips of paper two inches wide. After kids measure each other's spines, they measure the strip to the needed length by putting the paper against their partner's backbones. They cut off the extra inches and recheck the length. Then they can make the vertebrae by folding the strip in half lengthwise and carefully snipping cuts along the fold down the length of the paper to simulate breaks between the vertebrae.

The ribcage is made from a 12″ by 18″ sheet of white art paper folded in half to make a 6″ by 9″ rectangle. At the open side (opposite the fold), children draw a 1″-wide borderline from top to bottom parallel to the paper's edge. From the fold to their borderline left to right across the paper, they now rule eleven lines, one inch apart. (Many wooden rulers are exactly one inch, making it easy to trace the ruler's top and bottom for a quick way to rule two lines without moving the ruler). Kids are surprised to find that drawing eleven lines one inch apart gives them twelve ribs, exactly what they need. They cut on the lines from the fold to the border one inch from the paper edge and when finished, there are twelve paper ribs. The left and right borders bend to meet in the middle.

On a length of bulletin board paper, children lie on their backs for a partner to trace their body outline, head to toe. Inside the outline, some kids draw their hearts with the arteries and veins of the vascular system, the major internal organs, the lungs, stomach, and intestines. Others draw and color their facial features, leaving the rest of the tracing empty to be the background for a personal jigsaw puzzle of their bones, which when laid out, show a life-size paper model of their skeleton. Then by putting the bones and organs in their envelope, they fold the body outline and store everything in their encycloMEdia container box. Hereafter, they can easily assemble and disassemble their paper skeleton puzzle.

EXTENSIONS

His-Stories and Her-Stories Make History

Inside the word "history" is the word "story." History is a collection of stories containing and explaining the lives, struggles, achievements, and legacies of all the people who live or have ever lived along the world's roads, rivers, or desert, mountain, and jungle pathways. Learning the "his-stories" and "her-stories" of people—ordinary and notable—brings past and present alive for children, giving history relevance and meaning by connecting events with the human choices of the people who made those events happen.

Stories, relating our activities to others, are a way for kids to think of history as the minutes of their lives going by each day. Through their actions and choices, individuals create their personal, family, neighborhood, and community lives. What are commonly called national and world history are really the stories of individual decisions and group actions reverberating into other actions, extending into other lives, producing change on a grand social scale.

People have always tried to keep track of history. Ancient peoples looked to the heavens and read the cycles of the natural world. Many used art to tell the stories of their lives: drawings and illustrations on caves and walls, ancient stone clocks and calendars, baskets, jewelry, and household goods. Other people communicated through how they constructed dwellings and cities—aligned with the stars, nestled in rock cliffs, or positioned at the mouths of busy rivers.

The advent of written communications in pictures, glyphs, and texts produced a trail of history in print. Just as someone can imagine who came down a road, children can study history by moving backward in time, consulting written texts, maps, group stories, oral histories, personal memories, gravestones, cultural artifacts, and other primary sources to learn about the lives of people. Examined collectively, these records offer a glimpse into the different societies and cultures that have existed and vanished through time.

Vast, powerful, and awesome in its consequences is the chronicle of natural history. The earth makes its mark on humans as humans make their mark on the earth. Geologists, anthropologists, and archeologists are historians of the planet, examining rock formations, fossil remains, and the long-hidden artifacts of former civilizations in order to understand what life was like at different times in the past. Children, too, participate in learning about history by studying plants and animals, seasonal change, the weather, and other cycles in the natural world.

Discovering the hidden footprints of history lets young children connect past, present, and future stories. Since we cannot talk directly to those who lived hundreds or thousands of years ago, history is the way to connect with former generations. Each youngster is one of history's newest members engaged in doing what generations have done before and generations will do subsequently. For children, learning where we have been in the past is one guide to where we will be in the future.

Multicultural Memories

Historian Ronald Takaki (1993) has noted how alienating it is for Asian, African American, or Latino children to read history books and find so little information about their cultures and people. Their historical experiences, in writer, educator, and actor Bill Cosby's notable phrase, have been "lost, stolen, or strayed." To feel invisible in history contributes to feeling powerless in contemporary society. To learn about history, children from all backgrounds require accessible points of reference that connect people and events to their own lives and families.

Children's literature offers dramatic openers for teaching children about the multicultural history of our country through the memories of diverse peoples. Every event has multiple perspectives depending upon who is telling it. The following books present nonfiction accounts of people's lives based on oral histories and documentary records. There are many other titles listed in *Multicultural Voices in Contemporary Literature* and *Latina and Latino Voices in Literature* edited by Francis Ann Day (1994, 1997). *Children's Literature in Social Studies* as well as annual selections by the National Council for the Social Studies in its journal *Social Education* are sources for notable multicultural books.

- *Cuadros de Familia* (Family Pictures) by Carmen Lomas Garza, recalls the author's experiences as a young girl growing up along the Rio Grande River on the border between Texas and Mexico in the years after World War II. Each page describes an event from her youth in Spanish and English, with colorful illustrations. Through paragraphs of economical yet detailed descriptions, readers are transported into the middle of activities as the author and her brother, parents and grandparents go to the fair, pick oranges from the backyard tree, make chicken soup, and engage in other family times together.

- *Shortcut* by Donald Crews describes when he and his cousins decided to take a forbidden path along the railroad tracks, only to be trapped in harm's way by an oncoming freight train. The drama of the train's rapid approach and the youngsters' flight to safety is riveting and so is the author's confession at the end that they did not tell their mother or their grandmother what had happened and did not talk about it together for a "very long time." Said a second grader after hearing the book, "You mean he didn't tell anyone for forty years and then he told the whole world?" initiating a discussion of whether or not we always tell our experiences to our families.

- *Osceola: Memories of a Sharecropper's Daughter* collected and edited by Alan Govenar tells the story of Osceola Mays, growing up African American under the oppressions of slavery and segregation in rural East Texas around the turn of the twentieth century.

- *Nickommoh! A Thanksgiving Celebration* by Jackie French Koller describes the fall harvest ceremony of the Narragansett people who lived in present-day Rhode Island, a tradition that long preceded the Pilgrims' first thanksgiving.

Sometimes, people's memories are the foundation for imaginative historical fiction that locates the facts of the past within the structure of engaging stories.

- *Dinner at Aunt Connie's House* by Faith Ringgold features portraits of Sojourner Truth, Harriet Tubman, Mary McLeod Bethune, Fannie Lou Hamer, Rosa Parks, and other African American women describing how they contributed to the struggle for equality and justice throughout United States history.

- *Aunt Harriet's Underground Railroad in the Sky*, also by Faith Ringgold, uses the image of an actual railroad with Harriet Tubman as the conductor to highlight the heroic efforts of African Americans fleeing slavery in the years before the Civil War.

- *Ten Mile Day: And the Building of the Transcontinental Railroad* by Mary Ann Fraser focuses on how the transcontinental railroad was built in the 1880s in part through the labors of Chinese men, deliberately separated from their families by thousands of miles and subject to continual racial prejudice.

- *Baseball Saved Us* by Ken Mochizuki relays the memories of a young boy, confined with his family to the Japanese-American Internment Camp in Idaho during World War II, and how the game of baseball allowed moments of triumph amid the grim conditions of imprisonment.

- *Mailing May* by Michael O. Tunnell tells a story from the point of view of five-year-old May, whose parents spent fifty-three cents in 1914 to send her by railroad train across Idaho to visit her grandmother, long before automobiles and the interstate highway system made travel across distances easy.

- The "My Name is America" series features a diverse collection of historical fiction including *The Journal of Biddy Owens: The Negro Leagues* by Walter Dean Myers; *The Journal of Jesse Smoke: A Cherokee Boy, Trail of Tears, 1838* by Joseph Bruchac; and *The Journal of Wong Ming-Chung: A Chinese Miner* by Laurence Yep.

One Paragraph Memories and Little Memory Books

Multicultural history books show children ways to write personal memories to include in their encycloMEdia. Personal memories are often called autobiography; the assembling of many pieces of autobiographical writing in one place is a memoir. Descriptions of one's experience from one's own point of view—his-stories and her-stories—are written records from the life of the authors, male and female. They are important personal milestones that when added together with the writing of others build the larger history of a family, neighborhood, nation, and world.

Thinking about memories as personal his-stories and her-stories expands the definition of story writing for kids. While stories are generally discussed as a form of fiction writing, autobiographical stories are based in facts. They describe events that happened to actual people with real consequences. This is part of their great value as documents of history;

they give insights into people's lives as they lived them, not as someone else has imagined them to be.

Stories defined as personal history and written as memories from daily life become short episodes to enhance the scope of an encycloMEdia. Like the descriptions in *Cuadros de Familia*, any event can be a his-story or a her-story for a child's collection, as in the accounts by two kids of a special day in their lives (Figure 7.6).

Writing memories does not require lengthy essays or book style chapters. Personal his-stories and her-stories can be paragraph-length entries where every word plays an important role in communication. Since good paragraphs convey one idea clearly and concisely, one-paragraph memories serve as a practice for structuring writing into manageable segments that readers understand.

A one-paragraph memory can be expanded into longer narratives of his-stories and her-stories. *Stories Julian Tells* and *More Stories Julian Tells* by Ann Cameron are realistic fiction accounts of events in the family of the narrator, eight-year-old Julian and his family, father, mother, and younger brother, Huey. These funny, true-to-life episodes remind kids of similar occasions they have experienced. *The Bear That Heard Crying* by Natalie Kinsey-Warnock and Helen Kinsey chronicles the story of three-year-old Sarah Whitcher who in June 1783 was lost for four days in the woods beyond her home in Warren, New Hampshire. Her account, and those of community members who sought her, ascribe her survival

---

Mariah's Memory

Me and my friends Maritza and Brianna who I used to call Banana had a sleepover at Maritza's house. Maritza has a little brother that she thinks is a pest but he is not. He is a great friend to Kayla and he is not to me. At the sleepover, he ruined a lot of stuff. We told him and he kept on doing his rude stuff. We played with dolls for like the whole night but not for a whole night. In the morning we had soda and juice. Maritza and I went to Kayla, my sister's birthday party. There were sixteen kids in all and three grown-ups. We read the *Rainbow Fish*. Then we watched my cousin Ricky do magic. Then came the presents and cake and ice cream and rainbow changing tops. And then everyone left.

Elijah's Memory

On Friday, we went on a field trip. We went to a bunch of different places but first we went to the Lord Jeffrey Inn. There was a huge fireplace and a portrait of George Washington. Then we went to Jeffrey Amherst bookstore and Chris found a maze book, Jan found a King Arthur book, Jose found a book about the President and I found two books in the series of *The Secrets of Doom*. Then we went to a hardware store and I found some really cool pens. Jan and Jose found some comic books and Chris found an electrical violin. And finally, last but not least, we went to have a piece of pizza from a car dealership. Just joking! We went to what was a car dealership 20 years ago and what is now Bertucci's Pizza.

Figure 7.6 *Children's Special Day Memories.*

> On Sunday my family went to K-Mart. Then we went to this little place. Me and my brother got new shoes there. I looked at my shoes. They were colorful so I picked them.
>
> Before I had to help my Dad with the van and we had to buy an exhaust and new tires. Then we had to tighten the exhaust.

Figure 7.7   *Entries from Garrett's Little Memory Book.*

to the care of a grown black bear. Sarah was Natalie Kinsey-Warnock's great-great-great-great-great aunt.

A small spiral notebook with a colorful cover (found at many discount stores for a dollar or less) is one format to encourage kids to record personal memories and practice writing one paragraph at the same time. (Figure 7.7).

The design of such little memory books is inviting. They can be easily hand-carried and the small size invites short descriptions but does not preclude longer entries. Little memory books also expand the definition of an encycloMEdia beyond a single folder or notebook. An encycloMEdia can consist of writing and drawing that is collected in many different sources—scrapbooks, photo books, personal writing folders, little memory books, letters, and poems.

Inviting children to record memories requires great sensitivity on the part of adults. Many children have experienced events that they would rather not remember—painful, frustrating, heartbreaking times such as losing a loved one or facing danger or harm. Even a story like *Shortcut* reminds adults of times when they defied the rules, with frightening consequences. At the same time, memories are authentic occasions for writing and kids enjoy recalling pleasant things they have done and people they were with.

Before beginning memories, adults and kids may talk about the stories they plan to write. Some experiences are private, or best shared only among family members. Deciding to keep a memory private does not diminish its importance as a piece of personal history. It simply means that the writer has chosen to reduce the audience for that writing by not sharing it widely with classmates or others. Honest discussion about what personal stories to make public or keep private help kids to decide what to include in their encycloMEdia.

YOUNG WRITERS' BOOKSHELF FOR A CHILD'S ENCYCLOMEDIA AND MEMORIES

Journeys into the Past/Chronicles of Time

Time Train. Paul Fleischman. Illustrated by Claire Ewart. Scott Foresman, 1994. Children take a field trip through time backward to the era of the dinosaurs.

A Street through Time: A 12,000-Year Walk through History. Anne Millard. Illustrated by Steve Noon. DK Publishing, 1998. A record of people and events along the same street offers a unique view of the passage of history.

Roads and Rivers

Window. Jeannie Baker. Puffin Books, 1991. The view from the window of a house changes as the pristine natural environment is besieged by urban sprawl and blight.

Steamboat! The Story of Captain Blanche Leathers. Judith Heide Gilliland. Pictures by Holly Meade. Dorling Kindersley, 2000. The first woman to become a steamboat captain on the Mississippi River in the late 1800s.

A River Ran Wild: An Environmental History. Lynne Cherry. Voyager Books, 2002. The story of the Nashua River that flows between New Hampshire and Massachusetts from the time when Native Americans lived along its banks, through the impacts of industrialization, and its restoration in recent years.

River Town. Bonnie and Arthur Geisert. Houghton Mifflin, 1999. Life in eighteenth- and nineteenth-century communities that prospered along America's large rivers.

Books Cited in the Text

My Painted House, My Friendly Chicken and Me. Maya Angelou. Clarkson N. Potter, 1996 (out of print).

The Block. Langston Hughes. Collage by Romane Bearden. Viking Children's Books, 1995.

Children of Clay: A Family of Pueblo Potters. Rina Swentzell. Photographs by Bill Steen. First Avenue Editions, 1993.

Gabriella's Song. Candace Fleming. Illustrated by Giselle Potter. Atheneum, 1997.

EncycloMEdia

The Magic School Bus Inside the Human Body. Joanna Cole. Illustrated by Bruce Degen. Scholastic Books, 1990.

All about People: How We Grow, How Our Bodies Work, and How We Feel. Scholastic First Encyclopedia. Scholastic Books, 1995.

The Escape of Marvin the Ape. Caralyn and Mark Buehner. Puffin, 1999. Marvin the gorilla enjoys a whole new life after leaving the zoo.

Amazon Diary: The Jungle Adventures of Alex Winters. Hudson Talbott and Mark Greenberg. Putnam & Grosset Group, 1996. The fictional diary of a sixth-grade boy on his way to visit his anthropologist parents when his plane crashes deep in the Brazilian jungle where the Yanomani Indians live.

Memories

Cuadros de Familia. Carmen Lomas Garza. Children's Book Press, 1993.

Shortcut. Donald Crews. Mulberry Books, 1996.

Osceola: Memories of a Sharecropper's Daughter collected and edited by Alan Govenar. Jump at the Sun, 2000.

Nickommoh! A Thanksgiving Celebration. Jackie French Koller. Illustrated by Marcia Sewall. Atheneum, 1999.

Dinner at Aunt Connie's House. Faith Ringgold. Hyperion, 1996.

Aunt Harriet's Underground Railroad in the Sky. Faith Ringgold. Crown, 1995.

Ten Mile Day: And the Building of the Transcontinental Railroad. Mary Ann Fraser. Henry Holt, 1996.

Baseball Saved Us. Ken Mochizuki. Illustrated by Dom Lee. Lee & Low Books, 1995.

Mailing May. Michael O. Tunnell. Illustrated by Ted Rand. HarperCollins, 2000.

The "My Name is America" historical fiction series is produced by Scholastic.

The Bear That Heard Crying. Natalie Kinsey-Warnock and Helen Kinsey. Cobblehill Books, 1993.

The Stories Julian Tells. Ann Cameron. Random House, 1989.

Community Rules!

Writing Rules	TEACH	These Conventions *Unconventionally*
Writing Rules in Schools		Genre: Rule writing Persuasive writing
Sentences Communicate Rules		Types of sentences • Imperative • Interrogative • Declarative • Exclamatory
Reflective Writing about Rules		Reporting the facts/using details Point of view
Extensions: The Rules of Democracy		Democratic citizenship

Rules are a topic of great interest—and even greater contention—to young children since so much of their daily lives revolve around what they want to do and what adults say about it. Adults set limits and make rules, expecting that children will learn to obey them, but youngsters regularly challenge the parameters of whatever rules are in place.

At school, lists of what not to say, do, or wear are found in student handbooks and on classroom walls. Everyone is expected to maintain the building's code of conduct. Penalties, some unforgiving—"Three strikes and you are out!"—some predictable—"No homework done, no recess fun!"—await those who do not follow the established regulations.

Few people dispute the necessity of rules. Children need to be safe from harassment and harm, and all aspects of school days and family life function more smoothly when everyone acts harmoniously. Codes of conduct and discipline, when they are successful, make it possible for children and adults to live and learn together cooperatively and happily.

Getting rules to achieve their purposes requires wisdom, humor, and diplomacy by adults who must establish the basic guidelines of behavior and help children to assume ownership of and responsibility for whatever regulations are in place. Many times, adults create expectations for behavior either without involving children in the discussion or by sharing decision making as if kids were adults. Between these two points is a sensible middle ground where children can learn positive behaviors by helping set limits and fashion consequences.

When adults impose rules without children's involvement, the result is often counter-productive. "External control doesn't teach self control," noted one educator (Schimmel 5, 7). But even when "fair, participatory procedures" are used to develop rules, only if kids perceive that their interest is involved do rules become personally important to them.

This WOW shows how kids learn about rules by helping to formulate them—from imaginary regulations that stretch the boundaries of what is plausible or logical to actual codes for behavior choices. Creating fair-minded rules through a process that includes input and decision making by kids emanates from the history and social studies curriculum, including lessons about who made rules for whom and with what consequences throughout American and world history. Simultaneously, rule writing presents opportunities to discuss the roles of the four kinds of sentences, from imperative sentences that command orders to interrogative sentences that request compliance.

Writing Rules in Schools

Children associate rules with limits—not with freedom or fairness. They believe that rules always favor the rulemaker, not those who must follow them. But the purpose of rules is to persuade each of us who live, work, and go to school together that greater fairness, equity, and happiness result from supporting the common good instead of pursuing only our personal desires.

Kids easily recite the rules and easily disregard them in all types of situations. Although they want fair treatment, youngsters do not always treat others fairly—especially when they think someone else is breaking the rules. Rules and emotions are inextricably linked. Kids disbelieve the promise that rules will protect everyone equally because they have memories of times they feel they have been wronged or rules have been unfairly enforced. And most of the time, they do not believe they are wrong.

A thought-provoking analysis of why rules exist and why people make them can evolve after enjoying some preposterous, zany, hilarious stories and poems that galvanize kids' attention through humor. Discussions about these selections reveal kids' understandings of why rules exist and also their reasons for not wanting to abide by some of them.

- *The Dumb Bunnies* by Sue Denim describes a family of silly rabbits whose misadventures break every rule of common sense, including ice-skating at the bottom of a lake, playing baseball in the town library, and picnicking inside a car wash.
- "Rules" by poet Karla Kuskin warns against asking advice from snakes, yelling at mice, or taking a whale to visit a yacht. The results of such actions will not be welcomed.
- *Do's and Don'ts* by Todd Parr, offers a list of things kids ought and ought not to do—do give a dog a bath, but not with you.
- *The Stupids* by Harry Allard with illustrations by James Marshall describes the decisions of a human family aptly named for their ridiculous choices and madcap adventures.

After hearing or reading these selections aloud, kids want to reread them with friends, to laugh heartily at the obvious wrong choices of the characters. Writing "truly tall rules" follows reading these stories and poems. As a whole class, kids concoct impractical and obviously fictitious rules that could not possibly make sense: "I will ask the cafeteria to make what I want for lunch to serve to the school each day" or "We will have gym everyday and we will play only my choice of games."

Beyond exercising creative imaginations there are important reasons to think about actual rules by first writing implausible ones.

- Imaginary rule writing asks kids to consider the role of the rule and why it is included in codes of conduct. Rules exist to promote fairness, safety, and enjoyment for all. The necessity of rules to govern behavior is made clear when children describe how they feel if someone grabs, hits, kicks, knocks, pushes them or makes rude, meanspirited remarks. None of these actions are pleasant or desirable for anyone. When kids are part of the process of rulemaking, they can declare that certain unwanted behaviors will not be allowed in the classroom.

- When children are immersed in writing imaginary rules, they practice the successful group problem-solving interactions and teamwork behaviors that rules are intended to establish and maintain. Working together cooperatively and peacefully, children model the result of following codes of conduct. When the result of their efforts is pointed out—"You are experts at following the real rules. You are enjoying each other's ideas and behaviors as you collaborate on this activity"— kids begin to understand that they benefit from a fair and justified set of rules that informs how they behave every day.

- Kids can practice writing rules using styles they have not tried before: for example, tall tales about the adventures of characters who choose to do foolish things, poems about rules and their consequences, or cartoons that display rules in different situations and settings.

After inventing and displaying imaginary rules, young children are prepared to create actual classroom rules. Their efforts are remarkably thoughtful and insightful. They are well aware of the things that upset and frustrate them as well as their desire for safety and respect in the school, evident in the rules agreed upon by second graders shown in Figure 7.8.

Once rule writing becomes an important form of classroom communication and decision making, there are continual opportunities to formulate rules for particular activities such as constructing ramps in the classroom block area (Figure 7.9).

Moving from creating imaginary rules to writing actual rules requires empathy and problem-solving strategies from adults, and willingness to constantly support the building of a caring community for and with kids. The rationale for children making rules together with adults is that children learn the importance of consistent behaviors in order to maintain the standard of what is fair. After composing their classroom rules, second graders offered the following reflections during a discussion of the question, "What would school be like without rules?" (Figure 7.10).

It is easy to implement and sustain rules when everyone is calm, focused, and invested in an activity they enjoy. When emotions are triggered, children, and many adults, follow their feelings and ignore the rules—for example, pushing and shoving despite prohibitions against fighting or physical harm. Deciding the rules collectively, writing them down, and displaying them publicly gives everyone an agreed-upon standard of behavior to focus discussion when the heat of the moment subsides and the problem solving begins.

Child-written rules provide a context for group problem solving and individual choice of response to troublesome situations. Talking with kids provides a personal way to examine behavior and its consequences, but conversation alone does not possess lasting impact. Children still do what adults wish they would not do. Displaying classroom rules for everyone to see and revise provides a way for children and adults to work and learn together in a respectful community. Do rules prevent every problem? No, but they direct attention to the fact that individual actions have great consequences for the classroom society.

Figure 7.8 *Safety and Respect Rule Statements by Second Graders. Translations:*

Don't Say "I'm the prettiest girl" because everyone is pretty. No hitting EXIT signs at school. No running in front of a sled when a kid is in it. Do NOT play with matches at school.

Rules for the Block Area

No adding blocks.

No taking off blocks.

No rolling balls down the ramp without a block builder there.

Every child who is not a block builder may roll the ball down the ramp at least two times.

Figure 7.9 *Rules for the Block Area by second graders.*

Writing Rules in Schools

> *If everyone didn't follow the directions, it would be bad.*
>
> *Everyone would do something else.*
>
> *No one would care.*
>
> *Nothing would work for someone.*
>
> *That would mean there were no cars, trucks, ships, planes and other things.*
>
> *No one would learn.*
>
> *There would not be such thing as recess.*
>
> *The kids would sit down and do nothing instead.*
>
> *Music, arts and gym would not exist for us.*
>
> *We would be grounded a lot.*

Figure 7.10   *Reflections on rules by second graders.*

Sentences Communicate Rules

How do different sentences communicate rules to readers and listeners? Do all sentences deliver the message equally well? This is something that kids rarely consider. Writing rules provides the context for examining sentence types—imperative, interrogative, declarative, or exclamatory—to determine which best communicates a rule statement and why.

From the perspective of "role before rule," the choice of sentence depends on the writer's purpose in communicating and the power or urgency of the message. One way to discover the differences is to write the same classroom regulations using all four types of sentences so kids can judge for themselves how effectively each communicates information to an audience.

The following chart shows what happens to the meaning of the familiar admonition, "No running in the hall," when it is expressed using the four sentence types. An imperative statement commands someone to act while an interrogative sentence asks a question. A declarative sentence states facts straightforwardly while an exclamatory sentence includes emotion or urgency.

Sentence Type	Rule Statement
Imperative (issuing a request or a command)	No running in the hallway. You must walk.
Interrogative (asking a question)	Why are you running in the hallway? What might happen to you and to others?
Declarative (making a statement)	Everyone walks in the hallway because somebody might get hurt if people collide or fall.
Exclamatory (expressing strong feelings)	Please keep everyone safe! Walk!

By discussing how a message is delivered in different sentences, kids reflect about why rules are expressed as commands. In daily life, kids are expected to comply with many imperatives: "Time to get up," "Take a bath," "Brush your teeth," "Go to school," and "Look both ways before crossing the street," to name a few. They issue imperatives in everyday conversations: "No!" "Gimme!" "I'm first!" "Let me see it!" "It's my turn!" and so on. All these statements command performance; listeners are expected to do what is said or face the consequences.

Imperative sentences do not always successfully persuade people to follow the directives. People resent the imposition of regulations, especially those they have not participated in forming or adopting. An amusing way to illustrate this point is by giving one youngster a plastic crown and a royal cape to issue a self-chosen imaginary rule for the class. Assuming the royal garb, the child proclaims "The rule is . . ." The shock of no one following the directions is the ruler's surprise. This scenario could repeat throughout the school year, giving each child an opportunity to proclaim a rule. The result would not vary. If a rule does not make sense, or does not treat all fairly, others will ignore, forget, or proceed as if they had never heard it.

Attempts by kids to assert supreme power opens a discussion of history, not long past, when the imperial governments of kings and queens issued royal commands to their subjects that had to be obeyed. Such political systems were in sharp contrast to democracies where people make laws through argument, deliberation, and participatory decision making. Asking children if imperatives are the way they want a system of discipline to work initiates further discussion of how people treat each other, whether with fairness and respect or with disregard of mutual needs.

Interrogative sentences present regulations as questions, suggesting that compliance is voluntary. Stating rules as questions invites consideration and debate about whether this changes the purpose of having rules. "Is it okay to run in the hall sometimes?" "Is it acceptable to run whenever you want to?" "Then is it acceptable to roller blade, skateboard, or scooter through the hall or in the classrooms?" As writers, kids consider whether or not the rules of the classroom should be open to continual debate and personal choice. If not, they need a different type of sentence, not the interrogative.

Declarative and exclamatory sentences offer two other ways to state expectations for behavior. The former exudes less emotion than the latter, but both contain the essence of a choice, so a decision must be made about how much emphasis is needed to persuade people to follow a request. In some situations, especially where safety is involved, an appeal to emotions is an effective communication strategy. At other times, a straightforward declarative sentence will transmit the message by stating the facts in a more neutral style.

The purpose of experimenting with four sentence types to express rules is to understand how they are different and when each one suits a situation. For learning the roles of sentences, examining and writing rules is a powerful teaching strategy.

Reflective Writing about Rules

A playground swing rule states:

"Each rider may have 100 swings, then it's the next person's turn."

Trouble started one day when Bob, waiting in line, counted the number of swings for Dennis's turn. What occurred next is in dispute. Dennis claims that Bob counted by tens, instead of by ones, greatly shortening Dennis's ride. Bob countered that Dennis pushed him off as he tried to mount the swing, thereby ripping his pants and making him cry. When adults intervened, the boys were hollering and pushing each other.

To restore calm, Ruth asked the boys to write what happened. Writing offered a way for each boy to think about his actions and consider alternatives for resolving their dispute.

Sitting with the combatants one at a time, she asked each to explain the details of the argument. She took dictation, let each of them write some of the words of the text, and, when they were finished with their explanations, had them read their writing to one another.

As the story of Dennis and Bob suggests, when rules have been broken or are in dispute, asking kids to write is not a punishment, but a viable way for children to

- Recall what happened.
- Remember what they did personally.
- Reconsider the consequences of their actions for themselves and for others.

Writing changes interaction and communication. Instead of continuing an emotionally charged verbal or physical disagreement, which promotes anger, embarrassment, defensiveness, or stony-faced silence, writing provides a quiet release from the immediacy of the situation. Kids step out of the emotion of the moment to express their view of the situation. When using writing to solve problems and resolve conflicts, children and adults can pursue three communicative goals: "make it clear," "fix it now," and "focus on the future."

Make It Clear

Playground, classroom, or family disputes often become complex affairs when participants and bystanders add their points of view to each other's story. Layers of detail and conflicting descriptions make getting the particulars of the case seem impossible, resulting in confusion and frustration for all concerned.

Writing to "make it clear" asks kids to present their views of what happened using exact and detailed language. Many situations involving rules are ambiguous; there is usually more than one side to a story. By recording the details of what took place, a writer assists adults to resolve a situation quickly and fairly.

Writing to "make it clear" starts with kids stating on paper everything that they can remember about the situation. This type of writing is organized like a report from the specifics of "who," "what," "when," "where," and "why" as well as from the personal feelings generated by the incident. The purpose is for the writer to re-view the situation—to see it again—to describe what actually happened as closely as he or she can.

The parties involved read their writing to each other as a way of exchanging information and prompting memory in case somebody forgot to include something relevant. While they present their facts, children learn about differences in *points of view*. Each writer provides her or his perspective since that is all she or he can see.

Such descriptions must be accurate and inclusive of all relevant information. For example, "He hit me" may not reveal the fact that "First, I bumped him, and then he hit me." Without full disclosure of what happened, the situation remains unclear and unresolved. The goal of making it clear is not to make oneself look good or someone else look bad, but to state what happened, right and wrong.

Fix It Now

Writing to "fix it now" begins after the details of a rule-breaking incident are clearly described and known to all involved through "make it clear" communications. If someone has broken, bent, or reinterpreted the rules, she or he must decide how to straighten out or mend the infraction. "Fix it now" writing apologizes to those offended or harmed by misbehavior as well as to everyone in a class impacted by the situation.

Focus on the Future

"Focus on the future" writing asks children to set forth a plan of action for not repeating the behavior when similar situations arise. In the case of the disagreement at the playground swings, Bob wrote his plan to avoid further disputes, as shown in the chart below.

Make it clear: (Bob)	*Fix it now:* (Bob)	*Focus on the future:* (Bob)
I was counting as fast as I could to get my turn on the swing.	I am sorry I was unfair and rushed your turn.	I won't try to shorten somebody's turn. I will count fairly.

"Make it clear," "fix it now," and "focus on the future" give teachers and parents flexible options for addressing problems when disputes arise between kids or between kids and adults. Starting the process of conflict resolution on paper allows teachers the time to handle other pressing matters before turning full attention to the dispute. Situations occurring outside the classroom—on the bus, during a recess, or in the hall—can be addressed right away by writing about them rather than postponing oral discussion until time permits.

Sometimes it is not necessary to ask kids to write all three parts if problem resolution and behavior change do not require them. In some situations or with younger children, adults may want to use a combination of verbal and written responses. Adults may also want to space the writing over more than a day if time for reflection seems useful, or they may want to resolve a matter quickly so that everyone moves past a dispute.

Writing is a means of communicating between voices and viewpoints, letting children and adults think through problems and disagreements to the benefit of everyone involved (including the child who has broken the rules). Rather than being a punishment, writing remedies a wrong and addresses future behaviors. Many times children gain insights through reflective writing that gives them the forethought to abide by the rules the next time.

EXTENSIONS

The Rules of Democracy

The Day Gogo Went to Vote by Elinor Batezat Sisulu recounts the story of six-year-old Thembi and her great-grandmother as they journey together to the election polls on the day in 1994 when Black South Africans voted for the first time. The lines of voters are long, stretching as far as the eye can see in some places. For *Gogo* (meaning grandmother in the Xhosa and Zulu languages), voting is a momentous occasion, a culmination of more than two hundred years of struggle of indigenous Africans against white oppression. There are tears of joy and satisfaction as Gogo participates in making the rules of her country.

Sisulu's fine book opens the door to discussions of *democratic citizenship*—an essential topic in any social studies curriculum. In our country, citizens participate in making the rules (that is, setting public policies) through voting, engaging in peaceful demonstrations, writing letters to the editor and elected representatives, joining political parties or organizations, displaying signs and bumper stickers, or otherwise expressing views on the issues. In theory, when decisions are made, the majority rules, but every group has the right to make its case to the people.

Participating in making rules in a classroom connects kids directly to matters that are at the center of democracy as a form of government: the rights of individuals, the obligations of citizens, and the responsibilities of community members—in schools and society. From an historical perspective, democracy itself is a direct response to authoritarian rule-making by monarchs and despots. But, in the United States for more than two hundred years, African Americans, Native Americans, Latinos, women, Jews, and other people have struggled to achieve the rights guaranteed them under the Constitution. Today, Americans debate how to assure that everyone has sufficient education, health care, and income as well as how to counter threats to our rights and freedoms.

Nothing is more destructive to democracy than the idea that one's participation does not matter. In a classroom, everyone must be a contributing member or the community does not function well. If only some voices are heard, some children run the risk of being left behind. The same is true in society as a whole. For example, when people do not take steps to prevent special interests from dominating decision making, then the larger system will not succeed in maintaining individual rights and social fairness. Democracy requires open dialogue and discussion among everyone so that all views and visions can be heard as social choices get made.

For kids, asking thoughtful questions about who makes the rules is a natural entryway to the issues of democracy raised by events in history. For example, how do the words "with liberty and justice for all" pertain to kids' daily lives in the miniature society of a classroom? These questions initiate an examination of the Bill of Rights and the Constitution that govern the actions of the elected and appointed officials in our government. When one of Sharon's students asked the question, "What is a government?" the children's writing of the classroom rules provided the starting point for an answer.

Creating interest in questions about government offers an opportunity to simulate proposing and passing legislation by majority vote or committee compromise. School House Rock put the process of passing a bill into song lyrics so kids could recall the steps through singing. Many classes act out the legislative process with children being representatives and senators at work in the House and the Senate debating, compromising, and passing laws. *A More Perfect Union: The Story of Our Constitution* by Betsy and Giulio Maestro explains the history of those who wrote the masterpieces of our system of government.

Viewing segments of the movie *1776* sets the stage for discussing what might happen if children acted as representatives of different constituencies—girls, boys, short kids, tall kids, kids with glasses, kids who are not slender, kids who do not celebrate holidays or birthdays—to produce a classroom version of a Bill of Rights and a Constitution. Children meeting as committees compose paragraphs for the rights of their constituents, read these drafts aloud for debate and change, and finally vote for proposals by each group. Creating governing documents is not only an exciting process, it is the kind of talking and thinking work that adults rarely ask kids to do but that they always want to do. The documents can be displayed for all to see and used to mediate disputes.

When kids have knowledge of and understanding about a democratic process, and they are able to see that their actions make the contracts that are called rules, they perceive the importance of their own actions in a broader context. While the regular problems of childhood still occur—who will or will not play with whom, who said what to whom, who hit who first—the writing of governance documents address attitudes such as "Why are you blaming me?" "Why is it always me?" "It's not my fault!" with statements that all people deserve and receive fairness. If everyone cooperates with the classroom's governance policies—its Bill of Rights and Constitution—safety, personal comfort, and enjoyment for all result within the rules.

Young Writers' Bookshelf for Community Rules!

Making the Rules

David Goes to School. David Shannon. Blue Sky Press, 1999. A fast paced, hair-raising day in the life of David, who challenges the rules of his school. The cleverly written text in child-style font adds to the intensity of the story.

Never Spit on Your Shoes. Denys Cazet. Orchard Paperbacks, 1993. Arnie, a puppy, tells his mother about his first day of school, which features unruly classmates and new classroom rules like "No naps in first grade."

Who is the Boss? Josse Goffin. Clarion Books, 1992. An argument about who is the boss leads two friends into a power struggle, a calamity, and a compromise for cooperation.

The View. Harry Yoaker and Simon Henwood. Dial Books for Young Readers, 1992. Intense competition to build a house with a better view results in no one being able to see the beautiful countryside nearby.

Who Owns the Cow? Andrew Clements. Illustrated by Joan Landis. Clarion Books, 1995. A story of interdependence in a town where many people benefit from a cow and the milk it produces.

Don't Make Me Laugh. James Stevenson. Frances Foster Books, 1999. Two rules guide the reading of this group of stories: "No laughing!" and "Don't do anything you're told not to do, or you must return to the cover and begin again!"

The Stupids Step Out. Harry Allard. Illustrated by James Marshall. Houghton Mifflin, 1977. Other books include *The Stupids Take Off* and *The Stupids Have a Ball*.

Make Way for the Dumb Bunnies. Sue Denim. Pictures by Dav Pilkey. Scholastic, 1998. See other books in the series such as *The Dumb Bunnies* and *The Dumb Bunnies' Easter*. (Cited in the text.)

Do's and Don'ts. Todd Parr. Little, Brown, 1999. (Cited in the text.)

Voting and Democracy

The Ballot Box Battle. Emily Arnold McCully. Dragonfly, 1998. A young girl learns about the campaign for women's right to vote from her neighbor, Elizabeth Cady Stanton.

Granddaddy's Gift. Margaree King Mitchell. Illustrated by Larry Johnson. Troll, 1998. A young African American girl growing up in Mississippi in the 1950s accompanies her grandfather as he tries to register to vote, witnessing first-hand the prejudice of racial segregation and the courage of people in opposing discrimination.

The Araboolies of Liberty Street. Sam Swope. Pictures by Barry Root. Sunburst, 2001. A strange but good-natured family arrives and changes the established routine of a neighborhood.

The Day Gogo Went to Vote. Elinor Batezat Sisulu. Illustrated by Sharon Wilson. Little, Brown, 1999. (Cited in the text.)

A More Perfect Union: The Story of Our Constitution. Betsy and Giulio Maestro. Mulberry Books, 1990. (Cited in the text.)

Chapter Summary

Chapter Seven, "Social Studies," uses writing and its powers of self-expression and self-reflection as ways to advance children's thinking about themselves as history-making individuals who play roles as members of many different communities, including school. When kids compose entries for an "Encyclopedia of Me," they produce written records to share with others or keep for themselves. Personal encyclopedias feature memories—"his-stories" and "her-stories"—as records of important events in one's life and as connections to the multicultural experiences of people in diverse communities and cultures. Formulating rules of conduct for school classrooms demonstrates the power of sentences to communicate information to many audiences. Writing is integral to democratic classrooms where kids learn to express ideas, make proposals for change, and read the views of others.

References

Angier, Natalie. "Do Races Differ? Not Really, Genes Show." *New York Times* 22 Aug. 2000: Science 1, 6.

Ashton-Warner, Sylvia. *Teacher*. New York: Simon & Schuster, 1986.

Bryson, Bill. (1994). *Made in America: An Informal History of the English Language in the United States*. New York: William Morrow.

Chandler, David L. "A New Spin on Mars." The *Boston Globe* 23 June 2000: A1, A16.

Cogswell, David. (1996). *Chomsky for Beginners*. New York: Writers and Readers Press.

Cooper, Patsy. (1994). "Seeking Meaning in the Written Word." In National Storytelling Association (ed.). *Tales as Tools: The Power of Story in the Classroom* (pp. 71–73). Jonesborough, Tenn.: National Storytelling Association.

Cullum, Albert. (1967). *Push Back the Desks*. New York: Citation Press.

Day, Frances Ann. (1997). *Latina and Latino Voices in Literature for Children and Teenagers*. Portsmouth, N.H.: Heinemann.

Day, Frances Ann. (1994). *Multicultural Voices in Contemporary Literature: A Resource for Teachers*. Portsmouth, N.H.: Heinemann.

Der Manuelian, Peter. (1991). *Hieroglyphs from A to Z: Rhyming Book with Ancient Egyptian Stencils for Kids*. Boston: Museum of Fine Arts.

Esbensen, Barbara Juster. (1995). *A Celebration of Bees: Helping Children to Write Poetry*. New York: Henry Holt.

Fletcher, Ralph. (1993). *What a Writer Needs*. Portsmouth, N.H.: Heinemann.

Fox, Mem. (1993). *Radical Reflections: Passionate Opinions on Teaching, Learning, and Living*. New York: Harcourt Brace.

Gardner, Howard. (1999). *Intelligence Reframed: Multiple Intelligences for the Twenty-First Century*. New York: Basic Books.

Gardner, Howard. (1983). *Frames of Mind: The Theory of Multiple Intelligences*. New York: Basic Books.

Goodman, Ken. (1996). *On Reading*. Portsmouth, N.H.: Heinemann.

Haas, Monty and Laurie Joy Haas. (2000). *Read It Aloud! A Parent's Guide to Sharing Books with Young Children*. Natick, Mass.: The Reading Railroad.

Harwayne, Shelley. (1993). "Chutzpah and the Nonfiction Writer." In Bernice E. Cullinan (ed.). *Pen in Hand: Children Become Writers*. Newark, Del.: International Reading Association, 19–35.

Hopkins, Lee Bennett. (1987). *Pass the Poetry, Please!* New York: Harper & Row.

Inge, M. Thomas. (1989). *Comics in the Classroom.* Washington, D.C.: Smithsonian Institute Traveling Exhibition Service.

Johnson, David M. (1990). *Word Weaving: A Creative Approach to Teaching and Writing Poetry.* Urbana, Ill.: National Council of Teachers of English.

Kohl, Herbert. (1999). *A Grain of Poetry: How to Read Contemporary Poets and Make Them a Part of Your Life.* New York: HarperFlamingo.

Kohn, Alfie. (1999). *The Schools Our Children Deserve: Moving Beyond Traditional Classrooms and "Tougher Standards."* Boston: Houghton Mifflin.

Lane, Barry. (1999). *Reviser's Toolbox.* Shoreham, Vt.: Discover Writing Press.

Lane, Barry. (1993). *After the End: Teaching and Learning Creative Revision.* Portsmouth, N.H.: Heinemann.

Lunsford, Andrea and Robert Connors. (1997). *The Everyday Writer: A Brief Reference.* New York: St. Martin's Press.

Macrorie, Ken. (1984). *Writing to be Read.* (Revised Third Edition.) Upper Montclair, N.J.: Boynton/Cook.

McGee, Lea M. and Donald J. Richgels. "K is Kristen's": Learning the Alphabet from a Child's Perspective. *The Reading Teacher.* December 1989, pp. 216–225.

National Center for History in the Schools. (1996). *National Standards for History, Basic Edition.* Los Angeles: UCLA Press.

National Council of Teachers of English and International Reading Association. (1996). *Standards for the English Language Arts.* Urbana, Ill.: National Council of Teachers of English.

O'Conner, Patricia T. (1999). *Words Fail Me: What Everyone Who Writes Should Know about Writing.* New York: Harcourt.

Opie, Iona and Peter Opie. (1959). *The Lore and Language of Schoolchildren.* New York: Oxford University Press.

Padgett, Ron. (1987). *Teachers and Writers of Poetic Forms.* New York: Teachers and Writers Collaborative.

"Quality Counts 2001." *Education Week.* 11 January 2001: XX. 17.

Samoyault, Tiphaine. (1998). *Alphabetical Order: How the Alphabet Began.* New York: Viking.

Schimmel, David. "Traditional Rule-Making and the Subversion of Citizenship Education." *Social Education.* February 1997, pp. 70–74.

Shermer, Michael. (1989). *Teach Your Child Science: Making Science Fun for the Both of You.* Los Angeles: Lowell House.

Short, Kathy G. and Jerome C. Harste, with Carolyn Burke. (1996). *Creating Classrooms for Authors and Inquirers.* Portsmouth, N.H.: Heinemann.

Skolnick, Joan, Carol Langbort, and Lucille Day. (1982). *How to Encourage Girls in Math and Science.* Palo Alto, Calif.: Dale Seymour Publications.

Smith, Frank. *The Book of Learning and Forgetting.* New York: Teachers College Press, 1998.

Takaki, Ronald. (1993). *A Different Mirror: A History of Multicultural America.* Boston: Little, Brown.

Whitin, Phyllis and David J. Whitin. (2000). *Math Is Language, Too: Talking and Writing in the Mathematics Classroom.* Urbana, Ill.: National Council of Teachers of English.

Wilford, John Noble. "Finds in Egypt Date Alphabet in Earlier Era." *New York Times* 14 Nov. 1999: 10.

Index